WHAT'S GOOD ON TV?

UNDERSTANDING ETHICS THROUGH TELEVISION

JAMIE CARLIN WATSON AND ROBERT ARP

WILEY-BLACKWELL

A John Wiley & Sons, Ltd., Publication

This edition first published 2011
© 2011 Jamie Carlin Watson and Robert Arp

Blackwell Publishing was acquired by John Wiley & Sons in February 2007. Blackwell's publishing program has been merged with Wiley's global Scientific, Technical, and Medical business to form Wiley-Blackwell.

Registered Office
John Wiley & Sons Ltd, The Atrium, Southern Gate, Chichester, West Sussex, PO19 8SQ, United Kingdom

Editorial Offices
350 Main Street, Malden, MA 02148-5020, USA
9600 Garsington Road, Oxford, OX4 2DQ, UK
The Atrium, Southern Gate, Chichester, West Sussex, PO19 8SQ, UK

For details of our global editorial offices, for customer services, and for information about how to apply for permission to reuse the copyright material in this book please see our website at www.wiley.com/wiley-blackwell.

Library of Congress Cataloging-in-Publication Data

Watson, Jamie Carlin.
  What's good on TV? : understanding ethics through television/Jamie Carlin Watson and Robert Arp.
    p. cm.
  Includes bibliographical references and index.
  ISBN 978-1-4051-9476-1 (hardcover : alk. paper) – ISBN 978-1-4051-9475-4 (pbk. : alk. paper)
  1. Television broadcasting–Moral and ethical aspects. 2. Television broadcasting–Social aspects.
I. Arp, Robert. II. Title.
  PN1992.6.W395 2011
  170–dc22   2011009294

A catalogue record for this book is available from the British Library.

This book is published in the following electronic formats: ePDFs 978144434007; ePub 978144434014; mobi 978144434021

Set in 10/12.5pt Galliard by Thomson Digital, India
Printed in Malaysia by Ho Printing (M) Sdn Bhd

1   2011

CONTENTS

PREFACE

WHY WRITE A BOOK LIKE THIS?

We've been teaching ethics for a number of years at a variety of institutions (public community, technical, and four-year colleges and universities, and private colleges and universities) and one thing we've noticed in all our classes is that examples from popular culture help students understand abstract philosophical ideas more efficiently than textbook examples.

When presented with textbook examples, students' initial responses are often skeptical: "Well, but what else is going on in his life?" "Why is she on the trolley to begin with?" "Isn't there a phone nearby, so he could call someone?" "Isn't that against the law?" They are often more interested in how the case is set up than in the moral issue the case is attempting to elucidate. But with pop culture examples, students are more likely to recognize or identify with the characters, accept the back story, understand the circumstances, and more quickly focus on the moral issue. Even in cases where they aren't familiar with the TV show, film, or video game, students are generally more willing to accept the circumstances as given and press into the ethical issues.

Popular culture examples also have an ice-breaking effect, helping students to better connect with one another and the instructor through a shared understanding of a cultural icon. And, for instructors who are willing to keep up with a few trends, pop culture examples enrich the classroom experience, adding a degree of levity to otherwise serious debate.

WHY TELEVISION?

Focusing on the medium of television allowed us to fix our attention on one arena of culture that continues to have an immense effect on how we interact with one another. Television has been a notorious platform for expressions that challenge social mores (e.g., interracial kisses, bisexual kisses, wardrobe malfunctions, abortion, rape, drug use and abuse, etc.). And the increased popularity of reality television raises a host of ethical questions, not to mention a reconsideration of what constitutes "reality."

In addition to its controversial moral themes, focusing on television allows this book to be useful to a variety of people:

1. Students in cultural history courses, media history courses, philosophy and pop culture courses, television and media ethics courses, not to mention as a supplement to more traditional introductory ethics courses
2. Instructors of these courses who are always looking for new and interesting examples to make the difficult concepts of moral philosophy more accessible to their students.
3. General readers who are interested in ethics but who would see the pop culture approach as a less intimidating or more enjoyable way of engaging classical moral theories and concepts.

While this book is no substitute for primary texts, we hope it will provide a useful introduction to ethics for a wide variety of readers.

HOW TO USE THIS BOOK

Each chapter of this book includes a discussion of an issue in moral philosophy using examples from television shows, at least one suggested reading, which we summarize, at least one "case study" from a television show, and three suggestions for additional case studies on that topic. The chapters stand, for the most part, independent of one another, so that an instructor or reader can focus on the issues he or she is most interested in. In cases where an idea from another chapter is referenced, we have tried to make this explicit, directing readers to the relevant section of that chapter. Each television episode is available either free online, or through a popular medium, usually iTunes or NetFlix. We expect that the instructor interested in teaching ethics through popular culture would be familiar with these sources, and our choice of episodes was guided by the intent that the maximum investment of an instructor, even if she has to purchase 10 episodes, would not exceed $20. (For instance, the show *Cold Case* had interesting episodes on homosexuality and abortion, but they were difficult to obtain inexpensively, so we left them out of our primary discussions.)

The structure of the book is similar to a classic ethics textbook, beginning with metaethics, then discussing ethical theories (normative ethics), and finally moving on to a series of decisions in applied ethics. In addition to the standard issues in applied ethics, we include a special applied ethics section on the medium of television. Thus, we have arranged the book as follows (using terms like "pilot," "series," and "episode" to reflect our television theme).

In "The Pilot Episode," we discuss briefly the nature of ethics and offer a primer on basic reasoning, introducing students to helpful reasoning strategies and common fallacies to avoid when discussing moral arguments. These strategies and fallacies are referenced throughout the book and provide an objective standard against which to evaluate assignments. In "Series I," we review some basic questions about the nature and sources of value, including moral nihilism, normativity, and the relationship between God and morality. In "Series II," we review four of the most widely held ethical theories: relativism, deontology, utilitarianism, and virtue ethics. In "Series III," we review six discussions in applied ethics: environmental ethics, animal welfare, abortion, homosexuality, punishment and capital punishment, and physician-assisted suicide. And finally, in "The Epilogue," we raise some important moral questions surrounding television, including the influence of the medium on society's values and the ethics of reality television.

THE PILOT EPISODE: ETHICS AND POPULAR CULTURE

WHAT IS ETHICS?

In season 5 of *The Office* (US), human resources rep Holly Flax (Amy Ryan), attempts to organize an ethics seminar ("Business Ethics"). What sounds like an interesting and enlightening workshop (to some of us) turns out to be a laundry list of company dos and don'ts. After a few excruciating lines from the Dunder Mifflin Anti-theft Policy, Oscar Martinez (Oscar Nuñez) points out: "That's not ethics. Ethics is a real discussion of competing conceptions of the good."

Ethics is about the good

Humans have engaged in discussions about "the good" at least since ancient Greek philosophers began investigating reality. In one of these ancient dialogues, for example, Socrates argued that the search for *eudaimonia*, or the "good life," is the best possible human pursuit. Many agreed

What's Good on TV?: Understanding Ethics Through Television, First Edition.
Jamie Carlin Watson and Robert Arp.
© 2011 Jamie Carlin Watson and Robert Arp. Published 2011 by Blackwell Publishing Ltd.

with Socrates, though few could agree about what counts as "good." Socrates and Plato argued that the good life is the result of living rationally and in pursuit of justice. Aristotle argued that someone who has a fortunate life and who acts virtuously will eventually achieve a good life. Epicurus argued that the good life is only achieved by indulging in various sorts of pleasure.

Though some philosophers still investigate "the good" or "the good life" in a general or abstract sense, others have found it more productive to ask, instead, what makes behaviors or actions good. For example, David Hume argued that our passions are the only motivation for our actions, so to say that an act is good is to say that we are motivated by some passion for it. Immanuel Kant argued, quite differently, that a good act is one motivated by reasons independent of passions, that is, by *pure* reason. Around the same time, Jeremy Bentham echoed Epicurus and Hume, arguing that a principled cost/benefit analysis of the pleasures and pains resulting from an act reveals its moral worth. If an act increases overall pleasure and reduces overall pain, it is morally permissible; if doing anything else would reduce pleasure and increase pain, the act is obligatory.

Contemporary philosophers, with some exceptions, tend to follow this eighteenth-century model and investigate the moral value of human actions. Contemporary debates in ethics center around one of three questions: (i) Is there is anything like a "right" or "wrong" act?; (ii) if there are right and wrong acts, what makes an act right or wrong?; and (iii) if there are right and wrong acts, which acts are right and which are wrong?

Ethics is an investigation

What does Oscar mean by "a *real* discussion"? A real discussion is a dialogue with a purpose, an investigation. It is not simply sharing opinions or reading what someone else thinks. It is a rational consideration of the arguments for and against a particular moral claim or theory. It is a process that requires clarifying, evaluating, and either defending or critiquing candidates' answers to the three questions just raised.

In fact, we worry that the word "discussion" is a little too weak. As it is often used, people can discuss without making progress. But any academic study must have success criteria; that is, we must be able to identify our goals and know whether we have achieved them. We do not think your journey into ethics has to end with shrugging shoulders and frustration. In this book, we offer you a set of tools for evaluating moral claims objectively and rationally. No doubt, you bring to this book a set of moral opinions. Our goal is to help you evaluate those opinions and the opinions of others on rational and moral grounds. You may discover a handful of good reasons to keep the opinions you have, or you may find that your opinions are unjustified and must be rejected. Still yet, you may find that there is not enough evidence to make an informed decision either way, and so you may have to suspend judgment until there is some new evidence. Whatever the result, the tools for evaluating these opinions are available to anyone able to ask moral questions. These tools allow us to have more than a discussion about the "good": they help us make progress.

Therefore, while we appreciate the spirit of Oscar's definition, we will choose a slightly different definition for our study:

Ethics is the philosophical study of moral value

Philosophy is a method of investigating reality, very similar to science. In fact, most scientists throughout history considered themselves to be philosophers. Even Isaac Newton named his physical theory, *Mathematical Principles of Natural Philosophy*. The hallmark of a scientific/philosophical study is its heavy reliance on reason and logic. Scientists and philosophers reason about the nature of reality using a variety of evidence. However, contemporary philosophy is distinct from science in that, rather than conducting laboratory experiments, philosophers conduct thought experiments. Thought experiments involve either showing that the implications of a hypothesis are rationally unacceptable or constructing examples that reveal problems with a hypothesis. Since moral value is not the sort of topic that can be studied with microscope, test tube, or measuring tape, its investigation rightly falls to philosophers.

There are various kinds of value: moral value, aesthetic value, practical value, and truth value, among others. What "value" means in a particular situation depends, primarily, on the type of value under consideration. For instance, "practical value" refers to an act's function or usefulness; therefore, the more useful an act, the more practically valuable. Alternatively, "truth value" refers to a claim's veracity – that is, whether a proposition is true or false.

In this book, we are primarily concerned with "moral" value. Moral value refers to whether an act is obligatory (should be performed), permissible (may be performed), or impermissible (should not be performed). Moral value is also often expressed in polar terms (terms at the extreme ends of a spectrum), such as "right" or "wrong," "good" or "bad," "moral" or "immoral." Many times, however, "right," "wrong," "good," and "bad" are too broad to be informative. For instance, is it "right" or "wrong" to let someone cut in line in front of me? It seems morally permissible, but not explicitly "right." In some situations it may be morally better than not allowing them to cut (for instance, if you're at the supermarket with a full cart and the person behind you has only one item). But it is not morally obligatory that you let them cut in. And you are not morally wrong if you don't. Our point here is simply to encourage you to take care not to overstate moral claims.

Ethics is normative

Every claim that expresses value is, explicitly or implicitly, an "ought" claim: In X circumstances, a subject ought to do (ought not do; is permitted to do) Y. This means that ethical claims are "normative." A normative claim indicates the way things *should* be or *ought* to be. Note that "normative" is different from "*normal.*" Normal is the way things tend to be or have been for some time – you may have heard the expression, "That's just how things are," or "That's just how people are." Normative refers to the way things *ought to be* – the way people ought to act.

As we will see in Episode 2, ethical normativity is not the only important kind of normativity. If usefulness is your goal, then a belief or action's pragmatic value indicates what you ought to believe or do. We call this "practical normativity." If truth is your goal, then a claim's truth value, or the likelihood of a claim's truth value, indicates what you ought to do. We call this "alethic normativity" (alethic comes from the Greek word for truth: *aletheia*; some philosophers have argued that there is a moral obligation to follow alethic norms). If "goodness" or moral "rightness" is your goal, then a claim or action's moral value indicates how you *may* act, *ought* to act, or *ought not* to act. We call this "moral normativity," and it is the type we are most concerned with in this book.

The unique thing about normativity in ethics is that "goodness" does not seem to be contingent on any particular human goals. Whereas a true belief is valuable *only if* you are seeking truth and a pragmatic belief is valuable *only if* you are seeking usefulness, moral goodness is valuable regardless of what you are seeking. The standard we use to evaluate the moral value of an action is goodness itself; so, by definition, it is never morally good to do a morally bad thing.

Of course, different actions may be morally good or bad, and the same act may be good in one set of circumstances and bad in others. For instance, the act of jumping up and down seems morally permissible in many circumstances: on carpet, in the gym, on a trampoline. But it seems to become immoral in other circumstances, for example: on a baby kitten. Because of examples like this one, we might say that morality is "context relative." Nevertheless, the moral permissibility of actions is evaluated according to a standard independent of those circumstances.

Normative claims have important implications for how we interact with the world. This means we cannot take the process of determining what actions are morally permissible lightly. So, how do we figure out when an action is wrong?

Ethics involves theory

A statement about the moral value of an action is called a *moral claim*. A moral claim is a declarative statement about some moral feature of reality that is either true or false. For instance, "Rape is morally impermissible," or "It would be wrong for you to steal that pen." Grammatically speaking, moral claims are declarative sentences, and not questions or exclamations or commands. However, moral claims are often expressed as commands: "Don't do that!" "Stop stealing!" "Just give her the money you owe her." But commands are not true or false; they are not statements about reality. They are often *disguised claims*. Consider the reformulation of these commands: "You ought not to do that!" "You should stop stealing!" "You ought to give her the money you owe her." Reformulated as moral claims, we can now evaluate the truth or falsity of these statements.

We all have a list of actions we consider obligatory, permissible, or impermissible. These actions are expressed as moral claims. Many of us include the following moral claims on our list: murder is impermissible; stealing is impermissible unless what we're stealing is insignificant (paper clips, post-it notes); giving to charity is permissible and, perhaps, sometimes obligatory; caring for our children and aging parents is obligatory; keeping promises is obligatory, etc. The process of constructing a list of claims expressing the moral values of a set of actions is called "casuistry." Casuistry comes very naturally to us, but in order for our lists to perform the function we want it to (namely, to keep us from acting immorally or to help us act morally), we must ask two questions: (i) *Why does my list have the moral claims it does?* and (ii) *Are the claims on my list true?*

How we evaluate a moral claim – that is, whether and when a belief or action is considered morally permissible, obligatory, or impermissible – depends a great deal on our ethical "theory." Without an ethical theory, the items on our lists quickly become either inconsistent or self-serving. Consider another example from *The Office* (US). In "Sexual Harassment" (season 2), the corporate office had recently fired an executive for having an inappropriate relationship with his assistant and the Scranton branch is asked to review the company's sexual harassment policy. The boss, Michael Scott (Steve Carrell), takes this request personally, as an assault on his edgy sense of humor – the one thing (he thinks) that makes the office fun.

Unfortunately, Michael recognizes no distinction between "offensive" and "inoffensive" jokes, so he rebels by redoubling the number of crude jokes and email-forwards he distributes to his employees.

For most of the episode Michael stands firm. However, when his long-time idol Todd Packer (David Koechner) tells a joke that "crosses the line" by insulting an office worker, Phyllis Lapin (Phyllis Smith), Michael suddenly recognizes a moral reason to object.

Notice that, up to now, Michael has held the maxim, *All humor is morally permissible.* He says, "There is no such thing as an appropriate joke. That's why it's a *joke.*" Suddenly, however, he realizes that some jokes can hurt people's feelings. To illustrate the ugliness of a character in the story he's telling, Packer points at Phyllis. Kevin (from accounting) asks, "Phyllis?" Michael says, "No. No. No. No. That crosses the line." In stating this, Michael is revising his maxim to reflect an exception. We might formulate his new maxim as, *All humor is morally permissible except when it hurts someone's feelings.*

This might seem inconsistent, but changing your maxims to reflect new evidence is not a bad thing. When you have good reasons for doing so, you *should* revise your list of moral actions. It's part of how we make progress in ethics. But if we discover a serious inconsistency in our beliefs, we must appeal to a moral theory. Michael now seems to have a principled reason for revising his maxim. But since his revision is not being constrained by a moral theory, things go awry pretty quickly.

He suddenly finds that his revised maxim conflicts with his other long-standing maxim, *Don't do anything that will make people not like me,* because Packer asks, condescendingly, "Ex-squeeze me!?" In order to keep his belief that Packer's joke was wrong, while also avoiding further ridicule from Packer, Michael is forced, again, to revise his comment. He tries to relieve this tension by deflecting the blame: "Not you. Kevin. Just unwarranted. Hostile work environment, Kevin."

Now Michael holds the maxim, *There is a distinction between appropriate and inappropriate jokes, but only some people should be held responsible.* But it's obviously Packer's joke, so we really want to know "Why Kevin?" Michael needs some principled reason for implicating Kevin under this new revision. Attempting to point the blame in the right direction, Kevin responds, "Packer said it." Instead of following Kevin's intuitive suggestion, Michael attempts to justify his decision by invoking a distinction: "No, *you* said it. Packer pointed. A point is not a say."

To the audience, it seems obvious that Michael introduces this distinction (between "a point" and "a say") only to keep his maxims consistent. But the only reasons for keeping them consistent are self-serving. Michael saves face (that was the idea, anyway), but morality takes one in the loss column. Packer isn't held properly responsible for his actions, Phyllis isn't vindicated, and Kevin is punished for something he didn't do.

What does an ethical theory look like?

If an ethical theory is so important, how do we construct one? We'll see some of the details of theory construction in Series II, where we explain three classical ethical theories: virtue ethics, deontology, and utilitarianism. Here, we'll just highlight some of the rough details.

Constructing an ethical theory is very similar to constructing a scientific theory. Scientists begin in one of two ways. On the one hand, they can begin with particular experiences that need an explanation and then formulate hypotheses to explain those experiences, which, if they prove successful, become theories. Alternatively, they can begin with a working theory and evaluate some new experiences in light of that theory. If the working theory cannot account for the new experience, changes may be needed. The first approach is typically appropriate only when we are starting from scratch, with some really unique sort of phenomena; but few of us find such phenomena or are in a position to take on such an immense task. Therefore, scientists and ethicists typically begin with a working theory and attempt to revise it in the face of anomalies.

So, *begin with an assumption*. As an example, let's start by assuming that there are objective moral duties and those duties apply only to agreements among moral agents. So, for instance, I have a duty to pay you money only if I have explicitly entered into an agreement with you to pay you money. Similarly, I have a duty to save your life only if we live in a community where we have all agreed to help each other. To draw an analogy with science, let's assume that "heat" is a clear liquid-like substance called "caloric" and the more caloric an object has, the hotter it is. In addition, caloric moves from objects with more caloric to objects with less caloric, making the latter objects warmer. We'll call these our "working theories."

With these working theories in hand, we can now evaluate some phenomenon that needs an explanation. The next step, then, is to *clearly identify something that needs an explanation*. In science, this might be something like, "Why does a cold pan get warm when it touches something warm?" In ethics, it might be something like, "Why do I think it would be wrong for my spouse to have an affair?"

Next, *we form a hypothesis based on our theory to explain the phenomenon*. In science, this might be: "Since the warm pan has more caloric than the cold pan, the caloric from the warm pan flows into cold pan." In ethics this might be: "My spouse and I made explicit promises to one another that we would be monogamous, and promises (because they are explicit agreements) are morally binding."

Fourth, *we test this hypothesis against contrary evidence.* In science, this might be: "If the caloric theory is an accurate explanation, then two cold objects cannot become warm without making contact with something warm. Yet, two cold sticks become warm when rubbed together." In ethics, this might be: "If my spouse and I did not make explicit promises to be monogamous, it would not be immoral for her to have an affair. Yet, it still *seems* to me that, when I am in a relationship that just happens to be monogamous (there is no explicit agreement to be monogamous), there is a moral presumption that it would be wrong for my spouse to have an affair."

Fifth, *given contrary evidence like these, we may need to alter our theories or switch theories altogether.* In our science case, this might mean a change from the "caloric" theory of heat to the "molecular" theory of heat: "Heat is a function of the speed of molecules. When the molecules of an object are accelerated by some external manipulation (friction, electricity, etc.), the object becomes warm." In our ethical case, a competing explanation might be: "Some relationships confer special duties independently of any explicit agreement. Monogamous sexual relationships fall into this category."

Finally, *if this revised theory or hypothesis explains a larger number of similar cases and faces less contrary evidence than competing hypotheses, this hypothesis is the best explanation.* That is our working theory. We can now keep this theory and use it to resolve moral problems and guide our behavior until a better explanation comes along or until devastating contrary evidence is discovered. The molecular theory of heat explains all of heat's properties that the caloric theory explained, plus it explains why cold objects become warm when friction is applied. In our ethical case, the existence of duties not explicitly agreed to plausibly explains moral obligations in various sorts of relationships: a parent has an obligation to care for her child, but not someone else's, even if the child has not agreed; a teacher has an obligation to treat his students with respect, even if the students do not agree.

This illustration is just a skeleton of the process of constructing a moral theory. Steps 3, 4, and 5 may need to be repeated dozens of times before a plausible explanation emerges. Our moral explanation for the seeming immorality of having an affair may not be very compelling in light of other contrary evidence. These would need to be considered before settling on a working theory of special duties.

Ethics involves casuistry

Even if you are able to come up with a plausible ethical theory, you will still have to consider how to put it into practice. It is *not* likely that you will be able to hole up away from the world with a tidy ethical theory in hand; you will probably choose to live in a community of people who think in moral terms. To live with others productively and safely, you must construct a list of moral and immoral actions that guide your behavior and help you evaluate the behavior or others – for better or worse.

We can hear you now: "But who am I to *judge* other people? I don't want to *offend* anyone." Our first response is that this sort of attitude already expresses a moral sentiment, namely, that people are generally good and virtuous. Unfortunately for you, not everyone believes this. Therefore, by your very assertion, someone is wrong. *You will face moral conflict.*

Second, consider whether your attitude changes when your credit card company overcharges you. What about when your car is vandalized? Or when your college changes the rules on you without notice and now you have to take three more classes in order to graduate? Or when your mechanic lies in order to charge you *more* for the work he probably *didn't do in the first place?* What about when your roommate kills your fish or breaks your television or sleeps with your girlfriend/boyfriend?

Is anyone *wrong* in any of these situations? Have these perpetrators simply done something that you personally disagree with but which might be morally permissible for them? Have they simply acted according to their evolutionary tendencies? Can they really be blamed if they were raised in a very selfish home and don't care about your possessions or feelings or rights?

After serious philosophical consideration, you may come to the conclusion that there is no such thing as moral and immoral behavior, and, therefore, these questions do not disturb you very much. This is a viable position in ethics called "moral nihilism." But keep in mind that your behavior will reflect an answer to these questions as they confront you, regardless of whether you have drawn any conclusions about the nature of value. And your answers can be evaluated in terms of ethical theories. Therefore, even if you are a moral nihilist, if you are a member of a community of beings that can recognize moral reasons and your actions can be evaluated in terms of a moral theory, it is useful to understand the relationship between casuistry and theory so that you can adequately respond to those who would challenge the morality of your behavior.

HOW DO WE MAKE PROGRESS IN ETHICS ?

Recall Oscar Martinez's definition of ethics: a real discussion of competing conceptions of the good. We have talked about the good and what is required for an investigation into the good. But what about those "competing conceptions"? People invariably believe different actions are moral or permissible or immoral. People disagree. So how do we make any progress?

Ethical reasoning

The primary way to make progress in ethics is by *reasoning* about moral claims, that is, by constructing and evaluating arguments. Some people get nervous around the word "argument" because it brings to mind a heated emotional exchange, usually angry. Or it makes people think of mere disagreement, one person simply contradicting another. An old British television show called *Monty Python's Flying Circus* parodied this perception of an argument in a sketch called "The Argument Clinic" (episode 29), where a customer attempts to pay someone to have an argument with him:

CUSTOMER (C):	Ah, is this the right room for an argument?
ARGUER (A):	I told you once.
C:	No you haven't.
A:	Yes I have.
C:	When?
A:	Just now.
C:	No you didn't.
A:	Yes I did.
…	
C:	You did not.
A:	Yes I did.
C:	Did not.
A:	Yes I did.
C:	Didn't.
A:	Yes I did.
…	
C:	Look, this isn't an argument.
A:	Yes it is.
C:	No it isn't. It's just contradiction.
A:	No it isn't.
C:	Yes it is.
…	
C:	All of this is futile
A:	No it isn't.
C:	I came here for a good argument.
A:	No you didn't; you came here for an *argument*.
C:	Well an argument's not the same as contradiction.
A:	It can be.
C:	No it can't. An argument is a connected series of statements to establish a definite proposition.
A:	No it isn't.

C: Yes it is. It is isn't just contradiction.
A: Look, if I argue with you I must take up a contradictory
      position.
C: But it isn't just saying "no it isn't"
A: Yes it is.
. . .

In this sketch, the arguer thinks of arguments in terms of "contradiction," whereas the customer thinks of arguments the way philosophers think of arguments: reasons for thinking a claim is true. So, for our purposes:

An argument is one or more claims (called premises) intended to support the truth of another claim (called the conclusion).

We've noted that a moral claim is a declarative statement about some moral feature of reality that is either true or false. A claim in general is simply a declarative statement about any feature of reality that is either true or false; for instance: the barn is red; the field is grassy; the speed of light is 299,792,458 m/s.

In an argument, one or more claims (moral or otherwise) is being used as evidence for the truth of another claim. For instance, let's say someone made the claim: "Abortion on demand is wrong." As a critical thinker, you would want some reasons for thinking this is true. A classic argument for this claim looks like this:

1. A fetus has a right to life.
2. A person's right to life is stronger than a woman's right to decide what happens in and to her body.

3. Therefore, a fetus may not be killed on the grounds that a woman has decided she does not want the fetus.

(1) and (2) are claims providing support for (3), which says that because a woman decides she does not want a fetus (essentially: abortion on demand) abortion is wrong.

In order to evaluate this argument, we need to know what makes an argument good or bad (note: arguments are *not* true or false; only *claims* are true or false). In a "good argument," (i) the conclusion follows from the premises and (ii) the premises are true. A conclusion *follows* from the premises in one of two ways, either (a) if the premises were true, the conclusion could not be false (note: not that they actually are true, but, *if they were* – subjunctive mood), or (b) if the premises were true, the conclusion would be more likely than not. If an argument meets condition (i) because of (a), the argument is "valid." If an argument meets condition (i) because of (b), the argument is "strong."

An argument that is only valid or strong is not yet a good argument. We also need to know that the premises are true. If an argument is valid and has true premises, it is a "sound" argument. If an argument is strong and has true premises, it is a "cogent" argument. If either (i) or (ii) is not met or if neither is met, the argument is not good. If both (i) and (ii) are met, the argument is good.

Now, consider once again our argument against abortion. The conclusion follows from the premises in a way that, if the premises were true, the conclusion would have to be true, so it is a valid argument. Therefore, to determine whether it is a good argument, we need reasons for thinking the premises are true. For instance, why think premise (1) is true? Here's an example of an argument:

4.   A fetus is a person.
5.   All persons have a right to life.
_____
1.   Therefore, a fetus has a right to life.

Here we have another valid argument for the claim that a fetus has a right to life. We're making progress, but to know whether we have good reasons to believe (3), we still need to know whether (2) is true and whether premises (4) and (5) of the new argument are true. This can be a long process, but this is how arguments work, whether they are moral arguments, scientific arguments, metaphysical arguments, religious arguments, etc.

Four ways of evaluating moral arguments

In order to evaluate an argument, we need only to check to see whether it meets both conditions (i) and (ii) above. Of course, some arguments are very complicated and it is often difficult to see clearly whether both conditions are met. To help with this process, philosophers have discovered a handful of principles to help us evaluate moral claims and arguments.

1. The Principle of charity.   In season 1 of *30 Rock*, Jack Donaghy (Alec Baldwin) tells Liz Lemon (Tina Fey), "The Italians have a saying, Lemon. 'Keep your friends close and your enemies closer.' And although they've never won a war or mass-produced a decent car, in this area, they are correct" ("Blind Date"). Evidently Donaghy forgot the small matter of the Roman Empire. Nevertheless, we also think the Italians are correct (well, Mario Puzo anyway) because this saying highlights an important principle of reasoning, called the "principle of charity." Don't be deceived by its wimpy-sounding name; it will do more work for you than most other principles. It will keep you focused on the important parts of an argument.

The principle of charity directs us to be "charitable" to those who argue against our claims by presenting their arguments in the strongest way possible; it directs us to present *their case* in the best light. The idea is that, since we're after truth and not simply out to win an argument, it does not matter whether someone's original argument is weak or faulty, as long as a stronger argument in favor of their claim is available. An argument is good or bad independently of who offers it. Therefore, if we take the process of argumentation seriously, we are well advised to adhere to the principle of charity.

The principle has two dimensions: first, it allows us to determine whether our own claims are plausibly true (if the strongest argument against one of my beliefs is flawless, then I have a reason to change my belief), and second, it allows us to show, in the clearest and most objective manner, the flaws in our opponents' arguments.

It is probably clear to you that, for any belief you hold, there is a *chance* that that belief is false. In some cases, the chance you are wrong is incredibly small – for instance, a belief like $2 + 2 = 4$. Nonetheless, you must allow that a really intelligent mathematician could offer a proof showing that, however useful it is to believe $2 + 2 = 4$, it is not, strictly speaking, true. In most cases, on the other hand, the chances of being wrong are much greater: I won't die on this airplane; I won't get the flu this year; it's going to rain tomorrow; the universe is strictly guided by the second law of thermodynamics, etc.

A realistic perspective on our chances of being wrong should encourage us to take arguments against our beliefs all the more seriously. Nineteenth-century philosopher John Stuart Mill explains:

> He who knows only his own side of the case knows little of that. His reasons may be good, and no one may have been able to refute them. But if he is equally unable to refute the reasons on the opposite side; if he does not so much as know what they are, he has no ground for preferring either opinion. The rational position for him would be suspension of judgment. (*On Liberty*, ch. 2)

The idea here is that, to believe securely, or to be justified in our beliefs to at least some degree, we are well advised to seek out the opposition. Perhaps they are right and we are wrong. But we cannot determine which if we have not at least considered the best available evidence for the opposing claim.

The second dimension of the principle of charity assumes that, just as we could be wrong about our beliefs, so could our opponents. In order to show *convincingly* that an opponent's claim is implausible, an arguer must show *both* that the opponent's actual argument is faulty in some way, and that any similar or stronger argument for the same claim is faulty.

2. "Ought implies can" (though can doesn't imply ought).   Can you be held responsible for an act that you cannot possibly perform? Could you be morally obligated to jump over a building or run faster than a car? Could you be held morally responsible for breathing? It seems odd to think so. The principle of "ought implies can," often attributed to Immanuel Kant, means that, if there is some action you cannot possibly perform, we have a reason to believe you are not morally obligated to perform that act. For instance, people cannot change the color of their skin, so they cannot be morally responsible for being a certain race. This goes for a number of features of human psychology that have been the object of moral scorn throughout the ages. For instance, someone who has a genetic disposition toward being attracted to members of the opposite sex or the same sex, or toward alcoholism, or toward pedophilia, or kleptomania, according to this principle, cannot be held morally responsible for *having those dispositions*. This is because he has no choice with respect to *having* them. Of course, we do think he has a choice with respect to acting on them. We want the genetic alcoholic to refrain from drinking and the pedophile to refrain from performing acts of pedophilia, and both of these are moral concerns.

This principle is important because it helps us distinguish which aspects of certain behaviors are morally salient and can be used as evidence against any claim or argument that suggests that we are morally obligated to do something we cannot do. We just distinguished the genetic origins of an action from the performance of an action. Similarly, we can distinguish responsibility for an action at a given time from responsibility for a previous action. For instance, at the moment a drunk driver hits a pedestrian he could not have done otherwise, but he made a moral decision that led to this event by getting in the car drunk. Similarly, someone who takes out a loan who knowingly cannot pay it back makes a moral decision to defraud the lender.

This principle is controversial among philosophers primarily because there seem to be some obvious cases where it does not apply. If I borrow money, then accidentally spend all the money I have or, through no fault of my own, lose all my money along with the ability to make any more, the principle seems to suggest that I cannot be held morally responsible, since, in fact, I cannot pay back the loan. This, of course, would not be good for banks.

A standard response to this sort of case is that, if I have simply lost all my money, then, since I still have the capacity to make some, I am obligated to pay it back as soon as I do make any. But this doesn't quite save the principle. For example, if I agreed to pay it back on a certain day and just happen to have no money *on that day*, it seems the lender is right in holding me responsible for not doing so, even if I would have the money on the following day. And the same problem applies if I have lost the ability to pay it back (for instance, if I have lost my job).

Note that we could not solve this problem by pointing out that I made a promise in good faith that I would be able to pay it back. This is because now the action that I am unable to perform is keeping my promise. Yet, it still seems as if I am morally responsible for not making good on my word even if I cannot.

Nevertheless, the proponent of the principle may respond that, in cases where I am not morally responsible for either not being able to pay or not keeping my promise, the moral obligation to pay is lifted until I am able to pay it back. This response is plausible for two reasons: (i) it does not absolve the borrower of the debt; it simply acknowledges that the obligation cannot apply in cases where it is physically impossible for the borrower to repay. Note that this only holds if the borrower is not in this position because of negligence. If his actions caused his bankruptcy, he remains responsible for the debt just as someone who is drunk remains responsible for any unintentional actions that occur as a result of his drunkenness. And (ii) it does not leave it open that the borrower can remain destitute in order to avoid the debt; the moment he *can* take advantage of an opportunity toward making money, and, therefore, repayment of the debt, he is once again responsible for the debt.

Interestingly, the bankruptcy laws in the United States reflect this implication of the principle. A lender may take action against a delinquent borrower only until the latter can prove that he is physically unable to repay due to reasons outside his control. Under these circumstances, a borrower may file for bankruptcy and receive legal protection against his creditors. Therefore, we conclude that the principle of "ought implies can" is a plausible restriction on moral obligation.

Before concluding this section, it is important to point out that the converse of the principle, "can implies ought," does not hold. The counter-examples here are obvious, but they are worth noting given some advancements in medical science. The fact that we *can* drop atomic bombs on our enemies, have sex with multiple random partners, take hallucinogenic drugs, eat pie for 24 hours straight, stand on baby kittens, or harvest organs from perfectly healthy people against their will doesn't mean we *ought* to do so. In each of these cases, important moral questions must be answered before we are justified in believing they are permissible or impermissible. Interestingly, some argue that certain advancements in medical science – for instance, the harvesting of stem cells from fertilized embryos – is morally permissible simply because we *can* do it. Given the above examples, this is an insufficient justification.

To be sure, the most common argument for harvesting stem cells is the great good that it might do, and that this good outweighs any moral value attaching to a fertilized embryo. This might be right, but it is not a "can implies ought" argument. It more closely resembles a principle known as "the end justifies the means." We will discuss this principle in Episode 6, when we discuss utilitarianism, but it faces problems similar to those of "can implies ought;" for instance, harvesting organs from perfectly healthy people against their will might result in more healthy people overall. But in this latter case, the means do not seem to justify the ends.

3. Counterexample.   A useful tool for testing a claim or argument is called a "counterexample." A counterexample is an example used to show **either** that *a claim is false* **or** that *an argument is not good.* A counterexample to a *claim* is an argument showing that a mutually exclusive claim is true. Two claims are mutually exclusive if they cannot both be true at the same time – for instance, "the barn is red right now" and "the barn is blue right now"; "Michael Bluth has no sisters" and "Lindsay Fünke is Michael Bluth's sister." Therefore, if there is a better argument for the latter claim than the former, we have reason to believe the former is not true. Here's an example from ethics:

Argument I:	*Argument II – Counterexample to premise (1):*
1. Intentional killing is wrong.	4. It is not morally wrong to kill a mosquito.
2. Abortion is an intentional killing	5. Killing a mosquito is an intentional killing.
3. Therefore, abortion is wrong.	6. Therefore, some intentional killings are morally permissible.

Argument II highlights the inconsistency between the claims "Intentional killing is wrong" and "some intentional killings are morally permissible": both cannot be true. Since most people have good reasons to believe there is no moral harm in killing a mosquito, premise (1) is much too strong, and therefore we have a reason to reject it. If an argument could be made for protecting mosquitoes from intentional killings (that is, an argument that premise (4) is false), this counterexample would not work.

Note also that there would be no problem for premise (1) if it read, instead, "Intentional killing is *often* wrong," or "Intentional killing is *sometimes* wrong." If the arguer used either of these as a premise, the conclusion would also change to, "Abortion is often wrong" or "Abortion is sometimes wrong." But almost everyone could agree with the latter conclusion and many with the former (e.g., when it is against the mother's will, when the abortion would cause more harm than not having an abortion), so there would be little need for argument. The whole point is to determine the precise circumstances under which abortion is morally permissible and impermissible. This requires precise principles that help determine, for any particular pregnancy, if or when abortion is permissible.

Using the same example, consider a counterexample to the argument:

Argument I:	*Argument III – Counterexample to Argument I:*
1. Intentional killing is wrong.	1. Intentional killing is wrong.
2. Abortion is an intentional killing.	7. Killing bacteria with antibiotics is an intentional killing.
3. Therefore, abortion is wrong.	8. Therefore, taking antibiotics is wrong.
	9. But it is absurd to believe it is not wrong to kill bacteria.
	10. Therefore, there may be reasons for thinking intentional killing is not wrong in the case of abortion.

In this case, Argument III shows that inserting a different action into premise (2) yields an absurd conclusion, namely, that we are never morally permitted to take antibiotics. But if these premises lead to a conclusion we have independent reasons for thinking is false, something has gone wrong in the original argument. In this case, the first premise is the only feature that is the same in the counterexample; therefore, there must be something wrong with premise (1).

So, the problem with Argument I seems to be its first premise, and we now see two ways to show this: (i) argue directly that it is false (that is, offer a counterexample to a *claim*), or (ii) argue that accepting the claim in a different set of circumstances leads to an incoherent conclusion (offer a counterexample to an *argument*).

There are dozens of ways to offer direct arguments against a claim. These involve simply offering a set of premises in support of the conclusion that the claim is false. For instance, if we wanted to construct a direct argument that premise (1) of Argument I is false, we might offer an argument like the following:

Argument I:	*Argument IV – Counterexample to Premise 1:*
1. Intentional killing is wrong.	11. If intentional killing is always wrong, then life is the most valuable thing in the world.
2. Abortion is an intentional killing.	12. Life is not the most valuable thing in the world.
3. Therefore, abortion is wrong.	13. Therefore, intentional killing is not always wrong.

Additional reasons might be required to support the truth of premise (2), but if these premises are true, we have direct reasons for believing that the claim "intentional killing is (always) wrong" is false.

There are two general types of counterexample to an argument, one of which is called *The Technique of Variant Cases*. In this type, an argument is constructed that has *all* the same elements as the argument under consideration except the act in question. So, Argument III above is a Variant Case Counterexample; we just substituted "killing bacteria" for "abortion" to show that the one of the premises is incorrect. We have independent reasons for thinking that killing bacteria is not wrong. Of course, if someone could offer good reasons for thinking that taking antibiotics is morally impermissible or that taking antibiotics is not a case of intentional killing, this counterexample would not work.

The second general type of counterexample to an argument is called a *Bare Difference Argument*. In this type of counterexample, an argument is constructed that has *none* of the same elements as the argument under consideration *except* the act in question. Consider, one last time, Argument I:

Argument I:	*Argument V – Bare Difference Counterexample to Argument I:*
1. Intentional killing is wrong.	11. Killing in self-defense is not always wrong.
2. Abortion is an intentional killing.	12. Abortion when the mother's life is threatened is killing in self-defense.
3. Therefore, abortion is wrong.	13. Therefore, intentional killing is not always wrong.

In this case, we have changed the circumstances; now we are not simply considering killing, we are considering killing in cases of self-defense. In light of common-sense moral views about self-defense, some cases of abortion are morally permissible. Therefore, we have provided reasons for doubting the conclusion of argument I. If someone could show that killing in self-defense is always wrong or that we never need to perform abortions in defense of a mother (for instance, perhaps a doctor could always perform a Caesarian), then this counterexample would not work.

Keep these techniques in mind as you evaluate and construct moral arguments. They will help you discover the strengths and weaknesses of arguments. And understanding these strengths and weaknesses will help you construct arguments with more strengths than weaknesses and therefore, to make real moral progress.

4. The principle of caution.   Moral claims, if any are true, contribute to society in important ways. They help us express and explain why certain actions should not be performed, such as rape and murder, and they help encourage us to perform other actions, such as charitable and self-sacrificial ones. Ethical problems are often, as ethicist Tom Regan named one of his books, *Matters of Life and Death.* But in some cases, there doesn't seem to be enough evidence to make an informed judgment about the truth of a moral claim.

For instance, in the animal rights debate, it is not clear to many what it would mean for an animal to have moral "rights," or even moral value, independently of their relationship to humans (what are "rights" anyway?). Animals fight, kill, and eat one another, and there seems to be nothing good or bad, moral or immoral, about any of it – at least no more than a volcano erupting and wiping out a species 2,000 years before humans walked the earth. But just because it is difficult to determine whether animals have rights, since they might and since rights are morally significant, it seems we would be well advised to proceed with caution when it comes to how we treat them.

For instance, James Rachels writes, "there is no general answer to the question of how chimps may be treated. There are only the various ways of treating them and the various considerations that count for and against those treatments" (2008: 442). Similarly, there is very little consensus (and very little evidence to go on) about what conditions constitute "personhood," "welfare," or "happiness," or under what conditions it might be morally permissible to steal from the greedy, lying owners of a record label by illegally downloading their productions.

Nevertheless, we don't want to be murderers or thieves or cruel (at least we hope none of us wants to be those things). Therefore, with respect to ethical claims and arguments, it is advisable to err on the side of caution. Just as we would not want anyone in our contemporary society to say, "Well, the reasons given for and against the claim that Hispanics have the same rights as Caucasians sort of cancel one another out, therefore I am not rationally obligated to believe they have the same rights," we must also be careful with broad statements like, "Well, the reasons given for and against the claim that animals have rights are inconclusive, therefore I am not rationally obligated to treat them as if they do," or "The argument that an eight-week-old fetus is a person and has a right to life is seriously flawed, so I can treat my fetus however I want." It is true that if the reasons are really inconclusive, there is no *rational* obligation either way. But the principle of caution is not, strictly speaking, a rational principle; it is a pragmatic and moral principle. It may be that animals do not have rights and it may be that an eight-week-old fetus is no more morally significant than your fingernail, but the consequences of being wrong are very high. Therefore, a prudent reasoner will evaluate moral claims carefully and believe cautiously.

Six common fallacies in ethical reasoning

A "fallacy" is an error in reasoning. A fallacious argument seems good, but something has gone wrong. Either the premises only appear to support the conclusion or the premises only appear true. We briefly explain six common fallacies.

1. Argumentum ad populum *(appeal to the people).* What if everyone suddenly came to believe that Special Relativity is false or that God does not exist? Would everyone's *believing* these things *make* them true? Of course not. They are true or false independently of what anyone believes. Since someone's belief about a claim does not make it true or false, you will need a different sort of evidence to make a good judgment about its truth or falsity. If someone attempts to convince you to believe something or to do something on the grounds that large numbers of people believe it or do it, that person is committing a fallacy called *argumentum ad populum*, or "appeal to the people."

This fallacy is common in popular culture: everyone believes *the world is flat*; everyone believes that *premarital sex is morally permissible*; everyone believes that *driving after 9 pm is morally permissible*; no one thinks *you should drink and drive,* and so on. In each of these cases, the highlighted claim might be true or false. But the fact that everyone believes it or no one believes it does not constitute sufficient ground for believing it. Everyone could be wrong! You're mother even recognized these arguments as fallacious: "If all your friends jumped off a bridge, would you do that, too?"

Perhaps you have been tempted to think that a particular politician is doing a bad job because everyone else thinks he or she is doing a bad job. Or maybe you have been persuaded to believe there are objective moral facts, like "murder is always wrong," on the grounds that every culture in history has agreed on at least a few basic moral principles. There is a chance you have considered ingesting certain illegal substances, since "*everyone* has tried it" (and, heaven forbid you miss out). And you have probably even been tempted to buy something just because it is the "best selling *x* in America," or "mothers have been giving it to their children for 30 years."

All these arguments commit the *ad populum* fallacy. Make sure you recognize that, in each case, the conclusion – "I should believe *x*," or "I should do *x*" – may be true or false. There may really be objective moral facts. Some politicians really do a bad job. But evidence that "everyone believes x" or that "everyone does x" cannot help you make an informed decision about whether x is true.

Here are four more examples of appeals to the people:

(a) PenguinTears Shampoo – used by more salons than any other all-natural shampoo [Implied conclusion: Therefore, you should buy PenguinTears.]
(b) Reading – everybody's doing it! [Implied conclusion: Therefore, you should, too!] (This is from an actual PBS commercial during a block of children's programming.)
(c) "The majority of congressmen, including members from both parties, believe that Iran is a threat to the United States. Therefore, we should probably go ahead with the invasion."
(d) "Everyone on the board believes that the superintendent's policies are biased against male teachers. Therefore, we should not reelect her."

2. Argumentum ad misericordium *(appeal to pity/emotion)*. Is it *right* that you help starving kids in Ethiopia? Probably. Should you believe this because a television commercial with Sally Struthers makes you *feel bad*? Absolutely not. Your emotions have *nothing* to do with the truth of a claim. Just because you feel you deserve a new car for graduating, this does not place any moral obligation on your parents to buy you one. Just because you feel bad for criminals serving life in prison doesn't mean they shouldn't be there. Just because you don't like to go the speed limit doesn't mean you shouldn't. These arguments are fallacious because their premises are irrelevant to the truth of the conclusion. The conclusion might be true or false, but emotions cannot tell you which.

If someone tries to convince you that a claim is true by *appealing to emotions, especially negative emotions like pity,* she is committing the fallacy, *argumentum ad misericordiam,* or "appeal to pity." Appeals to pity show up in less conspicuous ways than in the starving kids commercials. Sometimes you can find talk shows where "noted" psychologists try to convince you and the audience that people who have committed horrible atrocities are not *really* bad at heart; they have just had a difficult childhood or poor role models. They try to convince you to feel sorry for them and to believe they should not be held to the same moral standards as those of us who did not share their experiences.

There is no doubt that, in some cases, a person's circumstances might mitigate blame or praise. For instance, if someone had a really awful childhood, we tend to consider her more praiseworthy if she becomes a productive and charitable member of society than someone who had a loving and encouraging childhood. Alternatively, we tend to regard someone who had a loving and encouraging childhood as more morally blameworthy if he becomes miserly and bitter – surely he knew better. But, these arguments are not appeals to emotion; they are appeals to psychological obstacles, or lack thereof, that help us sort out the extent of social or political punishment for immoral acts. There is no question as to whether the acts are immoral, even on the part of the psychologist offering the evidence; the arguer wants you to believe that the same moral standard does not apply *because* the victim's story is so tragic. This is an appeal to pity.

Here are four more examples of appeals to pity:

(a) "You'll say what I need you to, right? You wouldn't want us to lose our land!"
(b) *Student*: Please re-think my grade.
    Professor: But you did not answer the question.
    Student: My mom will kill me if I flunk History.
(c) "Don't fire Jack, even if he is incompetent. He has a huge family to provide for."
(d) "If I don't get this promotion my husband will leave me!" [Implied conclusion: Therefore, you should give me this promotion.]

3. Petitio principii *(begging the question; circular reasoning).*   If you listen closely, you will hear many people use the phrase, "that begs the question." But few use this phrase the way philosophers and logicians do. This is because the phrase has come to have two uses in the English language. One is rhetorical and the other is logical. The rhetorical use is the one you're probably most familiar with. The rhetorical use means to raise a question, to make a question obvious, or to make a question relevant. The other use is logical, and it means, in an argument, to assume in the premises something you are attempting to prove in the conclusion; it is also called a "circular argument." The logical use is the phrase's original meaning, but clever journalists have co-opted it for rhetorical purposes, and now it is standard to accept its rhetorical use. We, however, will only ever employ the term in its logical use – to mean a circular argument.

A circular argument is an argument that includes the conclusion in the premises. For example:

1. It is raining outside.
2. If it is raining outside, my car is wet.

3. Therefore, it is raining outside.

In this argument, the conclusion is already assumed in the premises. The arguer assumes that it is raining outside in order to prove that it is raining outside. Now, you might wonder: why in the world would anyone construct such a foolish argument? It's actually much easier to commit this fallacy than you might think. Consider the following, more subtle version:

1. The Bible says God exists.
2. The Bible is true because God wrote it.

3. Therefore, God exists.

In this argument, God's existence is assumed in premise (2). God could not have written the Bible if he did not exist to write it. But the whole point is to prove that God exists! The next example is even more subtle:

1. Murder is morally wrong.
2. Abortion is murder.

3. Therefore, abortion is morally wrong.

Why is this fallacious? It is not so explicitly, but implicitly, since almost everyone accepts that murder is morally wrong; premise (2) is really the claim that requires evidence. If we already thought premise (2) was true, we wouldn't be having the abortion debate in the first place. So, since the term "murder" means "immoral killing," we are assuming in the premises what we are trying to prove in the conclusion. Therefore, be careful not to beg the question in your own arguments, and watch that someone does not slip something by you by begging the question.

Here are four more examples of a circular argument:

(a)   "I believe Professor Arp that *X*. Look; it's even in his textbook on p. 322!"

(b)   "Of course the government should provide health care. The government is supposed to protect our rights and heath care is a basic human right."

(c)   "Cheating violates academic integrity. Therefore, it is wrong to cheat."

(d)   "It is wrong to assign grades according to relative student performance. But grading on a curve does just that! Therefore, grading on a curve is immoral."

4. Appeal to inappropriate authority.   People love to tell you that there is some scientific evidence behind their claims. Advertisements for shampoo, weight-loss supplements, cars, and painkillers all cite some form of "research" that supports some claim about their product. One commercial for a diet pill actually had a piece of paper in the background with the words, "Journal of Research," written in bold at the top while the announcer explained the "amazing results!" Just after the terrorist bombings in London in 2005, a CBN (Christian Broadcasting Network) news anchor interviewed a guest, whom they labeled, "Terrorism Expert," to explain just how serious the attacks were. Political pundit Glenn Beck said repeatedly, over the span of half an hour, that evidence for global warming is "false science."

What do all these sources of evidence have in common? *They are not authorities on the claim in question.* The "Journal of Research" does not exist, so it can't be an authority, and even if a journal with this name existed, it's not clear why it is a relevant authority on diet pills. It could be dedicated to agriculture or horticulture or veterinary medicine – who knows? Similarly, what is a "terrorism expert" and what college grants a degree in this field? Would a radical Islamic suicide bomber count as a "terrorism expert"? Pasting these words under someone's name does not establish his authority to inform a lay audience about terrorism. And finally, Glenn Beck is not a scientist, he did not interview scientists, he did not read scientific research on the air, he cited no independent source whatsoever – he simply authoritatively pronounced that a claim (made by scientists) is false.

To be clear, the diet pill may work, the terrorism expert may be legitimate, and global warming may, in fact, be a liberal myth. The problem is that you, as a critical thinker, have not been given *appropriate* evidence to think any of these claims are true. All three examples commit the fallacy of "appeal to inappropriate authority."

There are two ways an appeal to authority can be inappropriate:

- the authority can be *irrelevant*; or
- the authority can be *biased*.

If an authority is irrelevant, he or she is just not in any position to speak on the claim being evaluated. If an authority is biased, he or she pretends (knowingly or unknowingly) to be in a position of authority on the subject.

If your math teacher drones on and on about the deplorable character development in Jane Austen novels, it might be wise to take his opinions with a grain of salt. On the face of it, he is an *irrelevant* authority. Who cares what a mathematician has to say about literature? He might be right, but you should look for independent evidence. On the other hand, if you also learn that one of his long-time hobbies is nineteenth-century literature, you may take his claims a little more seriously. In this case, he is a relevant authority.

If a representative from the National Rifle Association (NRA) tells you that it is your constitutional right to own whatever gun you want, you should look for some independent evidence. Since the NRA is devoted to the promotion of firearm ownership, it is a potentially *biased* authority. This does not mean it is wrong; it just means that it has a *vested interest* in promoting certain claims. This vested interest can bias its testimony – that is, it could lead the NRA to exaggerate the truth or mislead you about a claim. This is tricky because it is not always the case. For example, the Environmental Protection Agency has a vested interest in promoting certain claims about the environment. However, it is better for it to be unbiased if it wants to keep getting funding.

Consider a more difficult case. What if a publication called *The Journal of New Testament Studies* publishes an article on Jesus of Nazareth? Whether it is an appropriate authority depends on what else you know about the journal. If it is a journal that publishes based on "blind reviews" (the reviewer does not know the author's name) and its editorial board is made up of well-respected scholars who study the New Testament, then it might be a reliable source. On the other hand, if all the editing scholars are known to have a certain take on the New Testament (say, that Jesus didn't exist), or that they only publish scholars who agree with them, the journal is less reliable – it is not an appropriate authority.

Jamie once saw a magazine ad with John Travolta wearing a Breitling watch. He immediately wondered: *Why should* this *make me want to buy a Breitling watch?* He decided there were two possible reasons, both fallacious. First, the ad might have been trying to convince Jamie that he should "be like Travolta," join an elite club of celebrities who wear Breitling. This would not be an appeal to inappropriate authority, but another fallacy, called appeal to snobbery.

Second, the ad might have been trying to convince Jamie that Travolta, being rich and famous, and having access to the finer things in life, has some *insight* into which things count as "finer," or at least as "fine timepieces." We are supposed to assume, implicitly, that Travolta is a connoisseur of fine watches (or at least fine things) and therefore, *recommends* Bretiling. But, John Travolta is an actor and a pilot. Acting and flying are his realms of authority. If Travolta recommended an airplane, then fine; he's an authority. But a watch? Hardly. It's like Whoopi Goldberg telling me to vote for Barak Obama, or the Red Hot Chili Peppers telling me to *Rock the Vote!* Who are these people to tell me *anything* outside their realm of expertise?

Here are four more examples of appeals to inappropriate authority:

(a) Actor Paul Newman says: "You should save the environment. Buy organic products." [Implied premise: You should do what Paul Newman says.]
(b) "The president of Ford Motor Company recently said that American cars are built better than any of their Japanese competitors." [Implied conclusion: Therefore, you should buy an American car (preferably, a Ford).]
(c) "The *Journal of Paranormal Research* says that 75% of people experience psychic phenomena on a daily basis. So, you have to believe there is at least some psychic phenomena in the world!"
(d) The *Sun* (tabloid) newspaper prints: "Monkey-boy is his own father!" [Implied premise: The *Sun* newspaper is a reliable news source.]

5. Slippery slope. In a slippery slope fallacy, an arguer inappropriately concludes that a series of unfortunate or undesirable consequences would follow if some claim, *p*, were true, therefore, *p* must be false. In *South Park* season 1, someone suggests that " "The Terrance and Phillip Show" is corrupting the minds of the children of South Park ("Death"). In response, Kyle's mom, Mrs Broflovski starts a protest: "Not allowing our kids to watch the show is not enough. We need to boycott the entire network. ... These boys' minds have been tainted by the garbage on television that they see and we are fed up!" The implication seems to be that what is on television will lead to negative consequences for kids and then society. Robert Arp has written that Mrs Broflovski's worry could be formulated as follows:

> If we allow a show like *The Terrance and Phillip Show* on the air, then it'll corrupt my kid, then it'll corrupt your kid, then it'll corrupt all our kids, then shows like this will crop up all over the TV, then more and more kids will be corrupted, then all of TV will be corrupted, then the corrupt TV producers will corrupt other areas of our life, etc., etc., etc. So, we must take *The Terrance and Phillip Show* off the air; otherwise, it will lead to all these other corruptions!!! (2006: 58)

The problem with this sort of argument is that it is not at all clear that all these negative consequences will follow from leaving "The Terrance and Phillip Show" on the air. In order to have a cogent argument, the arguer must give reasons for each particular consequence. To be sure, there is psychological evidence that continued exposure to violence tends to produce in children a more violent disposition. This means there might be some evidence that bad programming could have negative effects on children. But the further implications that shows like this will flourish until more and more kids are corrupted and other aspects of our lives are corrupted are unwarranted. Note: if all the causal connections between the p and the consequences identified in the argument can be established with good reasons, the argument does not commit the slippery slope fallacy.

Here are four more examples of the slippery slope fallacy:

(a) "The CEO's proposal will frustrate middle management, who will then take it out on the factory workers. When the factory workers are angry enough, they will go on strike and sink the whole company. Surely, we should not accept the proposal."

(b) "If we permit gay marriage, what is to prevent brothers from marrying sisters, or adults from marrying children, or, heaven forbid, a man from marrying his sheep? Thus, we should not permit gay marriage."

(c) "Censorship is immoral. If we censor one singer, we have to censor anything the public finds distasteful. Pretty soon we will be burning books and putting people in jail as instigators. This is a fast track to fascism!"

(d) "Religious belief is dangerous. First you're asked to believe an ancient text that we really don't know who wrote, on this basis you're asked to believe the interpretation of this text by someone who has been 'gifted by God' to do so, this leads you to give up your belief in the basic rationality of science and logic! Pretty soon you only believe a very narrow set of implausible claims. The more people become religious, the less rational society will be. Therefore, it is better not to be religious."

6. *The naturalistic fallacy (inferring an "ought" claim from an "is" claim).*   Recall that moral claims are normative, that is, they *prescribe* some action (e.g., you shouldn't steal, no one should lie to their mothers out of selfishness). Normal claims, on the other hand, are descriptive; they *describe* reality (e.g., the cat is on the mat, New York is north of Charlotte, etc.). Where does the normative force of a moral claim come from? Most philosophers agree that, wherever it comes from, we cannot infer normative claims ("ought" claims) from descriptive claims ("is" claims). To do so is to commit what is known as "the naturalistic fallacy."

For instance, you may know that plants need water to survive. This is a descriptive claim. But this claim tells us nothing about whether anyone should water the plant. The claim, "You should water the plant," does not follow from, "The plant needs water to survive." It is true that, *if* you *want* the plant to survive, then you have a normative reason to water the plant – you *ought* to water the plant. But even this sort of normativity (based on what you *want*) does not establish a moral obligation to water the plant. Rob may want to his daughter to grow up to be beautiful, and it may be a fact that if he gets her plastic surgery she will, but that does not mean he is under a moral obligation to get her plastic surgery. In fact, she will probably grow up to be beautiful even if Rob doesn't do something he knows will guarantee her beauty.

Not everyone agrees that it is irrational to derive an ought claim from an is claim. For example, some philosophers argue that the truth of the claim, "*X* causes pain," constitutes at least a *prima facie* reason to believe it is wrong to do *X*, even though "*X* causes pain" is a descriptive claim. But things here are not so tidy. These philosophers believe that increasing pain is essentially immoral. This means that, even though "*X* causes pain" is descriptive, since pain has moral implications, we have moral reasons not to do *X*. But on what grounds could you establish that increasing pain is immoral? Surely not on descriptive claims like, "brain state *x* is a pain state," or "smashing toes causes pain," or "I don't like pain." It seems plausible that we still need some moral claim to establish that pain is immoral. To be sure, this problem raises heated debates about where moral normativity comes from. Nevertheless, we feel it is safe to assume it does not derive from descriptive claims.

Here are four more examples of the naturalistic fallacy:

(a) "Bodies naturally break down over time, so exercise is just a struggle against nature. Therefore, you shouldn't exercise."
(b) "It's very natural for a child to lash out at her brother and hit him once in a while. You should just let her."
(c) "Animals eat each other, therefore, how could it be wrong for me to eat animals?"
(d) Homosexuality is a genetic predisposition, even if it cannot be linked to one specific gene. If homosexuals cannot choose whether to be homosexual, it cannot be immoral. Thus, homosexuality is not immoral.

WHAT DOES POP CULTURE HAVE TO DO WITH ETHICS?

Why do we think popular culture, especially television, is important to the academic study of ethics? There are two main reasons. First, pop culture is well positioned to make ethics more accessible. Philosophers have long relied on abstract examples, counterexamples, and case studies to highlight aspects or problems of a theory. For most philosophers, this is good fun. But for many students and non-philosophers, these abstract puzzles are not interesting, much less informative. Yet the bastions of pop culture have done a service to the philosophical community by presenting difficult philosophical problems in an engaging format.

For example, *Star Trek: The Next Generation* expressed many of the philosophical difficulties with defining the term "person," determining the relationship between the mind and body, and the logic of the preemptive strike. *Law and Order* continually raised questions about the relationship between God and morality, the moral responsibility of the mentally handicapped, and the morality of capital punishment. And the list grows as popular shows like *The Simpsons, House, M.D.,* and *South Park* go out of their way to address difficult philosophical and social problems.

Second, pop culture raises questions that philosophers are uniquely positioned to address. Our culture, locally, nationally, and globally, is informed, shaped, and lampooned by television. Some cultural biases and idiosyncrasies are best displayed in the types of television shows we watch and in the issues those storylines address. In the original *Star Trek* television series (think way back, the one with William Shatner and Leonard Nimoy), Captain Kirk, a Caucasian, kissed Uhuru, an African American – on national television – and this was a big deal!

In addition, many of the absurd aspects of our culture are expressed powerfully through television. Many will remember the *South Park* episode lampooning the religious organization Scientology ("Trapped in the Closet," season 9). After some controversy surrounding Scientologists' beliefs about psychiatry – beliefs promoted charismatically by actor Tom Cruise – many political and social commentators tip-toed around the less tasteful teachings of Scientology. But the creators of *South Park*, frustrated with the lack of serious, informed dialogue on the subject, wrote an episode ridiculing the religion and satirizing many of its famous proponents.

Philosophers are in a unique position to explain why *South Park*'s critique was apropos and to explain why we should recognize the absurdity of racial divisions. In addition, philosophers can integrate these expressions of pop culture into the context of ancient, modern, and contemporary investigations into the right and the good. Perhaps with a little effort on the part of philosophers, popular culture can begin, once again, to encourage the higher pleasures.

ADDITIONAL READING

The classics:

Nicomachean Ethics, Aristotle
The Principles of Morals and Legislation, Jeremy Bentham
Groundwork for the Metaphysics of Morals, Immanuel Kant
Utilitarianism, John Stuart Mill

The basics:

Moral Vision, David McNaughton
Ethics: Discovering Right and Wrong, Louis P. Pojman
The Elements of Moral Philosophy, James Rachels
Practical Ethics, Peter Singer

More advanced reading:

Explaining Value and Other Essays in Moral Philosophy, Gilbert Harman
Ethics: Inventing Right and Wrong, J. L. Mackie
Principia Ethica, G. E. Moore
Constructions of Reason: Explorations of Kant's Practical Philosophy, Onora O'Neill
Facts, Values, and Norms: Essays toward a Morality of Consequence, Peter Railton
The Right and the Good, W. D. Ross

SERIES I

IS ANYTHING "GOOD" ON TELEVISION?
THE NATURE OF MORAL VALUE

EPISODE 1: TRUTH AND NIHILISM IN ETHICS

INTRODUCTION

In Showtime's racy drama, *Californication*, Hank Moody (David Duchovny) tries to apologize to his daughter Becca (Madeleine Martin) for something he's done "wrong." But Becca responds: "There is no right or wrong, Dad, just the consequences of your actions. You taught me that" ("In a Lonely Place," season 2). Becca's claim is incredibly controversial. Can you imagine what the world might be like if she were right? Our condemnation of Hitler or Stalin or Pol Pot would just be a matter of – what? preference? We do not *prefer* someone like Hitler? We do not *care*

What's Good on TV?: Understanding Ethics Through Television, First Edition.
Jamie Carlin Watson and Robert Arp.
© 2011 Jamie Carlin Watson and Robert Arp. Published 2011 by Blackwell Publishing Ltd.

for Stalin's actions? Perhaps morality is just an agreement among people about how to act. That would mean that people in our group do not prefer that Pol Pot killed 21% of Cambodia – roughly 2.5 million people – for his selfish interests.

As strange as it may sound, some ethicists have presented arguments of this sort against the truth of ethical claims. The view that there are no true moral claims is called "moral nihilism." This is stronger than mere skepticism. "Moral skepticism" is the view that we do not know whether any moral claims are true. Moral skepticism is an epistemic thesis (a claim about what we can know). Moral skeptics admit that there might be objective moral facts, though it is not clear that we know what they are. Moral nihilism, on the other hand, is an ontological thesis (a claim about reality). Moral nihilists argue that there are no moral facts about reality. Since there are arguments for nihilism, given our commitment to the principle of charity (see "The Pilot Episode"), it is in our best interests to take them seriously.

To see how some moral philosophers arrived at nihilism, we need to know a little more about the nature of ethical theories. So, we'll begin with the traditional view that there are at least some true moral claims (e.g., you should not murder, you ought not rape, etc.) and then see how problems with this view lead to a version of nihilism that is growing in popularity among philosophers.

Most ethical debates begin with two assumptions: (i) moral claims are either true or false and (ii) humans can, for the most part, know the truth value of a moral claim. This view is known as "cognitivism." But in the twentieth century, some ethicists began challenging the coherence of (i). Claims about right and wrong are abstract, elusive, difficult to express clearly, and difficult to defend. Philosophers have faced many difficulties defining or explaining other abstract entities, such as properties (e.g., green, round, soft), relations (between, taller than), modalities ("x is necessary," "x is possible"), numbers, and language. But attempting to define or explain moral concepts is at least as difficult and perhaps more so. At least claims about numbers, language, and modalities can be meaningfully expressed using the formal rules of mathematics, grammar, and logic. And with properties, at least we can point to something like red or soft or smells-rotten-egg-like, even if we can't say exactly what it means for something to be a property. But what are we pointing at when we say an act is wrong? ("Surely, nothing in our sensory experience," so the argument goes). What tools could we use to speak meaningfully about moral claims? ("Surely, not our five senses"). But, it seems like moral claims are more important than claims about numbers. Everything we value is at stake.

Traditional ethicists like Aristotle, Kant, Mill, and Hume are cognitivists known as "moral realists." Despite their disagreements, they all accept (i) and (ii), and they also accept (iii) some moral claims are true. Different moral theories produce different (sometimes drastically different) results about which actions are morally permissible, but their disagreements do not entail that some moral claims are not objectively true and some objectively false. Their disagreement simply means that not all ethical theories are correct. If Kant is right, Aristotle, Mill, and Hume are wrong. If Aristotle is right, Kant, Mill, and Hume are wrong. And so on.

The writers of most TV shows assume at least some version of moral realism, given that most shows have a moral: don't cheat on Mr Woodman's tests (*Welcome Back Kotter*); don't steal from Bert and Ernie (*Sesame Street*); don't kiss your best friend's sister (every coming-of-age comedy); be honest, even when it is difficult (every episode of *Fresh Prince of Bel Air*); etc. But some TV shows challenge these traditional morality tales. For example, on the animated show *Family Guy*, the father of the family, Peter Griffin, is always extremely verbally abusive to his daughter Meg. Peter calls her ugly and fat, and sometimes even forgets he has a daughter. Unfortunately, the scripts never "make it right." To be fair, the show is a satire on the touchy-feely family drama. Nevertheless, the relationship between Peter and Meg is often portrayed as if Peter has done nothing wrong. And this sort of amorality pervades much of the show. What might justify this sort of attitude toward morality?

Difficulties like those mentioned above – whether talk about morality is meaningful – and difficulties with particular ethical theories have led some ethicists to reject (i), though they accept (ii). The view that (ii) is true, but (i) is false is called "non-cognitivism." The idea is that, though some sentences express "right" and "wrong," these expressions are not *claims*, they are not, technically speaking, propositions about reality that can be true or false. They may simply be expressions of our emotional states or prescriptions for action. Remember from "The Pilot Episode" that only claims can be true or false. Neither exclamatory sentences (e.g., "Ouch!" "Dammit!") nor imperative sentences (e.g., "Shut the door!" "Listen to me!") has a truth value. Therefore, if someone could show that all ethical claims were either emotive exclamations or commands, this would show that cognitivism is false and some version of non-cognitivism is the best account of morality.

One widely held non-cognitivist theory is called "emotivism" or "expressivism." Emotivists argue that moral statements are not claims, but are simply expressions of a particular attitude toward that action. For an emotivist, a moral statement like "murder is wrong" means something like,

"Murder, yuck!" There is no fact of the matter about murder or rape or child molestation; there are just attitudes of disapproval that are emotional in nature. Louis Pojman (1990: 145) explains A. J. Ayer's emotivism: "Moral statements are a type of nonsense, albeit a useful type. Even though they cannot be said to be true or false, they express our emotions." Pojman formulates Ayer's argument for emotivism this way:

1. A sentence is cognitively meaningful if and only if it can be verified.
2. Moral sentences cannot be verified.

3. Therefore, moral sentences are not meaningful.

If this argument is successful, the traditional cognitivist view that moral statements are claims is false; they are more like exclamations than claims. Therefore, we must find some explanation for the widespread use of moral language and its impact on culture and religion. If moral sentences are not meaningful in the same sense that a claim is meaningful, the best explanation for our moral language is that it expresses our emotions. It fulfills an important societal role because it allows us to express our feelings, to communicate strong preferences to others, and to persuade others.

Becca and Hank from *Californication* might be best described as emotivists. After Becca tells Hank she learned that there is no right or wrong from him, Hank says: "Well I guess I don't like the consequences of my actions very much right now." If morality is simply a matter of what we like or dislike, then emotivism is true.

Unfortunately for non-cognitivists, the problems for emotivism are at least as worrisome as those for cognitivism. The first premise of Ayer's argument was quickly shown to be false; it cannot meet its own criterion: premise (1) cannot be verified. In addition, there are strong reasons for thinking we can evaluate moral claims, at least in the same way we evaluate the axioms of arithmetic systems. We have strong intuitions that the axioms of arithmetic are true. All additional tests for their truth are evaluated against these intuitions. If no further intuitions contradict them – that is, they withstand attempts to construct counterexamples – their plausibility increases. The same seems true of moral claims.

Second, we seem to *mean* something different by moral claims than we do by emotive claims. If I say, "I like coffee," and you say, "Well, I don't. I prefer tea," we haven't disagreed about anything. What I have said does not contradict what you have said; both can be true. However, if I say, "Abortion is morally impermissible in all cases," and you say, "Abortion is sometimes morally permissible," then we have made statements that cannot both be true; we have disagreed. In the former statements (about coffee and tea), we both recognize that we are making statements about ourselves: it is true of you that you like tea. But in the latter statements (about abortion), it is much less clear that the statements are about ourselves. It seems we are making a claim about reality: it is true or false independently of me or you whether abortion is morally permissible.

Third, it seems emotivists cannot account for the universalizability of moral statements. For instance, I like vanilla ice cream. But it is easy to see that others do not and there is no particular reason they should. On the other hand, if I disapprove of *Johnny's* killing Susanne for no reason, I also disapprove of *George's* killing Susanne for no reason. And the same seems true for any name you put in place of Johnny's. It is the killing of Susanne for no reason that's wrong, and it is wrong no matter who does it.

Finally, according to emotivism, the value of a moral statement depends on your *attitude* toward an act. If this is right, then my causing you to have different attitudes would resolve many "moral disagreements." If I have a positive attitude toward murder, then perhaps I can get you to agree by manipulating your brain so that you find murder more tasteful. If emotivism is true, then manipulating your brain is tantamount to giving you good reasons for thinking murder is permissible. Nevertheless, it seems we have good reasons for distinguishing "behavioral manipulation" from "giving reasons." For instance, hypnotizing you so that you say, "Murder is good," any time you hear of one does not constitute a reason for you to think that murder is good. Since emotivism cannot draw this distinction, it is implausible.

Difficulties like these, plus those associated with cognitivism, have led some ethicists to accept both (i) and (ii), but to also argue we should add a further claim: (iv) all moral claims are false. Since these theorists argue that ethical claims *do* express claims about reality that are true or false, they are cognitivists. However, they also argue that all moral claims are false. Our ethical claims are meaningful, just as claims about unicorns are meaningful, but they correspond to nothing in reality, also like claims about unicorns; therefore, all moral claims are false. This view is commonly called "Error Theory" and it is becoming more popular among ethicists, especially among those who study evolutionary psychology. Error theory is a version of nihilism about ethics.

Although eighteenth-century philosopher David Hume is probably best categorized as a utilitarian, he anticipates many of the concerns of error theorists. Hume argues that our ability to reason is subject to our emotions. Because of emotion, we often attempt to manipulate reasons to justify our actions. In fact, Hume argues, the motivation for an action is never purely rational; there is always a trace of emotion. Reason gives us information; emotion gives us the will to act. He writes: "Since reason alone can never produce any action, or give rise to volition, I infer, that the same faculty is as incapable or preventing volition, or of disputing the preference with any passion or emotion" (*A Treatise of Human Nature*, Book II, Section III).

But Hume does not move from this conclusion to emotivism. Emotions lead us to make claims about reality and Hume thinks the most plausible explanation for what these claims are about is either pleasure or pain. So he defends a species of "utilitarianism" (for more on this theory, see Episode 6). Pain and pleasure are emotional motivations to perform or refrain from performing an action. Utilitarianism is a moral theory that says an act is right insofar as it tends to produce more happiness (in this case, pleasure) in the long run and wrong insofar as it tends to produce more unhappiness (in this case, pain) in the long run.

Error theorists argue that Hume's insights point in a different direction. They agree that they do not point to emotivism and they agree that emotions lead us to make claims about reality. However, they disagree that these claims track objective moral features of reality. In a famous paper, philosopher Michael Ruse and biologist E. O. Wilson write, "Beliefs in extrasomatic [body-independent] moral truths and in an absolute is/ought barrier are wrong. . . . The time has come to turn moral philosophy into an applied science" (2001: 421). A few pages later they explain that our study of evolution has revealed that "human beings function better if they are deceived by their genes into thinking that there is a disinterested objective morality binding upon them, which all should obey" (2001: 425). According to Ruse and Wilson, morality is just a useful fiction – we think we're talking about something real, but moral claims are no different than claims about unicorns.

Peter Griffin of *Family Guy* might espouse an error theory of morality. He seems to have no moral compass at all. In the episode, "Petarded" (season 4), Peter takes the MacArthur Genius Test and finds out he's legally mentally retarded. Peter discovers that his newfound legal immunity allows him "get away with anything." He kicks in women's bathroom stalls to see women on the toilet, he throws plates of food across the room, and he cuts in line, talks on the loudspeaker, and burns Lois with hot oil from The Fryolater at a fast-food restaurant, which results in Peter losing custody of his kids. Though he says he feels bad about burning Lois, he uses her bandages as toilet paper and tries to frame his friend Cleveland with prostitutes to get his kids back. At the custody trial, Peter doesn't argue that he deserves his kids back or that there is any moral reason he should have them; he simply says he *wants* them back. Someone who expresses no sense of right and wrong and acknowledges no moral reasons is a prime candidate for an error theorist.

It is important to note, however, that just because you hold an error theory doesn't mean you will act immorally. There are dozens of practical reasons not to act the way Peter Griffin does, none of which has any moral weight. An error theorist may act morally because it is easier to get along in society, because she doesn't want to go to jail or get sued, because she wants people to like and respect her, because she wants to keep her job, etc. So, holding an error theory doesn't entail anything about how someone will behave, but it does affect how someone answers moral questions, and how someone will behave if she thinks there are no other practical reasons for doing or not doing something (e.g., she won't get caught).

One of the foremost proponents of error theory is philosopher J. L. Mackie (1917–81). In the following passage, Mackie argues that if moral claims were true then they would be true about "non-natural" features of reality, that is, features of reality not available to the five senses or scientific experiments. Since there is no good way to make sense of non-natural features of reality, there is no good way to make sense of true moral claims. Therefore, all moral claims are, because of their purported subject matter, false.

THE CASE FOR NIHILISM

J. L. Mackie, "The Argument from Queerness," from *Ethics: Inventing Right and Wrong*

The opening line of Mackie's book is: "There are no objective values." With this sort of opening, it is difficult to miss that Mackie is a moral nihilist. More specifically, he defends an error theory. He agrees that (i) moral statements are either true or false and (ii) humans can generally know the truth values of these claims, so he is a cognitivist. But Mackie also argues that (iv) all moral claims are false.

Mackie's argument is largely negative; that is, he simply rejects objective moral truths on the grounds that it is not at all obvious how to explain them. He divides his argument into two parts, what he calls the "metaphysical" and the "epistemological." We can reformulate the metaphysical part as follows:

1. If there were objective moral values, they would be very strange, non-natural entities (different from everything else in the universe, for example, Plato's Forms).
2. We do not have evidence for any objects beyond natural entities, that is, entities we can perceive with our five senses, either directly or indirectly.

3. Therefore, it is unlikely that there are any non-natural entities.

This is an inductive argument (that is, the premises grant a certain amount of probability to the conclusion's truth). If there is no way to talk about moral truths without invoking supernatural language about objects not available to our senses, Mackie concludes that moral language must be like talk about vampires – interesting, but false.

We can reformulate the epistemological part like this:

1. If there are non-natural, objective moral values and we know about them, we need to explain some very special faculty for perceiving them.
2. The most plausible candidate for this special faculty is "moral intuition."
3. Moral intuition is implausible (for reasons Mackie does not specify).

4. Therefore, it is implausible to think we can know anything about non-natural entities.

This is also an inductive argument. Here, Mackie argues that, even if there were some mysterious, non-natural objects, we would need some access to them in order to make true claims about them. But what sort of access might this be? Some philosophers suggested we have a faculty of "moral intuition," something similar to our intuitions about mathematics (isn't it "obvious" that $2 + 2 = 4$?) and physics (when you see something flying at your head, you duck – even if you don't know what it is). But moral intuition has a bad reputation and, though it is gaining acceptance again in the philosophical literature, it had a particularly bad reputation when Mackie wrote *Ethics*. So, if the truth of moral claims is not available to our five senses (directly or indirectly) and moral intuition is incomprehensible, then it is plausible that our moral claims are not about anything in reality – they are false.

One of the most underrated responses to arguments like Mackie's comes from the author of *The Chronicles of Narnia*, C. S. Lewis (1898–1963). Lewis was academically trained as a literary critic and medievalist, but he was also a self-taught philosopher. It is likely that Lewis's argument is overlooked because it predates Mackie, but it could also be because it forms part of a larger, non-academic work on the nature of Christianity. Whatever the reason, we decided to include it here because it is a clear, concise response to error theory.

THE CASE FOR REALISM

C. S. Lewis, from *Mere Christianity*

Lewis begins by pointing out (1) that humans acknowledge a fairly uniform set of moral claims, and (2) that there is an obvious sense in which humans do not act morally. These are empirical claims, and Lewis offers some examples in support of them. Interestingly, Mackie and Lewis would probably agree at this point – there is some set of claims that humans roughly agree on and which are supposed to serve as a moral guide for our behavior, but which humans regularly ignore. The disagreement comes in the explanations for (1) and (2).

The first step in Lewis's explanation is to show that, by and large, people are not emotivists – they don't believe they are talking about preferences when they make moral claims. He points out that, in response to moral claims, the other person rarely says, "To hell with your standard." This latter sort of response would be perfectly appropriate if I told you, "You shouldn't prefer chocolate ice cream." You might be right to respond, "To hell with *your* preferences! *I* prefer chocolate." According to Lewis, "It looks, in fact, very much as if both parties had in mind some kind of Law or Rule of fair play or decent behavior or morality or whatever you like to call it, about which they really agreed" (1996: 18). Again, since Mackie is not an emotivist, he and Lewis would agree that, when people are speaking morally, they mean something about objective reality. Of course, for Mackie, this is like children talking about Santa Claus.

Next, Lewis responds to Mackie-like arguments. If language about objective morality is not true, then what could explain the power that moral claims seem to have over us? In chapter 10 of his book, "Patterns of objectification," Mackie hints at a possible explanation:

> Moral attitudes themselves are at least partially social in origin: socially established – and socially necessary – patterns of behavior put pressure on individuals, and each individual tends to internalize these pressures and to join in requiring these patterns of behavior of himself and of others. The attitudes that are objectified into moral values have indeed an external source,

though not the one assigned to them by the belief in their absolute authority.
... We need morality to regulate interpersonal relationships, to control some
of the ways in which people behave towards one another. (1977: 42–3)

The earlier quotes from Ruse and Wilson expand on this theme in
evolutionary terms. Biologically, humans function better if they think
they are obeying objective moral rules.

But Lewis gives three reasons for thinking this sort of response is not
sufficient. Keep in mind that Lewis is responding to error theory in terms of
the most up-to-date psychology of his day, which includes motivation from
"herd instincts" (desires to follow the crowd) and "instincts of self-
preservation" (desires to protect yourself). However, simply substitute
any contemporary evolutionary psychology terminology (e.g., selective
behavior, fitness, optimal functioning, etc.) and the point is the same.

First, we are able to distinguish our biological tendencies from our
moral code:

Supposing you hear a cry for help from a man in danger. You will probably
feel two desires – one a desire to give help (due to your herd instinct), the
other a desire to keep out of danger (due to the instinct for self-preservation).
But you will find inside you, in addition to these two impulses, a third thing
which tells you that you ought to follow the impulse to help, and suppress the
impulse to run away. (Lewis 1996: 22–3)

What is it that arbitrates these two psychological tendencies? If you respond
that it is simply another instinct, you've missed the point. Something tells
you that one instinct is *better* than another. But if it is simply another
instinct, it could not play this sort of authoritative role. "You might as well
say that the sheet of music which tells you, at a given moment, to play one
note on the piano and not another, it itself one of the notes on the
keyboard" (1996: 23).

Second, if all you experience are biological tendencies, then when you
experience such a conflict of motivation, the stronger of the two should
prevail. But it is at these times that the moral law seems to be telling you to
choose the weaker of the two desires. "You probably *want* to be safe much
more than you want to help the man drowning: but the Moral Law tells you
to help him all the same" (1996: 23). Therefore, there is something over
and above these basic motivations.

Third, if all you experience are biological tendencies, then we should be able
to pick out the "good" ones from the "bad" ones, so that we have an explanation for why we sometimes feel led to choose one desire over another,
especially a weaker desire. However, morality is not like this; for any particular

action, we can think of a time when it is morally permissible and morally impermissible. "There are also occasions on which a mother's love for her own children or a man's love for his own country have to be suppressed or they will lead to unfairness towards other people's children or countries. Strictly speaking, there are no such things as good and bad impulses" (1996: 24). Therefore, there is something over and above these tendencies that gives them the designation "right" or "wrong" in a particular context.

To sum up the argument to this point: we all feel a very strong weight of responsibility with respect to how we act toward ourselves, toward others, and toward the world. We identify this sense of responsibility as the force of the claims of morality. These claims could have subjective value (non-cognitivism) or they could be objectively true or false (cognitivism). There are reasons for thinking they are not simply subjectively valuable, and Mackie and Lewis would probably agree on these. Then, in response to philosophers like Mackie, Lewis offers three reasons for thinking they are objectively true: (a) we can distinguish biological tendencies from moral obligations; (b) something arbitrates our biological tendencies, often in favor of the weaker ones; (c) biological tendencies are not intrinsically good or bad, and so must get this quality from somewhere else. Lewis concludes, "Consequently, this Rule of Right and Wrong . . . or whatever you call it, must somehow or other be a real thing – a thing that is really there, not made up by ourselves. . . . It begins to look as if we shall have to admit that there is more than one kind of reality" (1996: 30).

Notice that this argument does not take the thrust out of Mackie's argument. Lewis has not offered a way to account for non-natural entities or moral intuitions. He simply offers an argument for the falsity of Mackie's conclusion. Recall that it is the very existence of a different kind of reality that leads Mackie to reject moral realism. Lewis is, in effect, saying, "However strange non-natural reality might be, there is more evidence that it exists than that it doesn't." We're reminded of the famous Sherlock Holmes line, "[W]hen you have eliminated the impossible, whatever remains, however improbable, must be the truth" (Doyle 2010: 54).

CASE STUDY: *The Office* (UK), "Work Experience," series 1

AVAILABILITY: **NetFlix, iTunes**

David Brent (Ricky Gervais), regional manager of the paper company Wernam-Hogg, has been trying to convince his staff there will be no redundancies (British for "layoffs"), though corporate executives have told him that one branch of the company is closing. He says: "I said there's not going to be redundancies and *that becomes gospel* – absolute trust." He lies about the possibility of their branch closing and gets offended when his honesty is challenged. What's more, instead of attempting to find ways of saving the company money and thereby increasing the likelihood that his branch won't be closed, Brent hires another part-time worker, Donna (Sally Bretton), as a favor to Donna's parents. Donna immediately becomes the object of all manner of sexual harassment. David pretends to play the protective uncle figure only to find out later that Donna enjoys the lewd attention and is a bit of a slut.

While he's introducing Donna around, David discovers an email depicting him as a woman in a sex act; he directs Gareth Keenan (Mackenzie Crook), a former soldier in the Territorial Army, to investigate. Gareth, as always, takes his duties much too seriously and begins police-style interrogations in the meeting room.

During the investigation, David's boss pays a visit to ask about his plans to make the branch more efficient. David lies to her about the changes he's made, about laying off an employee, and pretends he's making a call to fire another employee. Painfully, all his deceptions are uncovered, making Brent look more and more like a fool.

When it turns out that the inappropriate picture was created not by one of the office employees, but by Chris Finch (Ralph Ineson) – company representative and David's lewd friend – David suddenly changes his attitude toward the picture and evades allegations of favoritism.

Commentary: David Brent, the ultimate antihero

David Brent is one of the most amoral characters on television, alongside Basil Fawlty (John Cleese) and the gals from *Absolutely Fabulous* (is it a British thing?). There is so much deceit and pretense in "Work Experience" that many viewers are likely to double-check their own moral characters, asking themselves, "Why do I like this so much?"

How does this episode illuminate moral nihilism? If you watched the episode, it is likely that you felt a pang of embarrassment or discomfort as David Brent's lies were uncovered, one by one. If so, then you share a moral intuition with your fellow humans that there are ways you should not behave. Given this widespread attitude, we are challenged to give an explanation for it. This episode challenges us to consider which explanation best accounts for our embarrassment for David – Mackie's or Lewis's.

If Mackie, Ruse and Wilson, and other error theorists are right that there are no objective values, we have to accept the fact that Brent's apparently immoral behavior is nothing more than an aberrant result of millions of years of environmental pressures. There is nothing *really wrong* with his behavior at all; we simply *regard it* as wrong because it has been more useful to humans in the past to do so.

On the other hand, if Lewis, Kant, Mill, and other realists are right that there are some objective values, then it becomes clear that Brent is really acting immorally in being so deceitful and irresponsible in his position as manager. He should have known better and should be held responsible for his actions.

If your intuitions about this episode make it really difficult for you to believe Mackie's account of value – that is, if there is something either in the phenomenology of moral intuitions or in the role that moral claims play in our language that error theory cannot account for – then your intuitions constitute a *counterexample* to error theory. As we explained in "The Pilot Episode," a counterexample is an argument that constitutes a reason not to accept a claim or theory.

If you don't share this intuition, you probably have difficulty engaging in moral debates. It is likely that arguments about values do not carry much weight with you. If this is true of you, we don't know of any argument that could change your mind. We could offer example after example in an attempt to prime your intuition, but if you don't have it, you don't, and this might make ethics difficult for you to study. Keep in mind, however, that most ethicists throughout history do share this intuition and that the aim of this book is to introduce the major accounts of how various ethical realists explain what makes a moral claim true and how to apply those explanations to a variety of real-world moral decisions.

STUDY QUESTIONS

1. If you asked David Brent about his moral theory (and he knew enough to answer intelligently), do you think he would say he's a moral nihilist? Why or why not?
2. Do you think someone who holds an error theory about ethics can live a "moral" life? Explain your answer.
3. C. S. Lewis was a Christian and he ultimately argues that the most plausible explanation for how humans could have access to moral truths is that God shares them with us. Do you have to be religious to accept Lewis's arguments for moral realism?

4. List three other characters from television, movies, or books who seem amoral; that is, they seem to lack any concern for whether an act should or shouldn't be done. Explain why you chose each.
5. Do you find "non-natural" entities a problem for moral theories? If so, do you also find it difficult to accept scientific entities we have never experienced, such as dark matter, gluons, super strings, and gravity? If not, do you also think that paranormal activity, such as remote viewing, astrology, or Tarot cards, could have a place in the scientific community? Explain your answers.

ALTERNATIVE CASE STUDIES

1. *Absolutely Fabulous*, "Poor," series 2
    (Are Edina and Patsy moral nihilists?)
2. *Californication*, "Pilot," season 1
    (Does Hank have any moral intuitions?)
3. *The Office* (UK, "Judgment," series 1
    (Is David's lying immoral or simply irritating?)

EPISODE 2: NORMATIVITY – SOCIAL, LEGAL, AND MORAL

INTRODUCTION

In season 1 of *Arrested Development*, Lucille Bluth (Jessica Walter) interrupts a conversation with her son Michael (Jason Bateman) to complain to her fill-in housekeeper Lupe (B. W. Gonzalez) ("Charity Drive"). Lupe is cleaning the fireplace, and Lucille worries that she will track soot through the house, so she yells, "Tell me you've got an exit strategy!" Michael objects, "Mother!" but Lucille just says, "Oh, please. They didn't sneak in to this country to be your friends." Lucille's comments, here, both to

What's Good on TV?: Understanding Ethics Through Television, First Edition.
Jamie Carlin Watson and Robert Arp.
© 2011 Jamie Carlin Watson and Robert Arp. Published 2011 by Blackwell Publishing Ltd.

Lupe and to Michael about her Hispanic housekeepers, seem politically incorrect, even harsh. But are they *immoral?* Does being rude or obnoxious or prejudiced violate moral norms or do these actions merely break an implied social agreement on how people should behave?

In addition, Lucille implies that Lupe is an illegal immigrant, meaning that Lupe is breaking the law by living in the US and Lucille is breaking the law by hiring an illegal worker. Michael disapproves of the way his mother speaks to Lupe, but says nothing about the fact that she is breaking the law. Is breaking the law inherently immoral? In this Episode, we will examine "normativity" in greater detail and discuss how we might distinguish moral norms from social and legal demands.

In our "Pilot Episode," we explained that ethics is "normative." Normativity refers to claims about demands on our behavior. We also noted that there is more than one type of normativity. We distinguished "moral normativity" – if you want to do what's *right*, you *ought* to do *X* – from "practical normativity" – if you *want* to make more money at your hourly job, then you *ought* to work more hours – and "alethic (truth value) normativity" – if you want the *correct* answer to an addition problem, you *ought* to follow the rules of arithmetic. In addition to moral, practical, and alethic normativity, there are two other types of normativity: social and legal. These require special attention because they sometimes masquerade as moral normativity.

Social norms are the demands on our behavior determined by a person's culture. In the United States, for instance, it is considered "polite" to nod or say "hello" when you encounter a stranger on close terms (for example, in an elevator or on the stairs of a building, or jogging on the road); to say "thank you" when something is given to you, even if you are paying for it; to shake hands with someone when meeting for the first time or when someone extends theirs; and to hold the door for someone (male or female) when you both arrive at the entrance at the same time, or if the other person has packages or a heavy load. Social norms change over time. Sixty years ago, there were different cultural norms – such as removing your hat when you enter a building; whispering when in a church, even when it is not in service; and wives staying home to raise a family, while their husbands worked in full-time jobs. And the range of social norms varies. They may be national (take your hat off when the national anthem is played), regional (eat whatever is put before you, as in the American southeast), or familial (do not put your elbows on the table when you eat). No one from these cultures would regard you as *immoral* if you did not comply with these norms, just strange or impolite.

Legal norms are the demands on our behavior determined by a nation, state, county, or city's legislature. It is illegal to reside in the United States unless (a) you were born there, (b) you have a valid visa, or (c) you are in the process of (or have completed the process of) becoming a naturalized citizen. In the state of Florida, it is legally permissible to use deadly force if a stranger enters your home uninvited, but not if a stranger is merely on your property. In Union County, Georgia, it is illegal to sell alcohol. In New York City, it is illegal to smoke inside public buildings or restaurants. In most of these cases, no one would regard you as *immoral* for violating the legal norm. But doing so is certainly criminal.

To be sure, moral, social, and legal norms can overlap. For instance, in committing murder, in most places, you are violating moral, social, and legal norms. The difficulty comes when we try to tease these apart. Some people think of some social or legal norms as moral norms when really they are not. For instance, most of the research on marijuana shows that its negative side effects are negligible and reversible; and it even seems to have some medical benefit. Therefore, there doesn't seem to be anything essentially immoral about smoking marijuana, but it is still illegal and, in many places, continues to carry a negative social stigma. Similarly, some people think of certain acts as morally permissible when they shouldn't. For instance, it seems that some cultures (perhaps gang cultures or mafia cultures) would not regard some cases of murder as violating a social norm. Nevertheless, under most circumstances, it seems people are legally and morally prohibited from committing murder.

Why is it important to distinguish between these types or normativity? When we are studying ethics and evaluating moral claims, we want to be sure we are talking about moral reality and not social or legal reality. Since social and legal claims are often normative (e.g., "You ought to/ought not to do X."), they are easily confused with moral claims. In Episodes 4–7 we will discuss competing theories of the conditions that determine whether an act is permissible, impermissible, or obligatory, and this will enable us to clearly identify when a normative claim is moral. In the remainder of this Episode, we will discuss a classical problem about the relationship between moral, social, and legal norms.

Even though there are clear cases where social and legal norms can be distinguished from moral norms, there is, nonetheless, a difficult question about our relationship to society and the law. Do we *owe* (morally) our cultures loyalty to their customs and law? That is, even though putting your elbows on the table isn't considered immoral (in any culture, as far as we can tell), do we nonetheless have a moral obligation to keep social norms when we are in social contexts? Similarly, do we have a moral obligation to obey the law, even when particular laws have no obvious moral consequences (such as not stopping at a stop sign at 4 am, when no one else is around)?

In the case cited above from *Arrested Development*, it seems easy to think that Lucille Bluth is violating social norms. In many first world countries, we think it *rude* to speak harshly to hired help and *intolerant* to stereotype people from different cultures. In addition, it seems clear that Lucille is violating a legal norm by hiring an *illegal* immigrant. So, to restate our question in this context: Is Lucille somehow immoral for not keeping these social and legal norms?

In the next section, we will look briefly at two perspectives on this question, focusing primarily on legal norms. Whatever conclusions we draw for legal norms should apply similarly to social norms. First, John Rawls argues that there is a *prima facie* duty to obey the law, given that we tacitly consent to living in the society that has created that law. Second, philosopher John Stuart Mill argues, instead, that citizens have no more *prima facie* obligation to obey the government than the government has to protect the rights of citizens. Whatever duties citizens owe the government because of the benefits they receive are nullified if the government fails to respect citizens' rights. In our case study, we will examine the plausibility of each of these perspectives in light of *The Sopranos*.

YOU PROMISED TO PLAY BY THE RULES!

John Rawls, "Legal Obligation and the Duty of Fair Play"

We all tend to agree that promises are morally binding. Even if what is promised is morally insignificant (e.g., to pay you back 25 cents) or even immoral (e.g., to steal something for you), the promise itself is a moral contract, which, if broken, counts as an immoral act (though some would argue that there are exceptions, for example, if someone's life were in danger or when trying to catch a criminal). In addition, many of us (who have given it some thought), agree that we consent to the rules set up by our government (local, state, and federal). This is because (a) we are free to leave if we wish, (b) we pay taxes for governmental services (fire, police, military, courts), and (c) we call on those services when we need help. These establish what is known as "tacit consent." None of us has ever signed a contract with our governments, which would constitute "express consent," but if we stick around, take part in the process, and reap the benefits, we have tacitly agreed to live by the rules.

John Rawls argues that this tacit consent is like any other instance of promise-making: it establishes a moral contract to live by the rules set up by whoever you contract with. For instance, you are free to email whomsoever you please in your own time. But if you agree to work for someone (tacitly or expressly), and your boss forbids personal emails, then violating the prohibition constitutes a breach of contract on your part. You have broken your promise to play by the rules.

Rawls explains that breaking the law, in most cases, constitutes breaking a promise and is, therefore, immoral. He writes: "My thesis is that the moral obligation to obey the law is a special case of the prima facie duty of fair play" (1976: 370). His argument is motivated by two types of truths that, on the face of it, seem strange: "[F]irst, that sometimes we have an obligation to obey what we think, and think correctly, is an unjust law; and second, that sometimes we have an obligation to obey a law even in a situation where more good … would seem to result from not doing so" (1976: 371).

What justifies these apparent truths? Rawls argues that it is the duty of fair play. Given that we have consented to be governed by a certain constitutional system, we have obligated ourselves to play fairly by obeying that system's rules. He defines "the principle of fair play" as follows:

> Suppose there is a mutually beneficial and just scheme of social cooperation, and that the advantages it yields can only be obtained if everyone, or nearly everyone, cooperates. Suppose further that cooperation requires a certain sacrifice from each person, or at least involves a certain restriction of his liberty. Suppose finally that the benefits produced by cooperation are, up to a certain point, free: that is, the scheme of cooperation is unstable in the sense that if any one person knows that all (or nearly all) of the others will continue to do their part, he will still be able to gain from the scheme even if he doesn't do his part. Under these circumstances a person who has accepted the benefits of the scheme is bound by a duty of fair play to do his part and not to take advantage of the free benefit by not cooperating. (1976: 374)

In this paragraph, Rawls identifies a set of conditions that, if met by a government and its citizens, constitute a moral agreement – a contract – according to which it is wrong for the citizen not to obey. This is a version of what is known as a "social contract" theory of government. The idea is that, since people are inherently moral beings who can make decisions for themselves, the most efficient government is one that treats people as equal partners in a political contract. The government agrees (explicitly through a constitution) to protect citizens and their pursuits, and citizens agree (explicitly or implicitly) to cooperate with the government's regulations. Rawls doesn't mention this here, but social contract theory also implies that it is immoral for lawmakers to violate the contract.

To make this explanation clearer, consider an example. Imagine you live in a city with a fire department (perhaps not difficult). City (or county or state) taxes are levied to pay for the employees and equipment at the firehouse. In order to receive fire protection, enough people must pay taxes in order to cover the costs of running a firehouse. But if there is more than that number of people living in the city and paying taxes, there will be more than enough money to cover the costs. So, it is foreseeable that someone could refuse to pay taxes, yet still receive fire protection. Nevertheless, Rawls explains, since you accept the benefit, you have a moral duty to cooperate by paying taxes, even though you receive more goods by not cooperating (you keep your tax money *and* receive fire protection).

Though this seems reasonable enough, there is a problem in determining when a social or legal system meets these conditions. When is a governmental system mutually beneficial? Not when it produces the most goods for all – in some cases, a person can obtain more goods by not cooperating. Surely not when it produces fewer goods than the cost of the sacrifice. And what degree of cooperation is required? If I only make $20,000 per year, should I pay lower taxes than someone who makes $150,000 per year? If not, my sacrifice is greater, so my benefit-to-sacrifice ratio is lower than the person who makes more. If this is the case, would I face less moral blame for not cooperating? Therefore, if consent involves a contract that includes these conditions between citizens and a government, and the government does not meet the conditions, it seems citizens have no moral obligation to obey (though there may be strong practical reasons to obey, given, for example, a legal norm to pay taxes).

Many of these worries can be allayed by noting that citizens do not simply consent to receive benefits from a government; they also consent to abide by the results of a certain type of process of determining benefits, even if they don't always like the outcome. This is clear from civil court cases: instead of taking the law into their own hands, parties consent to have a judge hear their case. The plaintiff explicitly agrees (by signing a contract) to abide by the outcome of the process, even if she doesn't agree with the verdict, like the verdict, or think the verdict is morally correct. The same is true of living under a federal government with a constitution that defines the process by which benefits are distributed. Even I get less for my money than someone else, or am not completely satisfied with the benefits, or am not satisfied with the ruling of a fair court, I am morally obligated to obey the law.

But it still seems there are times when a government uses the agreed-on otherwise-fair process, but gets a morally disturbing result – a law that it seems immoral to obey. For instance, consider what are widely known as the Jim Crow laws. The Jim Crow laws were legal enforcements, passed in most southern US states after the Civil War, on racial segregation in public transportation, public schools, restrooms, and private restaurants. In this case, black Americans contributed to the system and implicitly agreed to a contract for benefits from that system, and it could even be argued that the system was (as it is the same system Americans share now), in general, fair. Nevertheless, the benefits distributed to black Americans were significantly fewer than those distributed to white Americans – and this inequality was enforced by law. Were black Americans obligated to obey these "separate but equal" laws?

Rawls considers an abstract version of such a case:

> [S]uppose there is a real question as to whether [a] tax law should be obeyed. Suppose, for example, that it is framed in such a way that it seems deliberately calculated to undermine unjustly the position of certain social or religious groups. Whether the law should be obeyed or not depends ... on such matters as (1) the justice of the constitution and the real opportunity it allows for reversal; (2) the depth of the injustice of the law enacted; (3) whether the enactment is actually a matter of calculated intent by the majority and warns of further such acts; and (4) whether the political sociology of the situation is such as to allow of hope that the law may be repealed. (1976: 377)

The point here is to identify the conditions under which a government violates the duty of fair play. If the constitution to which one assents is unjust – that is, it is organized in such a way as to enforce or encourage immoral actions – there is no moral contract. Similarly, if the "depth" of the injustice of a law is great, there is no moral contract. And if the unjust laws were intended by the majority to have these unjust implications, there is no moral contract. And finally, if there is little possibility that the unjust law will be rectified, there is no moral contract. If the government violates one of these conditions, Rawls explains, "a minority may no longer by obligated by the duty of fair play" (1976: 377–8).

The problem is that it can be argued that the Jim Crow laws did not meet any of these conditions, except, perhaps, the third. The constitution is generally considered just. The depth of injustice might not be considered that great when we consider that black Americans were not denied public transportation, education, access to water fountains, public restrooms, or restaurants. They were simply denied the ability to use the same facilities for these activities as white Americans. It was certainly possible that the laws were reversed; in fact, they were. It may be that the laws were intentionally aimed at restricting the rights of a segment of society, but Rawls would need to explain why this would render the law unjust. For instance, the law against pedophiles and child pornography is intentionally aimed at a very specific minority of the population; nevertheless, it is difficult to think that these laws are somehow unjust because of this. Therefore, one might come to the conclusion, based on Rawls's criteria, that the civil rights movement violated the duty of fair play.

There seems to be at least one further problem with Rawls's argument. For the moment, let's assume that our governments (federal, state, and local) meet his conditions for tacit consent. There is an additional problem that some of those who live under such a government *have not consented*, tacitly or expressly, to play by the rules. For instance, some people live in the US simply because it is easy to break the rules and flourish (e.g., sex traffickers, illegal immigrants, and tax evaders). These people don't pay taxes, they may not work, they do not contribute in any way; they simply freeload on the benefits. Are these people morally obligated to obey a government to which they do not even tacitly consent? Since Rawls's argument depends on the moral obligation of promise-keeping, and since these freeloaders have not made any promises, it would seem they are under no moral obligation to obey the law. Nevertheless, these freeloaders are basically stealing from taxpayers, which we generally regard as immoral.

Therefore, in order to ascribe moral blame in these situations, we cannot appeal to the fact that these people are breaking the law. We must appeal to an independent moral standard. But this suggests that legal obligation is not a subcategory of moral duty, but simply an instance of a moral contract, just like promise-making or buying a car. A car dealer is not a source of moral duty, but there is a moral duty, say, not to cheat the car dealer out of money. You have a moral duty to the car dealer, and the duty is derived from the contract. But it is recognized and evaluated as a duty on objective moral grounds.

In conclusion, it seems Rawls is right to argue that citizens, in tacitly consenting to government, have a moral obligation to obey the law. But the counterexamples we just noted indicate that there is further need to specify where this duty begins and ends. For a perspective on this, we turn to John Stuart Mill.

WHAT DOES MY NEIGHBOR HAVE TO DO WITH MY GOODNESS?

John Stuart Mill, "Of the Limits to the Authority of Society over the Individual" from *On Liberty*

Unlike Rawls, Mill does not think that society is based on a contractual agreement between a government and its citizens, though he often sounds like it. Consider the following passage:

> Though society is not founded on a contract, and though no good purpose is answered by inventing a contract in order to deduce social obligations from it, every one who receives the protection of society owes a return for the benefit, and the fact of living in a society renders it indispensable that each should be found to observe a certain line of conduct towards the rest. (2002a: 77)

Mill argues that there is a moral relationship between the government and the people, though he claims this is not established by a political contract. Nevertheless, he does treat this relationship as a *moral* contract, so we can compare the arguments in broadly "contractual" terms.

In this passage, Mill attempts to answer the questions: "What . . . is the rightful limit to the sovereignty of the individual over himself? Where does the authority of society begin? How much of human life should be assigned to individuality, and how much to society?" (2002a: 77). He begins, as we have, by distinguishing moral norms from legal norms: "The acts of an individual may be hurtful to others, or wanting in due consideration for their welfare, without going the length of violating any of their constituted rights. The offender may then be justly punished by opinion, though not by law" (2002a: 78).

He then argues that society has no right to infringe upon a person's action that "affects the interests of no persons besides himself, or needs not affect them unless they like . . . . In all such cases there should be perfect freedom, legal and social, to do the action and stand the consequences" (2002a: 78). Notice that Mill identifies the relevant freedoms as "legal and social." There may be immoral actions that a person should not commit, but most of these are not the province of law – for instance, it would be grossly impractical to make lying to your mother, or breaking a promise to your best friend, or refusing to recycle aluminum cans illegal, even if there are moral reasons to refrain from them.

Mill gives three reasons for this conclusion. First, he argues that society is not the best judge of what is right for a person. "[The citizen] is the person most interested in his own well-being: the interest which any other person, except in cases of strong personal attachment, can have in it, is trifling, compared with that which he himself has; the interest which society has in him individually ... is fractional, and altogether indirect" (2002a: 79). Society can only judge what is best for a person based on what is good for a person in general, and cannot evaluate a particular person's situation at a time. There is no one better to form a moral judgment in that situation than the person best acquainted with it.

Second, he argues that society has all of a person's childhood to train them morally and rationally, so additional legal coercion should not be required:

> If society lets any considerable number of its members grow up mere children, incapable of being acted on by rational consideration of distant motives, society has itself to blame for the consequences. ... [L]et not society pretend that it needs, besides all this, the power to issue commands and enforce obedience in the personal concerns of individuals. (2002a: 85)

Though society is not always successful, it is possible for it to produce a generation slightly better than itself. If it fails, it should bear the consequences of its actions, and not impose additional restrictions on individuals because of its failures.

Third, Mill says that the strongest of all of arguments for his conclusion is that, when government does interfere with "purely personal conduct," "the odds are that it interferes wrongly, and in the wrong place" (2002a: 86). As examples, he cites the disagreement between Christians and "Mahomedans" (Muslims) over the permissibility of eating pork, the disagreement between Catholics and non-Catholics over styles of worship, and the Puritan prohibitions on "music, dancing, public games, or other assemblages for purposes of diversion" (2002a: 90). If individuals, who are chiefly concerned with their own welfare, cannot easily discern what is in their best interests, government, which is at least at one remove from individual welfare, will not be able to clearly discern it.

In summary, Mill argues that any government infringement on activities beyond protection and regulation of fair play is arbitrary and constitutes a greater evil than any a person can enact on his own. Laws that infringe on personal freedom ascribe "to all mankind a vested interest in each other's moral, intellectual, and even physical perfection" and, Mill concludes, "[s]o monstrous a principle is far more dangerous than any single interference with liberty; [because] there is no violation of liberty which it would not justify" (2002a: 93).

We can draw parallels between Mill's and Rawls's arguments. Both argue that there are cases where a citizen (morally) owes obedience to her government, and both argue that there are cases where a citizen no longer owes her allegiance to that government. However, Mill argues that there are many more cases where an individual is justified in disobedience than Rawls would allow. Rawls argues that, regardless of the infringements on liberties, as long as the overall system is fair, and citizens consent to that system, citizens are obligated to obey. Mill argues that there can be no moral contract between citizens and a government that infringes individual liberties. He says this explicitly in chapter 5 of *On Liberty*: "[T]he individual is not accountable to society for his actions, in so far as these concern the interests of no person but himself" (2002a: 97). So, as soon as a government oversteps its bounds, a citizen is free from moral (though not legal) obligation.

In conclusion, there are times (perhaps many) when a law (even when made and carried out under the proper conditions) is immoral. In such cases, Mill argues that the government has overstepped its bounds and we are not morally accountable to society for our reactions. Though Rawls identifies a set of criteria that the government must violate before a citizen may justly rebel, and though these conditions may be sufficient for legally permissible rebellion, it is not clear that they are sufficient conditions for moral rebellion. Many of the episodes of the TV series *Law & Order* support these conclusions, in that a character known by the audience to be guilty of murder is found not guilty by the jury, but is then killed in the last minute of the episode. We, the audience, tend to regard the killing as the "right" outcome, even though (a) the justice system got it wrong, and (b) we accept that the person who kills the defendant should (legally, though perhaps not morally) go to jail.

CASE STUDY: *The Sopranos*, "College," season 1

AVAILABILITY: **NetFlix, iTunes**

Tony Soprano (James Gandolfini) and his daughter Meadow (Jamie-Lynn Sigler) are in Maine, where Meadow is interviewing at various colleges. Meadow has been suspicious of her father's involvement with organized crime and finally works up the courage to ask him about it. After a few not-so-careful dodges, Tony basically admits that some of the family income comes from "illegal gambling and whatnot" – a brief glimmer of honesty in the gangster's morally ambiguous life of half-truths and bald-face lies.

This moment doesn't last, however, because Tony sees a former gangster turned rat (police informant), who is now in the witness protection program. This begins a string of pretense and lies to Meadow, so he can make time to investigate and eliminate the snitch. A few years back, Freddy Peters (Tony Ray Rossi) turned over evidence against friends of Tony's organization, both of whom were killed in prison. In Tony's eyes, this betrayal warrants a death sentence, which he is able to carry out before he and Meadow leave Maine.

Meanwhile, Carmella Soprano (Edie Falco) is at home sick when her priest, Father Phil (Paul Schulze), arrives in the evening, during a rain storm, knowing that Tony is out of town, and under the pretense of getting some of Carmella's ziti. During the preparation of the meal, Tony's psychiatrist calls to cancel an appointment, and Carmella is surprised to discover that the doctor is a woman – something Tony failed to mention. Carmella and Father Phil eat and watch a movie together until Carmella breaks down under the guilt of being married to a gangster. Father Phil suggests confession and communion, and the intimacy of the ritual leads almost to infidelity, when suddenly Father Phil gets sick. He is forced to spend the night, though nothing sexual happens. When Tony gets home, Carmella confesses that the priest innocently stayed the night, just in case he hears anything from the neighbors about the car in the driveway. Tony is upset until Carmella asks why he didn't mention that his therapist is a woman.

Commentary: What's immoral *about Tony Soprano*?

Take a few minutes and try to list the norms at play in this episode. It seems clear that most instances of lying and promise-breaking in the episode (by Tony, Meadow, and Carmella) are unjustified. There are no greater moral goods (saving lives, preventing harm, etc.) that would outweigh a *prima facie* obligation to not lie. Though most of the lies are harmless, they don't produce a great deal of happiness, either. Therefore, they are most likely immoral.

What about Tony's business? He admits that some (though it is probably most) of his income is obtained illegally. Is this essentially immoral? Rawls and Mill would probably say yes. Tony benefits greatly from his society (at least national defense, police and fire protection in his neighborhood, public roads, and public education), and, in choosing to remain in the country and participating in these benefits, he is implicitly contracting with the government to play by the rules. In addition, the government is not violating any moral obligations to Tony or his family. Therefore, in not contributing (by not obeying the law, not paying taxes), Tony is violating his moral obligation to play fairly.

But what about Tony's killing Freddy? Freddy broke a promise not to snitch, and as a result of breaking this promise, two people died. It is clearly illegal for Tony to take the law into his own hands, and it is illegal to carry out a death sentence that has not been passed down by a jury selected to determine whether that punishment is warranted. Similarly, given Tony's mafia culture, it may be socially permissible to kill Freddy. But is it immoral?

In this case, the legal system worked exactly as it claims to do: Freddy is a bad guy, but he gets a little leniency for turning in additional criminals. If Rawls and Mill are right that Tony is immoral for ignoring the law in business, they are probably right that Tony is immoral to ignore the law in Freddy's case.

But let's imagine we can remove the legal considerations. Imagine Tony and Freddy and the two guys were on an otherwise uninhabited island. Freddy does something that saves his own life, but ends up causing the deaths of the other two guys. Would it be immoral, in this case, for Tony to execute Freddy? To adequately answer this question, we would need to know more about when it is morally permissible to execute anyone (see Episode 12). But it should be clear that there is now no legal prohibition against it – there is no law at all on the island. Also, the social norms of Tony's mafia culture remain the same, and would probably permit the execution. Even though we do not yet have the tools to answer this question, it is important to see that, even without the social and legal constraints, there remains the moral question of the permissibility of Tony's actions.

Now consider Tony's wife, Carmella. Does she violate any norms by allowing Father Phil to sleep over while her husband is away? Clearly there are several social norms violated, including the perception of Carmella's neighbors, her fellow parishioners, and the general view of the Catholic Church that such actions are inappropriate. But nothing sexual happened between them. So, technically, Father Phil didn't violate his vow of chastity and Carmella didn't violate her promise of marital faithfulness. And none of these actions has legal implications. Therefore, it would seem that Carmella and Father Phil have done nothing immoral or illegal.

STUDY QUESTIONS

1. List three *social* norms that your culture imposes on your behavior. List three *legal* norms you are forced to follow every day. What distinguishes social norms from legal norms?
2. Your boss tells you that you must wear a tie to work and that you will be fired if you refuse. Would not wearing a tie violate a social or moral norm? Explain.
3. Is Lucille Bluth immoral for hiring illegal immigrants? Is Lupe acting immorally by working illegally? Explain.
4. Given the arguments presented in this Episode, do you find the civil rights movement to abolish Jim Crow laws morally permissible?
5. Keeping in mind that Tony Soprano has a mistress on the side, if Carmella and Father Phil had sex, would Carmella have violated any moral norms?

ALTERNATIVE CASE STUDIES

1. *The Sopranos*, "Down Neck," season 1
   (Is it immoral of A.J. to drink the communion wine, or simply anti-social? Is he being immoral or simply illegal when he goes to school drunk?)
2. *Law & Order*, "Renunciation," season 2
   (Which of the schoolteacher's misdeeds violate moral norms and which violate social norms?)
3. *Family Guy*, "PTV," season 4
   (Does the FCC object to Peter's cable show on moral or on social grounds?)

EPISODE 3: GOD AND ETHICS

EPISODE OUTLINE

Introduction
What has Athens to do with Jerusalem?
 Plato, *Euthyphro*
Does God make the law or does he just let us in on it?
 C. S. Lewis, from *The Problem of Pain*
Case study: *Law & Order*, "God Bless the Child," season 2
Study questions
Alternative case studies

INTRODUCTION

In season 6 of *Scrubs*, Dr Kim Briggs (Elizabeth Banks) is pregnant with J.D.'s (Zach Braff) baby, and since their relationship is very young and they're afraid a baby will ruin their lives, they consider having an abortion. When the overtly religious nurse Laverne (Aloma Wright) overhears their conversation, she asks, disapprovingly, "Did somebody just say, 'abortion'?" Kim responds by saying it is none of her business, or Jesus's. Laverne says that Jesus might beg to differ and produces a statue of Jesus, which J.D. fantasizes coming to life, saying, "She's right, J.D. Every life is precious."

What's Good on TV?: Understanding Ethics Through Television, First Edition.
Jamie Carlin Watson and Robert Arp.
© 2011 Jamie Carlin Watson and Robert Arp. Published 2011 by Blackwell Publishing Ltd.

This scene raises an important question for ethical reasoning, namely: What role does the concept of God play in ethics? There are two ways to approach this question. On one hand, we might ask: (1) "Do moral claims make sense apart from some conception of a Divine Lawmaker?" On the other, we might ask: (2) "Assuming God exists (and is perfectly morally good), does God *make* moral laws or does he just follow them perfectly and give us the ability to know and follow them?"

Question (1) is about the meaning of a moral claim. Consider the moral claim, "It is always wrong to murder." If there is no morally perfect being to accurately judge people's behavior according to this claim, could it really be very significant? If there is no Divine Lawmaker, where would the moral *obligation* not to murder come from? Murder may be impractical, or too costly, but would it be *immoral*? This question also raises two more: question (1a): can we know what is right and wrong without acknowledging or being aware of God? And question (1b): even if moral claims make sense apart from God, does it matter whether we are ethical if there is no God?

Question (2) is about the relationship between God, if such a being exists, and morality. The philosopher Plato posed an interesting dilemma based on this question about the Greek gods' relationship to morality. If the gods make moral laws, couldn't they have made different laws from the ones they did make? For instance, couldn't they have made murder an obligation instead of prohibiting it? This would be strange, since then morality would be a matter of preference, and everyone knows the gods can be capricious. On the other hand, if the gods simply follow the same moral law that humans are held to believe in, then the gods cannot be "supreme" beings; they are under the same moral constraints as humans. This seems to diminish their worthiness to be worshipped.

In this introduction, we'll suggest some answers to these four questions. Then, in the following sections, you can evaluate our responses in light of some examples from television.

Question (1): Do moral claims make sense apart from some conception of a Divine Lawmaker?

By "do they make sense?," we mean, "are they meaningful?" or "can we even understand what a moral claim is attempting to communicate in the absence of God?" For a normative claim to make sense to someone, she must be able to understand that she is being directed to perform (or refrain from performing) some action on some moral authority, and she must understand what action she is being asked to perform (or refrain from performing). We find many examples of understanding actions and "being directed to perform an action" outside the context of religious language – for instance, at our jobs, in our families, and in our governments. So, the question really seems to concern the authority on which the action is being directed. Bosses, parents, and politicians are not *essentially* sources of moral authority – they may direct you to do immoral things, or to keep social or legal obligations without noting their moral implications. They may not even be *contingent* sources of moral authority – they do what seems right to them, but these actions are evaluated in terms of a standard that is independent of their motives.

So, where might moral authority come from? The authority of the normative claims of bosses, parents, and government derives from those who are willing to enforce them or from the practical consequences of not obeying them. The authority of natural laws (gravity, inertia, etc.) seems to derive from the laws themselves; they are essentially directive. Moral authority doesn't seem analogous to social or political authority; some actions seem wrong even if there is no one to praise or blame you for performing them. So, moral authority is derived *either* from practicality – it would be bad for you to do X, or it would be good for you to do X – *or* from something essentially moral.

If it derives from practicality, then understanding moral claims does not entail the existence of a lawgiver or require that someone accept the existence of a lawgiver. We will evaluate the plausibility of this view in Episode 4, but the fact that it is a *possible* source of moral authority shows that we can understand moral authority independently of God.

The same seems true if moral authority derives from something essentially moral. This essentially moral thing might be God, but it might not; it might be a moral law itself that exists abstractly, like a natural law. And even if the essentially moral thing is God, we could talk about this aspect of God without knowing anything else about him, just as we could study the concept of "omniscience" without accepting that an omniscient being exists – the concept makes sense even if we do not believe that any particular God exists. Therefore, we conclude that moral claims do make sense apart from some conception of God. There is a further question, however, of whether there is a *plausible moral theory* that does not depend on some conception of God.

Question (1a): Can we know what is right and wrong without acknowledging or being aware of God?

Scoffing at philosophers, the ancient Christian theologian Tertullian once asked, rhetorically: "What has Athens to do with Jerusalem?" Athens represents Greek philosophy and Jerusalem represents Judeo-Christian religious beliefs. The implication is supposed to be: They have *nothing* to do with one another! Tertullian believed that *reason* is a poor substitute for *faith* and that any genuine knowledge of universal truths must first be grounded in the knowledge of God. Therefore, if moral truths are to hold everywhere and always, then, in order to know moral truths, we must first know God.

However, most religious thinkers concerned with ethics have answered question (1) negatively: we do *not* need to know God to know what is right or wrong. The Gospel of Matthew records Jesus saying: "If you then, being evil, know how to give good gifts to your children, how much more will your Father in heaven give what is good to those who ask Him!" (NRSV). The implication is that even people who do not know God have the ability to distinguish right from wrong. This also seems evident in our daily lives. There are plenty of atheists who are kind and generous, and nice people to be around, even though they claim that God does not exist. It would be difficult to call these people immoral.

Question (1b): Even if moral claims make sense apart from God, does it matter whether we are ethical if there is no God?

If there is no God, does it matter whether we are ethical? It seems plausible that it might. But this is a question about motive, not the nature of morality. If utilitarianism is the most plausible moral theory, then being ethical increases overall happiness. This is independent of any considerations about God's existence. In order to live the happiest life I can, there are certain moral rules I must follow. Therefore, I might have reasons to be moral even if God doesn't exist. Similarly, if virtue ethics is the most plausible ethical theory and living a life of virtue contributes to an overall good life, then I have reasons to be moral independently of God's existence. Alternatively, if God exists and will punish me if I am immoral, then I have reasons for being moral (according to the most plausible ethical theory) independently of my own happiness or good life. Nevertheless, these are questions about moral motivation; the nature of right and wrong and our ability to do either seem independent of the existence of God.

It seems, then, that moral claims make sense independently of a conception of a Divine Lawgiver. This means that we can talk and reason about morality without first settling the issue of whether God exists. Of course, it might turn out that God does exist and has issued some behavioral mandates it would be immoral to ignore. For instance, given reason alone, homosexuality and sex outside of marriage may be perfectly morally permissible. But if God exists, is perfectly knowledgeable and good, and reveals to us that some relationships are immoral, then, given our new awareness of this moral demand, we are under a moral obligation to act in accordance with it.

It is possible, of course, that there are actions we are morally prohibited from performing even though, if we had no conception of God or divine revelation, we would not be aware of these norms. For instance, if God exists and tells us he created us for certain relationships and not for others, then we may be under an obligation to obey. If so, would this be a *moral* obligation, or would it be better understood as a legal norm? If God has certain *rights* over us in virtue of our being *his* creatures (as with a parent to a child), then it would seem we would have certain moral obligations to this being, including obedience. For these questions, it would be important to settle at least the plausibility of this sort of God and these sorts of commands in order to develop a comprehensive ethic. But this still doesn't imply that we need a particular conception of God to talk meaningfully about ethics. It simply means that to know some moral obligations we may need some additional evidence (e.g., divine revelation).

Question (2): Assuming God exists (and is perfectly morally good), does God make moral laws or does he just adhere to them perfectly and give us the ability to know and adhere to them?

But now consider our second question. This question is an old one and was entertained by Plato in his dialogue *Euthyphro*. Are the gods good because they are gods, so that whatever acts they prefer are good in virtue of their preferring them? Or are the gods good because they act in accordance with what is good? If the former is true, and if the gods were suddenly to prefer actions like rape and murder, these acts would be, by default, moral and good. If the latter, then we need not appeal to the gods as authorities on what is right and wrong; they are simply irrelevant to morality. This argument is known as the "Euthyphro Dilemma."

WHAT HAS ATHENS TO DO WITH JERUSALEM?

Plato, *Euthyphro*

A "dilemma" is simply an argument with a disjunction as a premise ("p or q"). The word "di-lemma" just means "two lemmas" or "two established assumptions." But often, dilemma is used to mean a disjunctive claim or argument where both the disjuncts are unfavorable. Being forced to choose between "a rock or a hard place," or "heads I win or tails you lose," would constitute dilemmas.

A popular example of a dilemma with this negative connotation is the "prisoner's dilemma." Imagine you have been arrested along with someone else and placed in separate rooms. You learn from your lawyer that if you rat on your partner, you'll go free, but your partner will get two years in prison and if your partner rats on you, he will go free, whereas you will get eight years. If each of you rats on the other, both of you will get four years. But if you both remain silent, you'll each only serve two years. The dilemma is whether to rat on your partner, hoping he doesn't do the same, and be released, or sit silently, hoping your partner also remains quiet, so that you both only get two years. Option 1 is unfavorable, because you risk getting four years in prison, even though you might go free, and option 2 is unfavorable because you risk getting eight years in prison; plus, you're guaranteed to get two.

In *Euthyphro*, Socrates poses a dilemma for the relationship between the Greek gods and morality. This argument is easily reformulated to raise doubts about the coherence of the Western monotheistic conception of God, so it is important for us to consider it here. Socrates is waiting to be tried for crimes against the state when he meets Euthyphro on his way to prosecute his father for murdering a former employee. Under most circumstances, in Greek culture, it is considered immoral to turn in a family member for a crime, especially for a crime against a stranger. Euthyphro, however, argues that the gods will favor him because he is righting an injustice and that this will outweigh any immorality associated with bringing his father to trial. Euthyphro's confidence that he is acting morally in prosecuting his father for murder leads Socrates to ask Euthyphro to teach him the nature of right and wrong, so that he may be better able to defend himself at his own trial.

After Euthyphro has dodged the question a few times, Socrates finally persuades him to commit to an account of right and wrong. Euthyphro says, "Then what is dear to the gods is holy, and what is not dear to them is unholy" (6e–7a). In response, Socrates notes that the gods often quarrel with one another about which actions are permissible and which are impermissible, so that there is a discrepancy even among the gods as to what is holy and what is unholy. Socrates suggests that maybe Euthyphro means to say: what is dear to *all* the gods is holy and what *all* the gods hate is unholy. Euthyphro accepts this definition, but Socrates challenges this one, as well.

Socrates argues that if we accept this definition, we must still answer a further question: "Is the holy loved by the gods because it is holy? Or is it holy because it is loved by the gods?" Euthyphro attempts to argue that "being holy" and "being loved by all the gods" mean the same thing. But Socrates responds as follows:

> But if in fact what is dear to the gods and the holy were the same, my friend, then, if the holy were loved because it is holy, what is dear to the gods would be loved because it is dear to the gods; but if what is dear to the gods were dear to the gods because the gods love it, the holy would be holy because it is loved. But as it is, you see, the opposite is true, and the two are completely different. For the one [what is dear to the gods] is of the sort to be loved *because* it is loved; the other [the holy], because it is of the sort to be loved, *therefore* is loved. (10e–11a)

Socrates is attempting to explain that Euthyphro's position is incoherent because of how language demands that we treat the terms "holy" and "what is dear to the gods." If the gods love something because it is loved, then there remains a question of whether they *should* love that thing. Basically, they like what they like. If they happen to like the holy, good for them. But this has nothing to do with what is actually holy – that is, with the nature of morality. On the other hand, if what the gods love is loved because it is holy (it is the sort of thing that *should* be loved), then there must be some independent way of determining what is holy. Either way, what is "holy" (read: morally good) is something distinct from what the gods love. The point is to show that morality must be understood independently of the gods.

Divine Command Theory

This rather abstract argument has been reformulated as an objection to the traditional Western monotheistic concept of God, namely, a single being that is all-powerful, all-knowing, and all-good. According to this picture, God is sovereign over all of reality, so that reality is the way it is because God created it that way – including the truths of math, logic, and morality. Interpreted a certain way, this view implies that acts are right or wrong because God has decreed them so. This view is known as Divine Command Theory. The idea is that, since God is the ultimate source of everything, including morality, to separate moral demands from the will of God (to claim that they exist independently of God) would detract from his power and perfection. After all, if God is subject to an authority distinct from himself, then he is not sovereign over all of reality; he is not all-powerful.

A problem with Divine Command Theory is that it seems to render morality subject to the arbitrary will of God. There is no right or wrong independent of God's will, so if God had, for whatever reason, decided that rape is permissible (or obligatory) instead of prohibited, then, according to Divine Command Theory, rape would be morally permissible (or obligatory). James Rachels explains that, according to this view, "Apart from the divine command, truth telling [or rape or torturing children] is neither good nor bad. It is God's command that makes truthfulness right [and rape and child torture wrong]" (2003: 51).

This implication seems unacceptable to many philosophers, and some have attempted to modify the Divine Command Theory in order to avoid it. Christian philosopher Arthur Holmes asks" "Do God's commands really make morality that arbitrary? Could God as well have commanded us to torture innocent children with relentless cruelty? Plainly not" (1984: 76–7). But why not? What would prevent it? Holmes continues: "[F]or we are not speaking of either a sadistic or an amoral deity, but of a God who is just and loving, both Creator and Redeemer, who by virtue of his own character would not do such a thing" (1984: 77). On the classical version of the Divine Command Theory, nothing would prevent God from making acts we now consider moral, immoral. But what about the following alternative?

Modified Divine Command Theory

Those, like Holmes, who find this implication of Divine Command Theory unacceptable, but who are still sympathetic to the classical picture of God, argue that the Euthyphro Dilemma uncharitably emphasizes the *will* of God over his *nature*. They argue, instead, that while morality depends on the commands of God, those commands are not arbitrary or whimsical; God's commands are constrained by his morally perfect and unchanging nature. This view is known as Modified Divine Command Theory. Norman Geisler summarizes the view by saying: "Christian ethics is based on God's will, but God never wills anything contrary to his unchanging moral character" (1989: 22).

Robert Adams elaborates, explaining:

> The modified divine command theorist agrees that it is logically possible that God should command cruelty for its own sake; but he holds that it is unthinkable that God should do so. To have faith in God is not just to believe that He exists, but also to trust in His love for mankind. The believer's concepts of ethical wrongness and permittedness are developed within the framework on his (or the religious community's) religious life, and therefore within the assumption that God loves us. (1996: 529)

Adams argues that Modified Divine Command Theory is the view that what is right and wrong depends not simply on God's commands, but also on those characteristics of God that motivate his actions in the first place. Since the traditional Judeo-Christian view takes God's love for humanity as fundamental to his nature, this love constrains the sort of commands God can reasonably will.

Unfortunately, Modified Divine Command Theory faces a problem at least as worrisome as that of classical Divine Command Theory. The problem with the classical theory is that it made morality arbitrary, subject to the whim of an all-powerful being. The problem with the modified theory is that it makes God's nature arbitrary. According to the modified view, God wills what is good because his nature is essentially good. But this means that there is no reason, beyond brute necessity, that God's nature is what it is. If, instead, his necessary nature had included the permissibility of rape or child torture, then his will would be bound to act in accord with that nature. God couldn't choose to act against his necessary nature, so whatever his necessary nature happens to be entails how he will act.

So, why is rape impermissible rather than permissible? Because it is immoral? No; according to Modified Divine Command Theory, it is because God's necessary nature happens to dictate that it is impermissible. If Adams is correct, God's nature happens to include a deep love for humans. This love may or may not include animals. If it does not, then torturing puppies may be morally permissible. It all depends on how God's essential nature is organized.

If this criticism is right, all talk of "God's *goodness*" becomes incoherent. This is because there is now no standard against which to evaluate the morality of his actions except his nature, and his nature is just whatever it happens to be – necessarily. So, the most we could ever say about God's actions is that they are either consistent with his nature or inconsistent with it (given that we knew his nature) – we could not say they are good or bad. Christian literary critic and lay philosopher C. S. Lewis explains this criticism in more detail in chapters 3 and 6 of his book, *The Problem of Pain*.

DOES GOD MAKE THE LAW OR DOES HE JUST LET US IN ON IT?

C. S. Lewis, from *The Problem of Pain*

Lewis's short book is aimed at answering the philosophical problem of evil posed as an argument against the existence of God. Lewis explains it this way:

"If God were good, He would wish to make His creatures perfectly happy, and if God were almighty He would be able to do what he wished. But the creatures are not happy. Therefore God lacks either goodness, or power, or both." This is the problem of pain, in its simplest form. (2001: 16)

But in responding to this perennial argument, Lewis addresses many of the fundamental assumptions humans make about what the world *should* be like and how we *should* be treated. And though he doesn't mention them by name (the names came a bit later), he addresses the classical and the Modified Divine Command Theories and the Euthyphro Dilemma.

In considering the classical Divine Command Theory, Lewis writes:

It has sometimes been asked whether God commands certain things because they are right, or whether certain things are right because God commands them. ... I emphatically embrace the first alternative. The second might lead to the abominable conclusion (reached, I think, by [William] Paley) that charity is good only because God arbitrarily commanded it – that He might equally well have commanded us to hate Him and one another and that hatred would then have been right. (2001: 99)

Lewis rejects the classical theory on the grounds we have mentioned – it makes morality arbitrary.

What about the Modified Divine Command Theory? Lewis is not sympathetic with this view, either. The motivation for the Modified Divine Command Theory is to preserve the absolute sovereignty over all things, including morality. But if God's essential nature determines what is right and wrong, then any conception of right and wrong we have apart from an understanding of God's nature would be nonsense.

[I]f God's moral judgment differs from ours so that our "black" may be His "white," we can mean nothing by calling Him good; for to say "God is good," while asserting that His goodness is wholly other than ours, is really only to say "God is we know not what." And an utterly unknown quality in God cannot give us moral grounds for loving or obeying Him. If He is not (in our sense) "good" we shall obey, if at all, only through fear – and should be equally ready to obey an omnipotent Fiend. (2001: 28–9)

Since we have a conception of morality independently of God, and God's nature may differ from ours, then it is unclear how we could make any accurate moral judgments. Even if we could understand the nature of God, since God's judgment differs so widely from ours, it is not clear that we would regard his judgment as "good." We could evaluate it as consistent or inconsistent with our own conception of good and bad, but this would be the extent of our moral language about God. Lewis concludes that, if goodness depends on God's essential nature, which may or may not be consistent with ours, we could never call God "good" in any meaningful sense.

In his defense of Modified Divine Command Theory, Robert Adams admits that God's nature is not subject to any independent standard of "goodness," but denies that this implies that the claim "God is 'good'" is meaningless. Adams confesses:

> The modified divine command theorist must deny that in calling God "good" one presupposes a standard of moral rightness and wrongness superior to the will of God, by reference to which it is determined whether God's character is virtuous or not. And I think he can consistently deny that. He can say that morally virtuous and vicious qualities of character are those which agree and conflict, respectively, with God's commands, and that it is their agreement or disagreement with God's commands that makes them virtuous or vicious. (1996: 535)

But Adams denies that calling God "good" loses all meaning. He argues that when humans call someone "good" they are often expressing a favorable emotion toward that person, or that the person is (in their perception) kind to them, or that the person exhibits qualities that humans generally consider virtuous. Humans may meaningfully call God "good" in all these senses.

Of course, the problem remains that these senses of "good" aren't *moral* senses. This puts Adams, a Christian, in a precarious place with respect to the traditional Christian doctrine of God, which says that God is all-powerful, all-knowing, and all-good. Whereas giving up the claim that what is moral depends on God's will seems to commit the theist to denying that God is all-powerful, Adams's Modified Divine Command Theory seems to commit the theist to interpreting the claim that God is all-good in non-moral terms. This may be equally unacceptable.

But what does Lewis argue? There must be some reason outside God's mere will that determines his commands, but is this his essential nature? Lewis says, no: "God's will is determined by His wisdom which always perceives, and His goodness which always embraces, the intrinsically good" (2001: 99). In wording it this way, Lewis is saying that "intrinsic goodness" is something distinct from the attributes of God, something to which we can compare the attributes of God.

There is some confusion here when Lewis writes that God's will is also determined by his "goodness." The source of God's goodness is the question we are asking, so to say his "good will" is determined by his "goodness" that embraces "intrinsic goodness" is a bit confusing. A plausible interpretation is that, by "His goodness," Lewis means God's "character." We might reword Lewis's sentence as follows: God's character is good because he embraces what wisdom reveals, namely, intrinsic goodness.

But Lewis was a Christian, so what does separating "goodness" from the essential nature of God do to his conception of God? According to the Euthyphro Dilemma, in accepting this horn of the dilemma, the monotheist seems committed to denying that God is all-powerful. Lewis doesn't say, but it may help to point out that, along with many other philosophers who believe in God, he believes that there are logical limits to God's power. God cannot make contradictions true – for instance, he cannot make $2 + 2$ anything other than 4, he cannot build round squares or create married bachelors, or make rocks too heavy for him to lift, or cease to exist. These philosophers take it as a virtue that God cannot do absurd things. In fact, if God could make contradictions true, we could validly derive both the existence and non-existence of God – which would clearly do more damage to the traditional conception of God than admitting that there are logical limits on his power. Therefore, if moral truths are necessary truths, like logical and mathematical truths, then the fact that God is subject to them is a virtue of his nature, and not a reason for doubt.

Turning back to our episode of *Scrubs*, it might seem, at first, that Kim is right that her decision about abortion is none of Jesus's business. First, the moral question of whether abortion is permissible is intelligible without a conception of a Divine Lawgiver. Second, even if abortion is impermissible, it is not likely that it is *because* some god says so. And third, if God does exist and reveals moral truths, then Kim already has access to all the moral evidence she needs to make her decision. Of course, humans are often poor reasoners, so if a perfectly moral God does exist and has spoken decisively on the issue, Kim would be wise to regard the revelation as relevant to her decision. *Scrubs* does a clever job of highlighting this possibility by having the Jesus figurine come to life in J.D.'s fantasy. However, even in the fantasy, Kim still thinks Jesus's opinion is irrelevant. God's commands may be irrelevant to the *truth* of a moral claim. But if Kim accepts that God exists, is morally perfect, and has clearly revealed moral truths, then she is wrong that the Jesus figurine's condemnation is irrelevant to her *decision*.

CASE STUDY: *Law & Order*, "God Bless the Child," season 2

AVAILABILITY: **NetFlix, iTunes**

How far do parents' rights extend? Can a parent allow a child to die because of their political or religious beliefs? In this episode of *Law & Order*, these questions are raised when a devoutly religious family is suspected of neglect after their housekeeper reports that their child is sick and the family refuses to permit medical treatment. When the child dies, the parents (the Driscolls) claim that their religious beliefs forbid them from using modern medicine, arguing that this exhibits a lack of faith in a god who has the power to heal.

In the state of New York at the time, according to Assistant District Attorney (ADA) Paul Robinette (Richard Brooks), the law allows "a single affirmative defense to endangering the welfare of a child: spiritual healing by an organized religion." In this case, the Church of All Saints directs its members to rely on faith for healing, and to reject modern medicine. Throughout the episode, Detectives Logan (Chris Noth) and Ceretta (Paul Sorvino) wrestle with the seeming conflict between religion and morality, while Executive ADA Ben Stone (Michael Moriarty) tries to find legal grounds to convict the parents of negligent homicide.

When police discover evidence that the parents doubted their own convictions – including testimony to an argument over how to treat the child and a 911 tape – Stone is able to convince a jury that they acted negligently.

Commentary: Could God command something inconsistent with morality?

Law & Order is a show about the interaction between the police and city prosecutors, and addresses a number of controversial social issues of moral and legal interest. But, as we saw in Episode 2, legality often overlaps with morality. Lying is immoral but legal, driving on the left side of the road is illegal but not immoral. Murder is both immoral and illegal. In this example, that line is blurred. In the state of New York (according to the show), there is a provision in the law exculpating parents of children who die from practices associated with "spiritual healing." However, there is also a moral and legal prohibition against a parent who neglects certain aspects of a child's care.

There are a number of difficult philosophical problems in this episode of *Law & Order*, not least of which includes questions about the extent to which the tenets of a religion should influence a legal decision and questions about how to determine the extent to which courts can legitimately pronounce moral judgments on the tenets of a religion. For our purposes, the most relevant question is: could the proponents of this set of religious beliefs (particularly, the Driscolls) be right? That is, could God command something that is morally atrocious to rational, moral people?

The housekeeper, Cora Amado (Socorro Santiago), seems to take the position that morality and religion cannot conflict, and if there is any apparent conflict, the tie goes to morality. She says, "My kids? They get sick? I pray for their souls. Their bodies? I call a doctor." Detective Logan agrees. In one scene, Logan and Ceretta are interviewing the church's pastor. The pastor says, "The loss of their daughter was terrible. But it is God's will." Logan responds by saying, "Most of us don't mind a little help from antibiotics." To which the pastor replies, "But some of us do." In a later scene, when they are interviewing the Driscolls, Mr Driscoll (Byron Jennings) says, "The rules are God's, not ours. . . . It's faith. That's what religion is." Logan immediately criticizes: "You call that religion? Neglecting a dying child? Now, you see, I call that irresponsible."

Ceretta, on the other hand, is more sympathetic to the Driscolls' perspective. When Logan asks a doctor about the state of mind of a parent who refuses treatment, the doctor says they "would have to be stupid, blind, or negligent." But Ceretta pipes in, "or very religious." Similarly, when Logan calls the Church of All Saints "wackos," Ceretta defends their right to their beliefs. "A lot of non-Catholics believe its wacko for priests not to marry. A lot of non-fundamentalists believe its wacko to take the Bible literally. To the Driscolls, losing this kid's soul is worse than losing this kid's life." However, Ceretta is clear about the law: "And if they had any doubts about prayer working and we can prove it, I'll be the first guy out with my cuffs."

But this is a lot of rhetoric and very little substance. And a person's right to his or her beliefs is irrelevant to whether their actions infringe on another's rights. So, are there any clear moral reasons for rejecting the Driscolls' defense? In court, ADA Stone echoes C. S. Lewis's objection to the classical version of Divine Command Theory. When the Driscolls' pastor says the government should protect freedom of religion, Stone asks:

"So that if a church doctrine called for beating children, or allowing them to handle poisonous snakes? What if a religious ritual called for leaving children naked in the snow?" He doesn't allow the minister to answer, but it's clear he's hoping that the moral intuitions of the person on the stand, and especially of the jury, will scream a resounding, "No, that's not right!"

Along with Lewis, Stone is effectively adopting the second horn of the Euthyphro Dilemma: if God exists and is good, he is good because he acts according to an objective moral standard. Where does this leave the classical Western theist (Jew, Christian, Muslim), who argues that God is essentially perfect in every aspect and the ground of all being? It will force them to think very hard about how to reconcile their picture of God with this rationally constrained picture of morality.

On the other hand, surely there is something to be said for an all-powerful deity. If the idea is not incoherent, isn't it at least possible that this being could be more concerned with a person's spiritual welfare than with their physical health? The Driscolls and the Church of All Saints argue, yes, because, as Ted Driscoll says, "The rules are God's, not ours." If Lewis is right, though, such a belief renders moral judgments meaningless. Interestingly, the jury seems to agree.

STUDY QUESTIONS

1. If morality is determined by God's commands, is there anything to prevent him from arbitrarily deeming acts like murder or genocide morally permissible?
2. If morality is not determined by God's commands, does this significantly affect the traditional Western (Jewish, Christian, Muslim) picture of God? If it does, explain how. If it does not, explain why.
3. What evidence do the Driscolls have for the truth of their religious beliefs about modern medicine? What evidence do the Driscolls have for believing that they should help their baby not to suffer in any way they can? Compare and contrast this evidence.
4. Which horn of the Euthyphro Dilemma does detective Logan seem to take? Ceretta? Give evidence for your conclusion from the episode.
5. Imagine you suddenly discover strong evidence that your fundamental beliefs about reality (whatever they are, atheist, humanist, Christian, etc.) logically entail that you should kill small children whenever you see one. Are you more sure that you shouldn't kill small children whenever you see one or that your fundamental beliefs about reality are true?

ALTERNATIVE CASE STUDIES

1. *Star Trek: The Next Generation*, "Justice," season 1
   (In what ways is the Edo's lawgiver like a Divine Lawgiver? What implications do these similarities have for their legal and moral code?)
2. *Touched by an Angel*, "The Face of God," season 7
   (Is Sarah misinterpreting God's will? What implications does the possibility of misinterpreting a Divine Lawgiver have for moral theory?)
3. *Joan of Arcadia*, "The Devil Made Me Do It," season 1
   (What if God asked you to do something that, at the moment, seems immoral?)

SERIES II
WHAT'S RIGHT AND WRONG?
ETHICAL THEORY

EPISODE 4: MORAL RELATIVISM

INTRODUCTION

In one episode of the 1980s television show *Cheers*, a mysterious patron comes into the bar acting very peculiarly ("The Spy Who Came in For a Cold One"). He walks cautiously, checks under the table before relaxing in his chair, kisses the waitress Carla (Rhea Pearlman) on the hand, and then, not-so-accidentally, tells her he's a spy. But when his story starts sounding fictitious, the culturally savvy Diane, another waitress (Shelley Long),

What's Good on TV?: Understanding Ethics Through Television, First Edition.
Jamie Carlin Watson and Robert Arp.
© 2011 Jamie Carlin Watson and Robert Arp. Published 2011 by Blackwell Publishing Ltd.

begins calling him on it. This leads to yet another conflict between Diane and the bar's owner Sam (Ted Danson).

When Diane suspects the mystery patron of lying, Sam says, "What? A customer in a bar is, uh, telling tall tales just to impress a cocktail waitress? Call *60 Minutes*." He explains, "In this bar, everybody gets to be a hero. Now what's the harm?" Diane continues her objection, noting that "any kind of lie is eventually destructive."

Sam seems to think that lying in a bar is not only permissible, but that bars are places set up so that people can "shoot their mouths off and get away with it." Bar culture is a culture that permits lying. Could Sam be right? Could there be cultural exceptions to moral rules so that moral truths are relative to certain times and places? In Diane's culture, by contrast, she was "raised to prize truth above all else." All cultures are bound by the same moral rules. Could Diane be right that moral claims are true everywhere and always? In this Episode, we will evaluate the arguments for and against the view that Sam seems to hold, which is known as moral relativism.

What do we mean when we say things like, "You *shouldn't* do that," "That was *wrong* of you," or "You're not *supposed* to do that"? Traditionally, moral philosophers have argued that there is some objective fact that makes these claims true or false. An "objective" fact is a fact whose truth depends on the way the world is regardless of whether any human exists. For instance, gravity would pull at the same strength and oceans would still be salty even if there were no humans around to know about it. Traditional moral philosophers have also argued that objective moral facts are true "universally," that is, they apply regardless of time or place. For instance, the law of gravity exists in the far reaches of space, though it acts differently out there. Nevertheless, the law holds universally, that is, throughout the universe.

Some philosophers, however, accept the objective character of moral claims, but argue that moral claims do not express universal facts – facts that are true always and everywhere; they express only, what we may call, "local," or "relative," facts – claims that are true only at certain times and places. For instance, when you say, "You should not murder," you are not expressing something about reality. You are simply expressing something about you or your immediate social group – *you* (or, you and your peeps) think murder is wrong. The claim that the truth of a moral claim is relative to a person or group is called "moral relativism."

Relativism is the claim that moral facts are true relative to the opinions or feelings of an individual or a group of people. The claim that moral truths are relative to individuals is known as "egoistic relativism." Egoistic relativists ("egoists," for short) argue that each person determines his or her own moral code, so an individual is morally obligated only to do what feels best. The claim that moral truths are relative to social, political, or cultural groups is called "cultural relativism." Cultural relativists argue that each culture determines its own moral code, typically on the basis of custom or tradition, but also on majority opinion. Cultural relativists argue that a person is morally obligated to keep or respect the moral code of whatever culture she is in, and that it is a mistake to pronounce moral judgments on other cultures because people in other cultures are not bound by your cultural norms. Sam from *Cheers* seems to accept cultural relativism, at least about truth-telling. For him, bar culture has its own unique moral code.

Moral relativism is very controversial, especially among ethicists. So, before we evaluate its plausibility, we should distinguish moral relativism from views that can seem very similar if you happen across them. These include the idea that moral truths are context relative, "ethical egoism" (also known as "objectivism"), and "psychological egoism."

As we noted in our "Pilot Episode," there is a type of relativity that applies to moral truths, called "context relativism." The idea is that different contexts affect whether certain actions are permissible, impermissible, or obligatory. For instance, some acts seem morally permissible in some circumstances (shooting a pistol *at a target*), but appear *really wrong* in others (shooting a pistol *at a 3-year-old child*). Examples like these show that the moral permissibility of an action can change depending on the circumstances under which that act is performed. But admitting that moral truths are context relative does not commit you to any version of moral relativism.

The difference is that moral relativists claim that moral facts are local, rather than universal – their truths are constrained to a specific time or place (individuals or members of a culture). But while contexts have particular implications for moral claims, it is possible that the moral fact of the matter can be evaluated at any time or place, that is, universally. For instance, telling a lie to your mother for your own selfish gain seems wrong, whether in the ninth century or the twenty-first. Similarly, telling a lie to protect an innocent person's life seems permissible, whether in ancient Rome or in Nazi Germany. This shows that context relativism is at least consistent with non-relativistic moral theories. So, someone who holds that moral truths are context relative could accept either relativism or some non-relativist theory.

Egoistic relativism is often confused with a non-relativist moral theory known as, "ethical egoism," or "objectivism." Ethicist and novelist Ayn Rand (1905–82) defended a moral theory according to which a person should always and only do whatever is in his or her best interests. At first, this sounds relativistic, because what is in someone's best interests is relative to that person.

But this is actually a version of consequentialism (see Episode 6), according to which an act is right or wrong depending on the consequences of the act.

Rand argues that an act is right if its consequences are in the actor's best interests and wrong if otherwise. This means there is an objective moral standard to which all actions can be evaluated – namely, what is objectively in a person's bests interests (regardless of what they decide or prefer). For example, if you decide that taking methamphetamines is what you want to do with your life, even if you like it, this is morally wrong, because it is not in your (or anyone's) best interest. This is not true for egoistic relativism. According to egoistic relativists, there are no objectively right or wrong acts. There may be acts that are wrong *for you*, if, say, you don't want to do them. But there is no objective fact determining what you should want. So, for an egoistic relativist, *you decide* what is right and wrong for you. If you decide that taking methamphetamines is the right course of life for you, then that's what's right for you, and no one can judge otherwise.

Egoistic relativism must also be distinguished from a descriptive (rather than normative) theory of human behavior that sounds similar, called "psychological egoism." Psychological egoism is a psychological theory about human behavior, and it states that individuals are incapable of acting in any way that isn't ultimately selfish. Notice, this is not a moral theory at all; it is not normative. Psychological egoists do not argue that you *should* only do what seems in your best interests; they argue that your brain is wired in such a way that *you cannot do otherwise*.

So, to summarize these differences, egoistic relativism is the claim that moral truths are relative to individuals. It is different from context relativism, which says that the objective truths of moral claims are determined, in part, by contexts, but are still evaluated in terms of a universal moral standard. It is also different from ethical egoism/objectivism, which says that there is an objective moral standard, namely, everyone should act in their own best interests. And relativism is different from psychological egoism, which says that humans actually cannot act in a way that they do not perceive to be in their best interests.

Egoistic relativism is often popularized in expressions such as, "Well, it's true for me; I don't know about you," or "I just want to find my truth," or "I can't judge whether that's right for you." Cultural relativism is expressed in similar statements, such as, "We have to respect other cultures," and "We cannot judge someone else's culture." But consider how strange these would sound if we spoke the same way about physics or mathematics: "Well, gravity is true for me; I don't know about you," "I just want to find the math that's true for me," "We have to respect other ways of doing chemistry," "We cannot judge someone else's mathematical system."

What is the difference between the claims of ethics and the claims of physics? Both are claims, so both are about reality and both are either true or false. If you're a nihilist (see Episode 1), and you believe there are no moral truths, then all moral claims are false (just like all claims about Dunder Mifflin employees outside the television show *The Office* (US)). If you think there are moral truths, then what would motivate this relativistic interpretation of what is right?

One powerful motivation is the widely agreed-upon claim that the truth of some claims *is* relative, and therefore it is at least possible that moral truths might be among these. For instance, the truth of preference claims, such as, "I like vanilla ice cream," "I don't care for eggplant," and "Bagpipe music is atrocious," depend on who utters them. Each may be true when Jamie says it, but false when Rob says it. Similarly, the truth of many perception claims, such as, "That music is too loud," "The wall color is 'eggshell white' not 'cream,'" and "The potatoes are not salty enough," depend on who utters them. We each have our own sense faculties, and these can be slightly different given variations in our genetics and the environments in which we were raised. So, couldn't moral truths be a subset of these subjective truths?

In the next section, we will look at a classical argument for cultural relativism from anthropologist Ruth Benedict. In the section following that, we will consider some reasons to reject Benedict's conclusion from philosopher James Rachels. We will then evaluate the plausibility of these arguments, as well as the plausibility of Egoistic Relativism, in light of *Deadwood*'s take on cultural sensitivity and *South Park*'s excellent spoof of politically correct morality.

ARE WE MERELY PRODUCTS OF OUR CULTURE?

Ruth Benedict, "A Defense of Ethical Relativism"

Anthropologist Ruth Benedict argues that moral norms are nothing more than social norms. There are no demands on our behavior beyond those imposed by various human cultures. She writes:

> Just as there are great numbers of possible phonetic articulations, and the possibility of language depends on a selection and standardization of a few of these in order that speech communication may be possible at all, so the possibility of organized behavior of every sort, from the fashions of local dress and houses to the dicta of a people's ethics and religion, depends upon a similar selection among the possible behavior traits. (2003: 424)

According to Benedict, the differences between claims of fashion, morality, religion, law, and architecture are determined only by the emphasis that a culture places on them. If she is right, then there is no significant difference between social, legal, and moral norms. As a majority of people in a culture adopt a belief system, this system becomes increasingly prevalent, and dissenters become viewed as "abnormal," and are stigmatized or ostracized. The majority determines which norms people should take seriously and to what degree.

How does Benedict arrive at this conclusion? She summarizes some of her work with various cultures and argues as follows. Different cultures generally categorize behaviors as "normal" or "abnormal." These categorizations reflect beliefs about morality, religion, fashion, architecture, eating habits, etc. Behaviors considered "normal" are always in the majority, and behaviors considered "abnormal" are always in the minority. Different cultures regard different, sometimes contradictory, behaviors as "normal." Therefore, human behavioral tendencies and beliefs about those tendencies are molded by culture. Therefore, the truth of any moral claim (or religious claim or fashion claim) is determined from within a particular culture.

What sorts of examples support this argument? Benedict gives several, but we will highlight only two. One example is a tribe in northwest Melanesia who regard behavior that we would probably consider extreme paranoia as morally obligatory:

> In this tribe the exogamic groups [groups that only marry outside their own clan] look upon each other as prime manipulators of black magic, so that one marries always into an enemy group which remains for life one's deadly and unappeasable foes. They look upon a good garden crop as a confession of theft, for everyone is engaged in making magic to induce into his garden the productiveness of his neighbors' .... Their preoccupation with poisoning is constant; no woman ever leaves her cooking pot for a moment untended. ... For some months before the whole society is on the verge of starvation, but if one falls to the temptation and eats up one's seed yams, one is an outcast and a beachcomber for life. There is no coming back. It involves, as a matter of course, divorce and breaking of all social ties. (2003: 422–3)

In this extremely paranoid culture, if someone "periodically ran amok and, beside himself and frothing at the mouth, fell with a knife upon anyone he could reach," the culture would simply regard this as a minor concern that will soon pass. But if someone was generous, kind, and altruistic, he was laughed at, and considered "silly" and "crazy."

Another, more extreme example, she explains, is that of the Kwakiutl civilization, on the North Pacific Coast of North America. She says that in last decades of the nineteenth century, this culture thrived better than many of its neighbors. However, their view of the value of human life differs remarkably from what we consider "normal":

> Among the Kwakiutl it did not matter whether a relative had died in bed of disease, or by the hand of an enemy, in either case death was an affront to be wiped out by the death of another person. The fact that one had been caused to mourn was proof that one had been put upon. A chief's sister and her daughter had gone up to Victoria, and either because they drank bad whiskey or because their boat capsized they never came back. The chief called together his warriors. "Now I ask you, tribes, who shall wail? Shall I do it or shall another?" The spokesmen answered, of course, "Not you, Chief. Let some of the other tribes." Immediately they set up the war pole to announce their intention of wiping out the injury, and gathered a war party. They set out, and found seven men and two children asleep and killed them. "Then they felt good when they arrived at Sebaa in the evening." (2003: 423)

The Kwakiutl people considered death an offense, when the universe has something against you, and this apparently demands retaliation in the form of another death. In this account, it is interesting that the soldiers considered the death of nine people successful reparation for the death of two people, as if the lives of the chief's daughter and sister were worth several times more than the life of one "commoner."

How should we interpret these examples? Should we conclude that these cultures are simply wrong in their moral judgments, or should we take them to indicate something deeper? Benedict argues that these examples "force upon us the fact that normality is culturally defined. An adult shaped to the drives and standards of either of these cultures, if he were transported into our civilization, would fall into our categories of abnormality" (p. 424). Since the majority of people regard a certain set of behaviors as normal, contrary behavior is regarded as abnormal and impermissible.

But what does "normal" and "abnormal" behavior have to do with morality? Benedict explains, "Mankind has always preferred to say, 'It is morally good,' rather than 'It is habitual,' and the fact of this preference is matter enough for a critical science of ethics. But historically the two phrases are synonymous" (p. 424). All these considerations come together in support of the claim that morality is culturally determined.

What are the implications of this view? Since everyone is a member of some culture, there is no objective standard of morality to judge behaviors by.

It would be nonsense to morally criticize another culture. Only the standards of a particular culture can be used to judge behavior, and these standards only apply within that culture. Therefore, the truth of any moral claim is relative to the culture in which it is made. "It is wrong to kill Jews" might be true in the United States in 2011, but false in Germany in 1940. "It is permissible to own slaves" might be false in Africa in 1800, but true in the United States in 1800. But given that our beliefs about behaviors are determined by the cultures in which we are raised, it is impossible to morally criticize another culture's moral standards. If Benedict is right, then Sam from *Cheers* could be right. If he is right that bars are designed so that people can lie and get away with it, then bar culture determines that lying is morally permissible.

The conclusion that it is impossible to legitimately criticize the moral judgments of another culture strikes many as odd. Nevertheless, Benedict offers evidence in defense of this claim, so we must respond on rational grounds, and not simply with our emotions. James Rachels argues that there are good reasons for thinking that Benedict's view is implausible.

RELATIVISM IS UNJUSTIFIED

James Rachels, "The Challenge of Cultural Relativism"

In this chapter from *The Elements of Moral Philosophy*, James Rachels reformulates arguments like Benedict's as follows:

1. Different societies have different moral codes.
2. There is no objective standard that can be used to judge one societal code better than another.
3. The moral code of our own society has no special status; it is merely one among many.
4. There is no "universal truth" in ethics – that is, there are no moral truths that hold for all peoples at all times.
5. The moral code of a society determines what is right within that society; that is, if the moral code of a society says that a certain act is right, then that action is right, at least within that society.
6. It is mere arrogance for us to try to judge the conduct of other peoples. We should adopt an attitude of tolerance toward the practices of other cultures.

Rachels argues that, while our judgments can be conditioned by our cultures, and while we should always be cautious about moral arrogance, and though there are some differences among cultural moral codes, there are reasons for thinking that premises (1), (2), (4), and (5) are false.

First, Rachels argues that premise (1) is not, strictly speaking, true. There is a sense in which premise (1) is ambiguous. It may mean, "Different societies differ in *some* of their moral codes," or it could mean, "Different societies have *completely* different moral codes." If cultural relativists mean the former, their conclusion does not follow. They need to show that each culture's moral standard is determined wholly within that culture. If there is a basic set of moral values that overlap, this would constitute a basic objective morality by which we could evaluate the behavior of people from other cultures. Therefore, the most plausible interpretation of premise (1), for cultural relativists, is the second: "Different societies have *completely* different moral codes." Is this plausible? Rachels argues that it is not.

Though there is a wide range of differences among cultural moral codes, there are a few basic moral standards that no culture can survive without. Rachels begins with an example similar to those offered by Benedict, of Eskimo culture's tendency to commit infanticide (killing infants). "They often kill perfectly normal infants, especially girls. We do not approve of this at all; a parent who did this in our society would be locked up" (2003: 24). Nevertheless, Rachels argues, environmental conditions force Eskimo people to make decisions that people in our culture do not face:

> An Eskimo family will always protect its babies if conditions permit. But they live in a harsh environment, where food is in short supply.... As in many "primitive" societies, Eskimo mothers will nurse their infants over a much longer period of time than mothers in our culture.... So even in the best of times there are limits to the number of infants that one mother can sustain. Moreover, the Eskimos are a nomadic people – unable to farm .... Infants must be carried, and a mother can carry only one baby in her parka as she travels and goes about her outdoor work. Other family members help however they can. (2003: 24)

Rachels also points out that males are preferred over females, one, because males are the primary hunters, and two, because the dangers of hunting often threaten the number of people able to hunt.

The point of this example is to show that, while Eskimos treat infants differently in their culture, their reasons for doing so are not fundamentally foreign to us. Rachels explains: "[A]mong the Eskimos, infanticide does not signal a fundamentally different attitude toward children. Instead, it is a recognition that drastic measures are sometimes needed to ensure the family's survival. . . . Killing is only the last resort" (2003: 25).

In fact, Rachels argues, there are a number of moral claims that no society could do without for any significant period of time. He asks us to consider a society that did not place any value on its children, or on truth-telling, or on prohibiting murder. He concludes, "*there are some moral rules that all societies must have in common, because those rules are necessary for society to exist*" (2003: 26; emphasis in original). And, in fact, social scientists have discovered these values in all viable cultures. Therefore, because there are some values shared by all viable cultures, it is false that different societies have *completely* different moral codes. Thus, premise (1) is false.

Second, Rachels argues, premises (2), (4), and (5) are implausible because there are rational grounds for rejecting certain moral claims independently of any cultural considerations. Rachels asks us to consider the case of female circumcision, called "excision," in which a female's genitals are permanently disfigured so that she is incapable of sexual pleasure. Justifications for this practice include: it will make females less promiscuous; there will be fewer unwanted pregnancies in unmarried women; and wives will be less likely to be unfaithful. But despite any arguments that might be offered in response to these reasons, is it permissible to condemn this practice on moral grounds?

Rachels argues that, whatever we might think of these arguments, they have something in common: they attempt to "justify excision by showing that it is beneficial to society." This is a moral reason we all consider worthy of consideration. Therefore, cultures that condone excision do not seem to have a dramatically different moral compass from ours; they just apply it differently. If there are moral considerations that suggest their application is seriously morally deficient, they have a reason to stop excising women. We can challenge their practice by asking, with Rachels, "*whether the practice promotes or hinders the welfare of the people whose lives are affected by it*. And, as a corollary, we may ask if there is an alternative set of social arrangements that would do a better job of promoting their welfare" (2003: 28; emphasis in original). But if we can have this sort of moral discourse with cultures that condone excision, it seems there is a culture-independent moral standard to which we can appeal to praise or blame practices in other cultures. Rachels concludes, "But this looks just like the sort of independent moral standard that Cultural Relativism says cannot exist" (2003: 28). If this is right, then premises (2), (4), and (5) are false, and the conclusion that moral truths are culturally relative is unjustified.

What about premise (3)? It is important to acknowledge that many of our cultural norms are simply culturally conditioned social norms with no moral content. We express normative claims that will simply not translate into vastly different cultures. However, this does not undermine our reasons for thinking that some of our cultural norms have objective moral content. If this is right, then premise (3) is also, strictly speaking, false. Therefore, if Rachels is right, Diane from *Cheers* is right. There seem to be universal moral standards, at least a common set, from which we derive other moral claims.

Other philosophical reasons for rejecting cultural relativism

In addition to Rachels's criticisms, there are at least three others worth mentioning.

1. Cultural relativists commit the "naturalistic fallacy." The naturalistic fallacy is committed when someone draws a conclusion about the way things *should be* from premises about the way things *are*. For instance, someone might argue that it is perfectly permissible for a child to lash out violently because that is a very normal thing for children to do. The premise of this argument is that it *is* very normal for children to lash out violently, and the conclusion is that they *should*, or, at least, *it is morally permissible* that, they act that way. But, of course, this conclusion doesn't follow. And we can see this using a variant case counterexample. It is very normal for mosquitoes to bite me, or for viruses to attack my immune system, but these are not good reasons for permitting mosquitoes and viruses to assault me.

Now consider the argument for cultural relativism. Even if Rachels were wrong about the widespread agreement about moral claims – that is, if every culture held a completely different set of moral standards – this would not support the claim that cultural relativism is true. Even if people held wildly divergent moralities, it is possible that there is one objective moral standard and, therefore, that lots and lots of people simply act immorally. Of course, this argument shows only that examples of cultural differences are not sufficient for establishing cultural relativism. If there were other considerations in its favor, we would be obliged to consider them. But since Benedict's reasons depend on examples of cultural differences, it is a fallacious argument.

2. Benedict's conclusion does not explain the difference that cultures draw between "social" and "moral" norms. Though Benedict argues that humans prefer to call behaviors "moral" rather than "habitual," citizens of various cultures still make distinctions among social, legal, and moral norms.

For instance, we know of no culture where eating with your elbows on the table is considered "immoral," though there are plenty where it is considered to be "impolite."

What determines these differences within a culture between social, legal, and moral prohibitions? Benedict says that, historically, they are synonymous. The problem with this claim is that cultures do not *treat* them synonymously; in fact, most cultures give priority to moral claims over social claims. This means that, even if cultures determine moral truths, they do not determine them completely. Some other considerations must be invoked to explain the differences in emphasis and priority given to moral claims over social claims.

More sophisticated cultural relativists may point to evolutionary considerations and argue that the longer a set of beliefs about behavior is entrenched in a culture – for example, those behaviors that helped our pre-human ancestors survive in their various environments – the more morally significant they might be to that culture. There are two problems with this response. First, since culture does not fully determine a culture's moral code, this moral theory is no longer cultural relativism. Second, it is not obvious that this avoids the naturalistic fallacy we noted above. Just because a set of behaviors helped a species survive, does not entail that those behaviors are morally permissible.

3. Cultural relativism is self-defeating.   The most worrisome objection to cultural relativism is that the view seems to entail its own falsity. By "entails its own falsity," we mean, "if you assume it is true, for the sake of argument, you can derive its negation." We call claims like this "self-defeating." In the history of philosophy, there are a handful of famous self-defeating claims. For instance, some academic skeptics have claimed, "We humans cannot know anything." Of course, if they *knew* this, it would be false, because they know at least one thing. Similarly, some logical positivists have argued that we should not believe any claim that is not self-evident, evident to the senses, or incorrigible. Don't worry about what this means, other philosophers were quick to show that the claim, "We should only believe claims that are self-evident, evident to the senses, or incorrigible," was not self-evident, evident to the senses, or incorrigible. Therefore, we shouldn't believe it. There is a worry that cultural relativism is also self-defeating.

Cultural relativists argue that we are fundamentally incapable of making judgments about the moral value of the actions of those in other cultures because we are irreversibly conditioned by the moral values of our own culture. But someone like Benedict is writing from within a culture that is shaped predominantly by the Judeo-Christian ethic, which says it is morally permissible to praise or blame the actions of people in other cultures. Therefore, in her culture it seems morally wrong to not judge the moral claims of other cultures. If cultural relativism is true, it is false for her culture. And if it is not true in her culture, then it is not true for all cultures. Therefore, cultural relativism is not true for all cultures. But since it is a claim about all moral claims in all cultures, if it is not true in one culture, it is not true in any; it is self-defeating.

CASE STUDY 1: *Deadwood,* "Childish Things," season 2

AVAILABILITY: **Netflix, iTunes**

HBO's *Deadwood* chronicles the lives of citizens in the mining town of Deadwood, South Dakota in 1876. Among corruption, crime, and tragedy, citizens such as Wild Bill Hickock and Seth Bullock attempt to drag order out of lawless chaos.

Early in the episode "Childish Things," one of the town's businessmen Cy Tolliver (Powers Boothe) discusses the welfare of his prostitute employees with the town physician Doc Cochran (Brad Dourif), who is on Tolliver's payroll to treat them. Cochran urges Tolliver to let him also care for the newly arrived "Chinese whores," who are starving to death. In response, Tolliver presents an argument for ignoring the women's need on the basis of Cultural Relativism.

Tolliver explains:

I ain't one, Doc, [who] holds [that] the white man's path is the sole and only path. I strive to tolerate what I may not agree with. Those people's culture . . . their women are disposable. They . . . they ship 'em unfed; replace 'em when they expire. They dose 'em with opium, I know, which I gather eases their pangs.

Doc Cochran doesn't find this argument satisfactory and threatens to quit treating any of Tolliver's prostitutes unless Tolliver allows him to treat the Chinese women *pro bono*. Tolliver agrees, this time feigning cultural sensitivity: "Well, Jesus Christ. Here, too, let me tolerate a different point of view."

Commentary: Cy Tolliver on moral tolerance

Notice that Tolliver is not defending cultural relativism. He is assuming it is true, and is using it as a premise in his argument. If we reformulated the argument, it would look something like this:

1. Cultural relativism is true.
2. Chinese culture treats Chinese women as disposable.
3. Therefore, I should treat Chinese women as disposable.

Tolliver seems to think that he is somehow respecting Chinese culture by treating women under his care the way they would be treated in their own culture.

Does this conclusion follow? To adequately answer this question, we must answer another. Assuming cultural relativism is true, do cultural norms transfer from one culture into another? That is, if we meet someone from another country, are we obligated to treat them according to their norms or are we obligated to treat them according to our norms? We do not treat people from other cultures according to their legal or social norms (we expect them to stop at our stop signs, drive on our side of the road, speak our language, and use our greeting methods – shaking hands, bowing, etc.). Therefore, it would seem strange to think that their moral norms would obligate us, when they are in our culture. If this is right, Tolliver is under no moral obligation to treat the Chinese prostitutes as their countrymen would.

But cultural relativism has implications for more than simply obligation; it also has implications for moral permissibility. It seems perfectly permissible to respect other cultures by speaking their language or greeting them according to their custom. So, is it permissible for Tolliver to treat the Chinese prostitutes according to their custom? Interestingly, for the cultural relativist, that depends on the moral code of his culture.

Doc Cochran seems to think there are moral considerations that apply independently of culture. Chinese prostitutes deserve treatments just like white American prostitutes. If this insight is merely a function of Cochran's 1870s American culture and moral relativism is true, then Tolliver's tolerance argument doesn't hold up. His culture prohibits his treating Chinese prostitutes differently from American prostitutes while he is in his culture. If Cochran's insight is an objective moral prohibition against refusing medical treatment to those who are suffering and cultural relativism is false, then Tolliver's argument doesn't hold up. The only scenario in which Tolliver's argument would work, it would seem, is if Tolliver were a brothel owner in China.

CASE STUDY 2: *South Park*, "Death Camp of Tolerance," season 6

AVAILABILITY: NetFlix, iTunes, www.southparkstudios .com/episodes

South Park is an animated comedy that challenges many cultural norms and stereotypes with intentionally controversial exaggeration. We think it is one of the most important sources of social satire in contemporary culture.

At some point in the past, Mr Garrison, one of South Park Elementary School's teachers, was demoted from teaching third grade to teaching kindergarten because the school administration thought his openly gay lifestyle might negatively influence some of the children. Principle Victoria apologizes for this discrimination and offers Mr Garrison the opportunity to teach fourth grade. "We in administration now see that you are an individual with your own preferences, and we respect that." Mr Garrison is skeptical, but Principle Victoria reassures him that, "with all of the new laws, we could never fire you for being gay now; you would be able to sue us for millions of dollars." Mr Garrison decides the money is worth more than the job and decides to do whatever it takes to get fired for being gay. He begins exaggerating his lifestyle in class. He starts using sexually suggestive phrases ("It will be long and hard."); he hires a sadomasochistic teaching assistant, Mr Slave, who dresses in leather and chains; he pinches Mr. Slave's butt, and bends him over a desk and paddles him in front of the children.

When the students express their disapproval over this behavior to their parents, they are accused of being intolerant and are taken to the Museum of Tolerance. When Mr Garrison puts Lemmiwinks the gerbil up Mr Slave's behind, the kids quit going to school. Their parents are so upset that they send the kids to "Tolerance Camp." At Tolerance Camp, which looks suspiciously like a concentration camp from Nazi Germany, the kids are forced to work "every hour of every day until [they] submit to being tolerant of everybody." The leader of the camp explains, "Here, intolerance will not be tolerated."

Because of the discrimination he has endured, Mr Garrison is honored with the "Courageous Teacher Award." Since the kids didn't get him fired, Mr Garrison decides he needs to show the parents what a "sick queer" he is. So, he and Mr Slave come up with a highly inappropriate stage act for the award ceremony. Nevertheless, the parents in the audience keep saying, "He's so courageous" and "What an amazing human being." Finally, Mr Garrison can take it no longer and begs to be fired because he's gay. Rather than being fired, Mr Garrison is sent to Tolerance Camp because he is intolerant of his own behavior.

Commentary: "Intolerance will not be tolerated!"

The writers of *South Park* have a knack for highlighting the absurd aspects of contemporary culture. In this case, their target is "tolerance." It is currently very politically correct to praise "tolerance" and to revile "intolerance." But those who use the word "tolerance" rarely explain what they mean by it. As it is commonly used in political speeches and teen-oriented television shows, tolerance seems to mean that we should accept everything anyone else believes or does without judgment. This might pass in the land of politicians and 14-year-olds, but it quickly becomes problematic in the real world, where people steal, murder, and genuinely disagree about the answers to significant moral questions.

At the Museum of Tolerance, the boys go through the Tunnel of Prejudice, where they are called racist and religiously discriminatory names. The tour guide picks on one of the boys, Cartman, as an example, explaining: "You must be tolerant of his differences as well. If he chooses to eat fatty foods, that's his life choice." In general, the guide explains, "[w]e have to accept people for who they are and what they like to do." Unfortunately, of course, many people are highly selective of when they want to be tolerant. As a point of irony, when the tour group walks out of the Museum, the tour guide gets very angry at someone who is smoking, yelling, "Get out of here you filthy smoker!" And, of course, she doesn't criticize the boys' parents when they call the smoker intolerant names, like "dirty lungs," "tar breath," and "dumbass."

The irony escalates to absurdity when Mr Garrison starts talking about "licking balls" and being the asshole for Mr Slave at his award ceremony while the parents in the audience fully accept his "life choice." Finally, Mr Garrison cannot take the absurdity any longer and draws a moral distinction that the crowd doesn't seem to recognize: "Just because you have to tolerate something, doesn't mean you have to approve of it. If you had to like it, it would be called the Museum of Acceptance."

How should we treat others who are different from us? Other rational beings have the same access to moral reality we do, so we should respect their judgments. This goes hand-in-hand with the principle of charity we noted in our "Pilot Episode." However, we also have access to moral reality and can evaluate whether others are applying moral rules appropriately. So, while we have good reason to tolerate the considered judgments of others (that is, to live alongside those who disagree with use), we do not have good reason to accept any judgment they arrive at (they could be wrong, and their judgments could lead to harm). And we shouldn't even tolerate those that lead to harm, such as the beliefs that pedophilia, child pornography, rape, and murder are morally permissible.

In our discussion of *Deadwood*, Cy Tolliver assumes cultural relativism is true in order to defend his right to treat the Chinese prostitutes however he wants. But if the general sentiment in this episode of *South Park* were correct, that tolerance entails acceptance, then egoistic relativism would be true. Individuals would determine which moral claims are true. Cy Tolliver made a life choice about how he wants to treat prostitutes and we must respect that *as true*. Similarly, Mr Garrison made a life decision to put Lemmiwinks up Mr Slave's ass in front of a class of fourth graders, and therefore we must respect his belief that this is permissible as true. We take it that these examples constitute variant case counterexamples to egoistic relativism.

We can conclude, then, that two people can disagree about, say, the moral permissibility of homosexuality, but tolerate one another as citizens, neighbors, co-workers, and even friends, without accepting each other's beliefs. How is this relevant to our discussion of moral relativism? One motivation for moral relativism is the belief that we have an obligation to tolerate those different from us. This episode of *South Park* shows us that tolerance doesn't entail acceptance. If this is right, then it is possible to respect someone's moral beliefs without also accepting those beliefs as true.

STUDY QUESTIONS

1. List some non-controversial claims whose truth seems relative to individuals. How might these types of claims motivate moral relativism?
2. What is the difference between egoistic relativism and ethical egoism? What is the difference between egoistic relativism and cultural relativism?
3. Explain one argument for cultural relativism. Does this argument justify Cy Tolliver's treatment of the Chinese prostitutes?
4. Explain one argument against cultural relativism. How might this resolve the dispute between Sam and Diane in the *Cheers* episode we discussed?
5. What is the difference between "tolerance" and "acceptance"? List some behaviors that you tolerate but do not accept. List some behaviors that you neither tolerate nor accept. Should Doc Cochran tolerate Cy Tolliver's treatment of the Chinese prostitutes? Should he accept it?

ALTERNATIVE CASE STUDIES

1. *The Andy Griffith Show*, "Opie's Hobo Friend," season 2 (What are the social implications of moral relativism?)

2. *30 Rock*, "Believe in the Stars," season 3
    (Is Jack a moral relativist or a moral nihilist?)
3. *South Park*, "200," season 14
    (Is moral relativism significantly different from religious or social relativism?)

EPISODE 5: DEONTOLOGY

INTRODUCTION

In the popular daytime court TV show *Judge Judy*, Judge Judith Sheindlin arbitrates small claims lawsuits with quick wit and razor-sharp reasoning. But in addition to administering justice, she also dishes out plenty of moral and practical advice to people who have made consistently bad decisions. Some of her recurring phrases include, "If you tell the truth, you don't have to have a good memory," "If it doesn't make sense, it's probably not true"

What's Good on TV?: Understanding Ethics Through Television, First Edition.
Jamie Carlin Watson and Robert Arp.
© 2011 Jamie Carlin Watson and Robert Arp. Published 2011 by Blackwell Publishing Ltd.

(though she doesn't always include the "probably"), "What you feel is irrelevant," and, in some formulation or other, "If you can't afford to have kids, you shouldn't have had kids."

Consider the last catch phrase. Judge Judy was a family court judge for 24 years and she has strong feelings about how parents should raise their children. Her opinions actually aren't very controversial: parents should provide for their children's needs and protect their interests. But this is no weak moral consideration, Judy seems to regard it as a moral absolute: parents have a *duty* to raise their children a certain way.

Could this be right? If moral claims are not relative (as we considered in Episode 4), are they automatically unfailing and absolute? Immanuel Kant argued that they are, and that we can derive all true moral claims by reasoning about them.

KANT'S THEORY OF MORAL DUTY

Immanuel Kant, from *Groundwork of the Metaphysic of Morals*

Prussian philosopher Immanuel Kant (1724–1804) is one of history's most influential and prolific thinkers. His work in ethics sets him apart as the foremost proponent of the moral theory called "deontology." The term "deontology" is a melding of two Greek words: *deontos*, which means "duty," and *logos*, which means "the logic of" or "the study of." Kant argues that whether an act is good or bad, moral or immoral, permissible or impermissible, depends wholly on one's *duty* concerning that action. He argues, further, that if a person's motivation for an act includes any psychological state other than a respect for the law of duty (what Kant calls "inclination," e.g., pleasure or pain, taste or distaste, desire, etc.), that act cannot rightly be called "good." This is not to say that such an act is bad or immoral (it may be consistent with duty, that is, it may *accord* with duty). However, if a subject cannot separate motivations based on inclination from motives based on duty, a subject cannot *know* whether the act is good (it was not committed *from* duty). We will look at each of these arguments in turn. But first, we need to clarify some of the terms Kant uses.

According to Kant, what things are "good"?

The only plausible candidate for something that is *intrinsically* good is a good will. By "will" Kant apparently means a human's ability to rationally intend something for reasons. If a will can recognize purely rational reasons (as opposed to practical or emotional reasons), the will is "good," so we will also refer to the good will as the "rational will." Therefore, whereas an animal may be able to intend to do something for a reason (e.g., eat because it is hungry), only humans can intend for purely rational reasons.

The word "intrinsic" means "essential to" as opposed to "incidental to." For instance, your DNA is intrinsic to you – part of what you are, essentially, is a certain DNA code. Your haircut, on the other hand, is extrinsic to you – it is incidental to you that you have the hairstyle that you do (*it* could be different without *you* being different). An intrinsic "good" is something good in and of itself, without qualification or context – sort of like vanilla ice cream (who doesn't like vanilla ice cream?). An extrinsic "good," by contrast, is something that is good only in some circumstances or for some purpose – sort of like Tylenol; in certain circumstances it cures pain, but too much damages your liver.

So, for Kant, the rational will is intrinsically good and the *actions of* the rational will are, at best, extrinsically good. For instance, Kant identifies two types of abilities we have that are not essential to us – they are "gifts": *gifts of nature*, which include intelligence, wit, judgment, courage, and perseverance, and *gifts of fortune*, which include power, wealth, and honor. These gifts can be used for moral good or for moral bad; therefore, they are not good in themselves. In addition, since they require a rational will for their use – that is, the values rational will is *prior to* the use of these gifts – the gifts cannot *make* that will good. Any value the actions of the will has is derived from the fact that the will is intrinsically good. It is because the rational will is good that we can be morally blamed for doing something immoral. Therefore, for one of our gifts to be used for good, a rational will must use them from the right motivation – that is, from duty.

Why does Kant call the will "good" in itself?

A rational will is required for performing good or bad acts, but why does Kant think this will is *intrinsically good*? A rational will is intrinsically good because it is the only thing in existence that can both (a) recognize the difference between a right and wrong act and (b) choose between right and wrong acts. Kant writes:

> A good will is good not because of what it effects or accomplishes – because of its fitness for attaining some proposed end: it is good through its willing alone – that is, good in itself. Considered in itself it is to be esteemed beyond comparison as far higher than anything it could ever bring about merely in

order to favour some inclination or, if you like, the sum total of inclinations. (1964: 62)

No animal or object, corporeal or incorporeal being, can be called intrinsically good unless it has these abilities. To put it slightly differently, a will's "goodness" does not depend on the acts it actually performs, but simply on its *ability* to choose to act in a good or a bad way (or at least, it is *the sort of thing that could* have this ability – Kant would probably include coma patients in the set of things having a good will, but he definitely would not include trees).

Since it is the only thing that can recognize acts as right or wrong and choose to act one way over another, the rational will is the only thing in existence that can be the recipient of moral praise and moral blame. Because of this ability to choose for the sake of duty (even if it does not choose to act for the sake of duty), the rational will is valuable in itself; it is intrinsically good.

Wouldn't that mean a good will could never perform a wrong act?

Quite the opposite: since it can recognize and choose a wrong act, the good will can be blamed for performing a wrong act – and it is the only thing that *could* be blamed for performing that act. This means a good will can perform a wrong act. Of course, other things might perform acts that are wrong: robots, computers, dogs, roosters – but these do not have the capacity to recognize their actions as bad; only rational wills have that. Because rational wills can choose between right and wrong, rational wills are morally responsible for their actions.

Perhaps Kant's theory would have been better served if he had called the will "intrinsically valuable" instead of "intrinsically good." It seems easier to say that someone who wills heinous acts has some sort of fundamental value in virtue of his ability to choose in a morally significant way than it is to say that person's will is "good." But Kant doesn't make room for a "*bad* will" and doesn't use the more general "value" to describe the will; he calls it "good in itself." Later in the *Groundwork*, Kant does mention an "absolutely good will," by which he means a rational will that always wills what is right and good, and never what is evil. He writes, "The *will* is *absolutely good* if it cannot be evil – that is, if its maxim, when made into a universal law, can never be in conflict with itself" (1964: 104). Presumably, according to what Kant says in other places, the only being with an absolutely good will is God.

So, when is an act "right" or "wrong"?

An act is "right" or "wrong" insofar as it fulfills or violates some law of morality. If there is some moral law that good wills are supposed to keep, then a robot could violate that law and, technically, would commit a "bad" act. But, according to Kant's requirements for moral responsibility, these laws apply only to rational wills, so a robot is under no obligation to keep a moral law – it can't even recognize an action as moral or immoral. Kant's idea is that, if there were no rational wills, there would be no recognition of duties, and therefore no right or wrong acts. Remember, everything that is "good" is good extrinsically, except the good will. Without a good will to act out of pure goodness (from duty), no act would be right or wrong, good or bad.

A good will does what is "right" insofar as the action is performed *from duty* or *according to duty*. An act is performed *from duty* if that act fulfills a duty (she *should* do it) and the good will's *only* motivation for that act is "respect for the law of morality" (that is, I do it because it's right) and *has no inclination toward that act or its effects* (that is, I don't do it because I want to or because the consequences are good). Kant argues that, if your motivation for performing an act includes an inclination toward that act (emotions, desires, etc.), you cannot be held properly praiseworthy for doing your duty – you haven't acted purely from duty. You haven't acted wrongly, because you still recognized your duty and acted in accordance with it, but since it was not your only reason for acting, you should not be praised for that act.

A good will does what is "wrong" insofar as a moral duty is violated – that is, the action is not performed from duty or even in accord with it. "When I deviate from the principle of duty, this is quite certainly bad" (1964: 70) – others translate "quite certainly bad" as "beyond all doubt wicked" (e.g., Kant 2008). Recall Judge Judy's phrase, "If you can't afford kids, you shouldn't have kids." She is expressing a moral duty: you have a moral obligation to support your children; therefore, if you cannot support them, you should not have accepted that responsibility. Would Kant be happy with this duty? To answer this question, we need to know a bit more about duties.

What is a duty and how do we recognize one?

A "duty" is a moral imperative. An "imperative" is a "practical law" (Kant 1964: 80–1) or command, that is, a rule that dictates how we should behave. In contemporary ethics we would call a duty a "moral principle" or "moral rule." A duty is "practical," according to Kant, not because it is useful (as we would typically think), but because it refers to *practice* (action or behavior).

Duties are commands or *imperatives*, but not all imperatives are duties. It is important to identify which type or types of imperative dictate our behavior morally. Kant distinguishes two general types: "categorical imperatives" and "hypothetical imperatives."

Categorical imperatives tell us we should act a certain way no matter what – that is, they dictate absolute obligations. Categorical imperatives are derived from reason alone, independently of any circumstances or personal concerns. If a rule dictates an action, and any contrary rule (dictating the action not be done, or that not doing it is permissible) would lead to logical self-defeat of the rule or a contradiction, then the rule is a categorical imperative.

Hypothetical imperatives, on the other hand, tell us we should act a certain way if we have certain goals. You may have what Kant calls "problematic" or "skilful" goals – for instance, if you want to get something off a high shelf, you should get a ladder; if you want to repair a broken mug, you should use superglue. Similarly, you may have what Kant calls "assertoric" or "prudential" goals – that is, goals that further your happiness or well-being. For instance, if you are sick and you want to feel better, you should go to a doctor; if you are hungry and want to be full, you should eat.

Now, in order for a command to be morally binding, according to Kant, two conditions must be met: first, everyone it binds must be able to know the command, and, second, everyone who knows the command must be able to evaluate any action in light of it. The first condition is an expression of the principle "ought implies can." If you cannot know or recognize a moral principle, that principle cannot condemn your actions. A rock cannot recognize a moral imperative, therefore a rock is not morally responsible even if it rolls off a mountain and kills someone. The same goes for a mentally handicapped person who does not have the ability to recognize moral reasons.

The second condition is the claim that all moral commands must be universal – that is, they must hold for all rational beings at all times and in all situations. Kant argues that hypothetical commands depend on temporary, contingent circumstances. For Kant, moral values are abstract truths like those of mathematics. If mathematical truths hold necessarily, we cannot derive them from contingent truths. This is because we could never amass enough contingent truths to establish even one necessary truth. Similarly for moral value: since we cannot know all possible contingent circumstances, we cannot derive a system of moral values from contingent reality; we must derive it a priori.

According to Kant, we have a moral imperative (duty) to do something if doing anything else will violate the laws of good *reason*. Duties are derived from reason because reason is available to all good wills (it is consistent with the first condition above) and reason dictates beliefs or actions categorically, which means it is relevant to every possible situation (it is consistent with the second condition above). Rational laws of action are duties, and because duties are rational, they apply to every being that can reason and they apply in every situation.

Some types of actions will have duties that perfectly correspond to them; for instance, "Should I have children if I cannot afford them?" "Should I eat off my date's plate while she's in the bathroom?" "Should I illegally download music?" But Kant recognized that not every action will have a duty perfectly corresponding to it; for instance, "Should I tell my sister that her husband has been having lunch with the cute cashier at his work even though nothing has happened?" To account for this discrepancy, Kant makes a distinction between two types of duties: perfect and imperfect.

Imperfect duties are derived from evaluating particular "maxims" (i.e., rules for action; for instance, "Do not make a promise you do not intend to keep unless you really need money") in particular situations in light of categorical imperatives. Maxims are evaluated by checking to see if they violate a categorical imperative. If a particular maxim does not violate a categorical imperative, the action dictated by the maxim is permissible. On the other hand, if not performing some action violates the categorical imperative, the action is obligatory, and is a perfect duty.

Kant argues that there is only one categorical imperative, though there are three ways to formulate it. The first formulation reads: "Act only on that maxim through which you can at the same time will that it should become a universal law" (1964: 88). The second formulation reads: "Act in such a way that you always treat humanity, whether in your own person or in the person of any other, never simply as a means, but always at the same time as an end" (1964: 96). The third formulation reads: "A rational being must always regard himself as making laws in a kingdom of ends which is possible through freedom of the will – whether it be as member or as head" (1964:101).

It is controversial whether these principles are really different formulations of the same categorical imperative or three independent principles. For our purposes in this section, we'll focus primarily on the first formulation. We will look briefly at the second formulation and evaluate the plausibility of both through the case studies below.

The first formulation says you should act only in such a way that you could command everyone to act that way. You can imagine contemplating whether to do something and asking, "What if everyone did this?" But the question is not whether you would be comfortable with everyone doing it (remember, acts that are motivated by taste or preference cannot be called "good"), and it is not whether everyone could get away with it or whether bad consequences will follow (what makes an act right is not the consequences of that act, but whether it is dictated by some duty). So, what Kant wants you to think about when you ask "What if everyone did this?" is whether the maxim would be self-defeating, that is, whether it would entail its own falsity. Let's look at an example.

Kant asks us to consider the following scenario:

> A man feels sick of life as the result of a series of misfortunes that has mounted to the point of despair, but he is still so far in possession of his reason as to ask himself whether taking his own life may not be contrary to his duty to himself. He now applies the test "Can the maxim of my action really become a universal law of nature?" [a practical command, not a "natural" law like gravity]. (1964: 89)

Is it a violation of the categorical imperative to commit suicide when the rest of your life may involve more bad than good? Kant says, yes:

> It is then seen at once that a system of nature by whose law the very same feeling whose function (*Bestimmung*) is to stimulate the furtherance of life should actually destroy life would contradict itself and consequently could not subsist as a system of nature. (1964: 89)

The idea seems to be that the good will, in virtue of its intrinsic goodness, is compelled to preserve itself. This drive to preserve life could not, without contradiction, will something that ends life. Thus, any decision to commit suicide is inherently irrational, and is therefore, a violation of the categorical imperative.

The Kantian method

So, how do we use Kant's ethical theory? Several Kant scholars have suggested a strategy for understanding Kant's reasoning process (O'Neill 1975, 1990; Rawls 1989, 2000). The following example is from Robert Johnson (2008):

1. Formulate a maxim that identifies your reason for acting.
2. Reformulate the maxim as a universal law of nature governing all rational agents.

3. Consider whether your maxim is even conceivable in a world governed by this law (does it entail a contradiction?).
4. If it is not conceivable, it is morally impermissible.
5. If is conceivable, ask yourself whether you could rationally will to act on your maxim in such a world.
6. If you cannot, the act is morally impermissible; if you can, it is morally permissible.

So, would Kant be happy with Judge Judy's view that anyone who cannot afford children should not have them? This seems consistent with the first formulation of the categorical imperative: if it were required of everyone, no contradictions would result. It is also consistent with the second formulation: supporting children would result in fostering their ends. And it may be obligatory on the second formulation: a person's inability to support them would treat someone else (taxpayers) into supporting them, thereby using them as a mere means. If this is right, Kant would agree with Judge Judy that people should only have children if they can afford them.

To highlight some of the details of Kant's theory, we will discuss two case studies. In an episode from *Arrested Development*, we discover reasons for thinking that lying is impermissible even when the consequences are good. In an episode of *Friends*, we are given some interesting reasons to believe that we can never act completely without inclination.

CASE STUDY 1: *Arrested Development*, "Not without My Daughter," season 1

AVAILABILITY: **iTunes, NetFlix, Hulu.com**

In "Not without My Daughter," the protagonist and voice of reason Michael Bluth (Jason Bateman) attempts to be a role model of honesty and responsibility for his niece Maeby (Alia Shawkat). Maebe's father, Tobias (David Cross), is now unemployed and has reverted to the carefree lifestyle of many college freshmen (sleeping and watching television – not that we're against watching television). In order to encourage Maeby toward a virtuous life of honesty, Michael offers her $50 if she can go all day without lying, to which she agrees on the condition that Michael also participates. Being the bastion of moral fortitude that he is pretending to be, Michael agrees.

Unfortunately, when faced with the prospect of going to jail over the sudden disappearance of his father's former assistant Kitty (Judy Greer) (whom he fired then threatened), Michael discovers several practical reasons for not telling the truth, the whole truth, and nothing but the truth, including the information that Kitty was on the family yacht that his brother Gob (pronounced "jobe"; Will Arnett), blew up in one of his magic acts. In front of Maeby, Michael virtuously keeps his promise, responding honestly to an officer's questions. But behind her back, he tells his lawyer, "If I lie in front of her, I lose fifty bucks. I *do* think we should lie." And in the interrogation room, when questioned about having evidence of Kitty's whereabouts, Michael responds, "I ... have no idea. None."

In the end, lying actually helps bring the truth to light. Maeby lies to get into the evidence room where she discovers Kitty, alive and well, and finds out that the police have been using her supposed disappearance to leverage Michael into testifying against his father George Sr. (Jeffrey Tambor) (who is in jail and under investigation for defrauding shareholders). A dash of the truth and Michael is free to go, so all ends well – except that Kitty has lots of evidence against George Sr. and thinks Michael tried to kill her.

Commentary: Michael Bluth on lying

According to the first formulation of Kant's categorical imperative, a person who lies for the sake of convenience acts in contradiction to the dictates of the categorical imperative; it is impossible to will that everyone lie for the sake of convenience. Kant offers the following example: "Take this question, for example. May I not, when I am hard pressed, make a promise with the intention of not keeping it?" (1964: 70). Kant argues that this deceitfulness violates the categorical imperative:

> I then become aware at once that I can indeed will the lie, but I can by no means will a universal law of lying; for by such a law there could properly be no promises at all, since it would be futile to profess a will for future action [express my intention] to others who would not believe my profession or who, if they did so over-hastily, would pay me back in like coin [by doing the same to me]. (1964: 71)

And later, in response to an almost identical case, Kant explains that a universal law of lying "would make promising, and the very purpose of promising, itself impossible, since no one would believe he was being promised anything, but would laugh at utterances of this kind as empty shams" (1964: 90).

The idea is that universalizing lying would lead to the breakdown of trust between moral agents. Remember, this cannot be a worry about the *consequences* of lying, first, because Kant doesn't argue that all people might choose to lie for convenience thereby leading to these consequences, and second, because Kant rejects the method of discerning moral principles by their consequences. Kant argues that universally prescribing lying under certain conditions entails a contradiction. The inconsistency results from asserting that it is morally obligatory to lie to alleviate distress, since then the lie could not, once universalized, achieve its intended goal of alleviating distress. If that law were universalized, no one would take an assertion under distress to constitute a moral contract; logically, the contract would be null and void from the outset.

In "Not without My Daughter," Michael Bluth wants to be a good role model for Maeby. When questioned by the police, he is, with only a slight bit of trouble, completely honest with the officers. But, though his actions *accord with his duty* to be honest, he is not acting *from duty*. He is constantly aware of Maebe, who is scrutinizing every claim, and he has to rephrase several statements so that they are not bending the truth. If he were acting from duty, Maeby's scrutiny would not motivate Michael's honesty. He would tell the truth because it's the right thing to do.

Later in the episode, Maeby tries to get into the evidence room at the police station and gets caught by one of the detectives. She tells the man she is Detective Fellows's daughter (because it's Take Your Daughter to Work Day). The detective is convinced and gives her the code to the evidence room door. The consequences of this lie are very good. Maeby discovers Kitty, which means Michael was not really in any trouble because of Kitty's disappearance, and everyone goes home happy. However, Kant argues that even lies that have good consequences violate the categorical imperative. Maeby could not will her lie to become a universal law because no one would accept claims made for the sake of convenience as morally binding.

This is, admittedly, difficult to see in cases like Maeby's. If the consequences are so good and the consequences of not lying would have been much worse, why not lie? First, there was no way to predict whether the consequences would be that good. Maeby had no indication that Kitty was in the back room. The consequences could just as easily have been bad. Therefore, it seems right to think, as Kant suggests, that contingent reality is not a reliable guide to moral truth.

And second, Kant thinks something much more fundamental is at stake than simply logic. This is clearer when we evaluate Maeby's lie in terms of the second formulation of the categorical imperative.

As noted above, the second formulation reads: "Act in such a way that you always treat humanity, whether in your own person or in the person of any other, never simply as a means, but always at the same time as an end" (1964: 96). This version of the categorical imperative implies that a person who lies out of self-interest uses other rational beings only as a means to some end and not also as an end in themselves. Why should we recognize others as ends in themselves? Because everyone recognizes him or herself as an ultimate end – that is, as intrinsically valuable. How do you know? Just ask them. All rational beings regard themselves this way; it is an objective fact (an "objective fact" is a fact true for everyone, like gravity, and not just for some, like a preference for coffee):

> *Rational nature exists as an end in itself.* This is the way in which a man necessarily conceives his own existence: it is therefore so far a *subjective* principle of human actions. But it is also the way in which every other rational being conceives his existence...; hence it is at the same time an *objective* principle. (1964: 96; emphasis in original)

If being an "end in itself" is entailed by being rational, then humans certainly count as ends in themselves. Of course, Kant only says that rational beings *regard* themselves as ends in themselves, so it is unclear that this really justifies his claim that all rational wills are objectively intrinsically valuable. If they are, Maebe has violated the categorical imperative (at least, she violated the second formulation) by lying, because she was using the detective as a means to an end (getting in the evidence room) and not also as an end in himself.

How do we know whether we are using someone as means only? Kant says you respect someone as an ultimate end if that person is in a position where she could offer her assent to be used in that way. For instance, you use a cashier at a store as a means to an end (to pay for your stuff). But he has consented to be there on the condition that he will be compensated as a result of your purchases. Neither you nor anyone else is forcing him to be there against his will. Therefore, you are respecting him as an end in himself.

In addition, he is using the owners of the store as a means to some end, but he is respecting them as ultimate ends by providing a service for the money he is being paid. This sort of assent (whether tacit or explicit) is the only way to respect others as ultimate ends, that is, as intrinsically valuable beings. To use someone only for your own ends (slavery, deceit, rape, etc.) is to deny their intrinsic goodness, which is, by definition, bad. Therefore, despite all the good that comes from Maeby's lie, since the detective was not in a position to consent to be lied to, it was still her duty to be honest.

CONTEMPORARY DEONTOLOGY

Some moral philosophers are sympathetic with the general outlines of Kant's theory, but admit that it leads to some strange consequences. For instance, if there is an absolute duty against lying and an absolute duty "to help others where one can" (Kant 1964: 66), what happens when those duties conflict? What would Kant tell someone in Nazi Germany who is hiding Jewish people in her attic and the Gestapo comes to the door and asks whether she is hiding Jews? Surely, lying is permissible in this case. But Kant's original theory does not seem to allow for this.

Therefore, some contemporary Kantians focus on the second formulation of the categorical imperative (treat people as an end in themselves and not merely a means), and argue that this formulation establishes a set of *prima facie* duties that can be balanced against one another in cases of conflict. For instance, Onora O'Neill argues that there are two main categories of duties: duties of justice and duties of beneficence. Duties of justice are prohibitions against coercing and deceiving people. These tend to be closer to absolute duties. "When we act on such maxims, we treat others as mere means, as things rather than as ends in themselves" (2009: 80). Duties of beneficence are obligations to help others achieve their ends, for instance by encouraging or funding or adopting some of their goals. O'Neill admits, however, that "we cannot seek everything that others want; their wants are too numerous and diverse, and, of course, sometimes incompatible. It follows that beneficence has to be selective" (2009: 80). These duties are much more flexible.

CASE STUDY 2: *Friends*, "The One Where Phoebe Hates PBS," season 5

AVAILABILITY: **NetFlix**

Joey Tribbiani (Matt LeBlanc) has just been hired as, what he thinks is, co-host for a PBS telethon. As it turns out, he's only taking pledges. "A little, uh, good deed for PBS. Plus, some TV exposure. Now that's the kind of math Joey likes to do." But when he expresses excitement over "co-hosting" the telethon, Phoebe Buffet (Lisa Kudrow) remarks, disgustedly, "Ugh! PBS!" When asked "What's wrong with PBS?" Phoebe says, "Oh, what's *right* with them!?"

As it turns out, years ago, just after her mom killed herself, Phoebe wrote to PBS, but all they sent in reply was a keychain. Needless to say, her opinion of the network is not positive. After this heart-wrenching tale, the following dialogue ensues:

JOEY: I'm sorry, Phoebs. I just – you know, I just wanted to do a good deed, like – like you did with the babies.
PHOEBE: This isn't a good deed. You just want to get on television. This is totally selfish.
JOEY: Whoa, whoa, whoa! What about you having those babies for your brother? Talk about selfish.
PHOEBE: What are you talking about!
JOEY: Uh, well, yeah, it was a really nice thing and all. But it made you feel really good, right?
PHOEBE: Yeah. So?
JOEY: Well it made *you* feel *good*, so that makes it selfish. Look, there's no unselfish good deed. Sorry!

After coming up short in the example department, Phoebe sets out to find a selfless good deed. Her first attempt falls flat. She sneaks over to her neighbor's house and cleans up the leaves on his front stoop. "But he caught me and force-fed me cider and cookies. Then I felt wonderful. That old jackass!"

Unfortunately, her next attempt fares no better. Phoebe goes to the park and lets a bee sting her so that the bee can "look tough in front of his bee friends." Phoebe explains: "The bee is happy and I am definitely not." Of course, Joey informs her that the bee probably died after stinging her, thus foiling another attempt.

Once more, Phoebe tries to do something selfless by giving $200 to PBS. It's a significant amount of money for her, so it's a sacrifice, and it's going to a network she has reasons to not like. But, while it starts out completely selfless, Phoebe's pledge leads to a record-breaking pledge total, and, since Joey took the call, Joey gets on TV. Phoebe says, "Oh, look-look, Joey's on TV! Isn't that great? My pledge got Joey on TV! Oh, that makes me feel – oh no!"

Commentary: Can Phoebe act solely from duty?

There are two general difficulties with Kant's theory of moral duties. The first is that, though Kant's categorical imperative is supposed to hold always and for everyone in every situation, it is very difficult to find an example that does not have an exception. It seems there are times we would want someone to do something even though we would not want to make it a moral mandate that everyone do it. If someone is going die unless he receives medical assistance and there is only one doctor in the room, we want to say that, most of the time, there is a moral duty that attaches to that person being saved by the doctor. But we don't want to universalize that: for instance, maybe the only option is a lethal injection and, although the doctor is the only one who could save the person, he should not do so, for the sake of justice. Alternatively, perhaps the doctor is a neurosurgeon and the person is suffering from kidney failure. In this case, it would seem the doctor has no more duty than anyone else in the room.

But perhaps we could alter our maxim accordingly. "Only save someone I can save if I am a specialist in the field relevant to their malady and only if the person is an innocent victim." But now our maxim is much too narrow. We could easily come up with a dozen reasons not to universalize it. In addition, it depends too much on circumstances. Remember, Kant argued that we should not derive morality from contingent reality, but only from categorical considerations.

The second difficulty is that Kant's theory provides no real guidance for constructing hypothetical imperatives. This leads to lots and lots of arbitrary maxims. For example, I might have as my maxim, "I should not lie for the sake of convenience." According to Kant, this is consistent with the categorical imperative. But what about, "I should not lie for the sake of convenience or to people with red hair and green eyes." It would seem that, if the first maxim is consistent with the categorical imperative, the second one is. But the second one is just arbitrary. Without some further qualification, it seems our theory would become unruly or simply arbitrary.

In our *Friends* episode, we find a third difficulty with Kant's ethical theory. The question is whether you can come up with any purely selfless acts. Did Mother Teresa act selflessly when she gave her life to the poor and outcast? Someone might argue no, because, since she was a Christian, she had eternal happiness in heaven to look forward to in return for her service. What about stepping in front of a bullet for someone? If you're reasonably sure you won't die, you might do it for the accolades – getting your name in the newspaper, being called a local hero, having the person and his or her family in your debt. If you thought you were likely to die and you believe in an afterlife that rewards moral sacrifice, you may be acting from a selfish desire to be rewarded. So, is the only selfless act laying down your life for someone while not believing in an afterlife?

Why does any of this matter? If Kant is right that we only act from duty when there is no selfish motive involved, and if it is also the case that there are no selfless acts, then, according to Kant's theory, no one can ever act morally. Surely, something has gone wrong. It would seem that either Kant has to give up this feature of his theory or we have to give up the idea that anyone ever acts morally.

It is interesting to note that H. J. Paton, a famous Kant scholar, argues that this interpretation of Kant is too naive. "Kant's doctrine would be absurd if it meant that the presence of a natural inclination to good actions (or even of a feeling of satisfaction in doing them) detracted from their moral worth" (Kant 1964: 19). Paton argues that, though Kant's language allows for this interpretation, "we must remember that he is here contrasting two motives taken in *isolation* in order to find out which of them is the source of moral worth" (Kant 1964: 19; emphasis in original). The idea is that, as long as an agent can distinguish which motive dictates her actions, it is perfectly permissible that she feels a sense of satisfaction or pride in doing the right thing.

But there remains a problem. Imagine a mother who, although she recognizes that mothers have a duty to their babies, cares for and nurtures her new baby primarily from inclination. Now imagine another mother who cannot stand children and really regrets having a child, but who recognizes that mothers have a duty to their babies so, purely from a sense of duty, she cares for and nurtures her child. Notice that the consequences are the same, yet we have a different moral sentiment for the first mother than we do for the second. Even according to Paton's reinterpretation of this tenet of Kant's theory, we are to regard the second mother as more morally praiseworthy than the first.

Perhaps this is not so implausible. The first mother found it much easier to care for her baby, so there was not much moral fortitude required. We might say that the second mother is more morally praiseworthy for doing the right thing *because* it was more difficult for her.

STUDY QUESTIONS

1. Why does Kant think lying violates the categorical imperative?
2. What's the big deal about lying if the consequences are good?
3. Does the episode of *Arrested Development* raise any criticisms of Kant's view of lying?
4. In the case where Michael tells the truth to the police, he is acting in *accordance* with duty (he knows he has a duty to tell the truth), but not *from* duty (he would rather lie). In trying to be a good role model for Maeby, are there any duties that he might be acting *from* rather than just *in accordance with*?

5. In the cases where Maeby lies, are there any duties that override her duty not to lie?
6. Explain the difference between acting from duty and acting in accordance with duty.
7. Why does Kant think a motive has to be completely rational for an act to be right?
8. Can you think of any absolutely selfless acts?
9. Despite what Kant says, do you think an act can be good even if it is not completely selfless?
10. What might become of Kant's theory if we left out the requirement that all motives be purely from duty?

ALTERNATIVE CASE STUDIES

1. *The Simpsons*, "Lisa the Iconoclast," season 7
   (Is it permissible to defend a lie in order to preserve an overall sense of well-being?)
2. *Star Trek: The Next Generation*, "Justice," season 1
   (Is it plausible to think there are any absolute moral rules?)
3. *24*, "Torture: 9PM – 10PM," season 5
   (When does the well-being of the many outweigh the well-being of a few?)

EPISODE 6: CONSEQUENTIALISM

INTRODUCTION

Jack Bauer (Keifer Sutherland) is the main character on the TV show *24*. Bauer works for a government organization called CTU, Counter-Terrorism Unit. He is known for breaking the rules to get the job done. He apparently thinks that, in many cases, the rules get in the way of what "should" be done. Recalling Episode 2, we might say that Bauer regards "the rules" more as social norms than as moral norms. And he gets

What's Good on TV?: Understanding Ethics Through Television, First Edition.
Jamie Carlin Watson and Robert Arp.
© 2011 Jamie Carlin Watson and Robert Arp. Published 2011 by Blackwell Publishing Ltd.

results, so he's not fired. Bauer has even been known to torture suspects to get some piece of information that he hopes will save the lives of many innocent people (and, luckily for him, it usually does).

For example, in the second season, he uses techniques that might reasonably be described as "torturous" to gather information in order to stop terrorists from detonating a nuclear bomb in Los Angeles ("Day 2: 10pm–11pm"). In fact, Bauer uses a variety of interesting torture techniques – both physical and psychological – in some 65 scenes during the first five seasons of *24*. He will sometimes even kill a person if it means saving the lives of others. In other words, he will use virtually *any means necessary* to achieve his goals.

Are these actions morally justified? Do these ends justify these means? Do desired or morally good consequences make undesirable or horrendous actions morally permissible? If you tend to think so, you share the moral intuitions of many moral philosophers known as "consequentialists." Consequentialism is the view that an act is morally permissible if the consequences are morally good. What counts as "morally good" depends on which consequentialist you ask. Consequentialists who are "utilitarians" hold that a morally good consequence is increased happiness for the greatest number of people. Consequentialists who are "ethical egoists" hold that a morally good consequence is increased happiness for the individual performing the action. We will begin with a reading from one of the most famous consequentialist moral philosophers, John Stuart Mill (1806–73), who defends a version of utilitarianism.

MILL'S THEORY OF UTILITY

John Stuart Mill, from *Utilitarianism*

Utilitarianism is the view that an act is right insofar as it produces more pleasure for more people in the long run and wrong as it produces more pain for more people in the long run. John Stuart Mill is one of the foremost proponents of utilitarianism, but he is certainly not the first. Utilitarianism can be traced to ancient Greece, to philosophers such as Epicurus (341–271 BC) and Aristippus (435–356 BC). These ancient versions are known as "hedonism," and we know little about them. It seems they may not have been well developed. Jeremy Bentham (1748–1832) offered the first comprehensive account of the view that happiness is the primary moral good, which he called "utility." Bentham heavily influenced Mill's theory, and Mill is probably the first to use the term "utilitarianism" to name the view.

According to Mill, what things are "good"?

Mill begins by stating the thesis of his version of utilitarianism, and then defends it by responding to a series of objections. He argues that actions are evaluated according to "the Principle of Utility," which Mill also calls, "the Greatest Happiness Principle," which is the thesis that "actions are right in proportion as they tend to promote happiness, wrong as they tend to produce the reverse of happiness" (2002b: 239).

"Utility" refers to the moral value of the outcome of an action. The word "utility" typically means "usefulness," but in Mill's theory it has a more specific, moral meaning. If an outcome produces lots of happiness, it has high utility and the action that brought it about is morally good; if an outcome removes lots of happiness, it has low utility and the action that brought it about is morally bad. If an action produces an outcome with null utility – that is, if happiness is neither increased nor decreased – the action is morally neutral, and probably permissible. For Mill, the production of utility is the production of happiness.

Happiness, then, is what ultimately makes an act right or wrong. But "happiness" is both vague (it has no clear boundaries) and ambiguous (it can refer to a lot of different things), so what is happiness? Mill explains: "By happiness is intended pleasure, and the absence of pain; by unhappiness, pain, and the privation of pleasure" (2002b: 239). So, happiness means experiencing more pleasure than pain. Combined with the Principle of Utility, Mill's theory says that an action is morally right insofar as it increases pleasure and reduces pain. Mill explains: "[P]leasure, and freedom from pain, are the only things desirable as ends; and that all desirable things (which are as numerous in the utilitarian as in any other scheme) are desirable either for the pleasure inherent in themselves, or as means to the promotion of pleasure and the prevention of pain" (2002b: 239–40).

Mill seems to mean that every action a person performs has personal pleasure as *the* ultimate motive. After a little consideration, this is fairly intuitive. It's easy to see when it comes to the pursuit of pleasures associated with eating, drinking, and one-night-stand kind of sex. Why do we eat good-tasting food, drink good-tasting wine, or have sexual intercourse with someone we barely know? Because it brings us (at least, we hope) pleasure.

Are all *our actions motivated by pleasure?*

But what about other human activities and interactions? Why do parents love, teach, and protect their kids? Because parents want their kids to grow up to be well-adjusted people who live fulfilling lives. But why do parents want *that* for *their kids?* Ultimately, because parents want the pleasure of knowing they have been good parents and are loved by their kids, and don't want the pain of being considered a horrible parent, or being hated by their kids. Why did Mother Teresa do what she did? To help others, to ease their pains, to bring them pleasure, to bring herself the pleasure associated with knowing that she helped them and did the will of some god, so she could get into heaven, the ultimate pleasurable experience for herself. You can do this "tracing back to pleasure as the ultimate goal" for any action anyone performs. Why make advances in medicine and technology? To help people, to ease burdens, to streamline processes, to ... produce pleasure and eliminate pain. Why give your own life to help others? To ... produce pleasure (the pleasure associated with knowing you are giving you life to help others) and eliminate pain.

So, the promotion of pleasure and the alleviation of pain are the ultimate goals of any moral decision the utilitarian makes, pure and simple. And, it seems, further, that personal pleasure is what is valued in life such that we should all be personal pleasure-seekers. On the face of it, then, it might seem that Mill would approve of the lifestyle of, for example, plastic surgeon Christian Troy (Julian McMahon), on the show *Nip/Tuck*. Troy is notorious for his pursuit of sex, food, money, power, and the like. For example, in the episode "Ricky Wells" (season 5), a music montage flashes back and forth between Christian's awkward "significant" other, Liz (Roma Maffia), trying on clothes and Christian having sex with numerous women. The implication is clear: Christian changes sex partners as easily as Liz changes clothes. And why does Christian do this? Surely not in fulfillment of some duty, or to contribute virtue to the world – no, he does it for pleasure.

Similarly, Samantha Jones (Kim Catrall), the fun-loving public relations consultant from *Sex and the City*, is known not for her business prowess (which she has), her humanitarian efforts (which she doesn't), or her overall kindness (ditto), but for her numerous one-time affairs with gorgeous men (and sometimes couples). In the earlier seasons, Samantha doesn't believe in monogamy, in relationships, or real estate agents ("The Monogamists," season 1). In addition to her sexcapades, Samantha also pursues the pleasures of fame and money. In "The Man, The Myth, The Viagra," (season 2), she dates a 72-year-old millionaire who buys her diamond jewelry and offers to "make it worth her while" to spend the next 10 or 12 years with him. She justifies the prospect of having sex with the older man by saying, "All cats look the same in the dark."

So, according to utilitarians, if you want to know what the right thing to do is in a situation, *at a minimum*, you have to make sure that your action likely will bring about happiness. Mill calls this the "Greatest Happiness Principle," or the "Principle of Utility." Jack Bauer actually brings about the happiness of thousands, perhaps millions, of people by preventing them from suffering and/or dying as a result of a nuclear blast. And Samantha Jones attempts to bring about her own happiness through numerous sexual encounters. In addition, it is probably no accident that if you ask the average person on the street what they ultimately want in life for themselves, their parents, their kids – or even complete strangers – they will say: "to be happy." Everyone wants to be happy.

Doesn't pursuing pleasure make for poor morality?

We need to be careful here. Even if pleasure is a primary moral good, it seems we have reasons for thinking it is not the *only* moral good. We don't want a society full of people who only seek their base, animal urges. Does this mean utilitarianism is implausible? Well, it turns out that Mill would probably not approve of most of the actions of our pleasure-seeking plastic surgeon friends and our non-monogamous public relations consultant. How can this be?

Like happiness, *pleasure* is a pretty vague term and can refer to a lot of different things. What does Mill have in mind? To allay this worry, Mill defends two further claims: (1) there is more than one kind of pleasure, and (2) the morally better pleasure is not the "animal urge" kind of pleasure.

Mill distinguishes two types of pleasure and pain. There are pleasures and pains associated with the body, which Mill calls "lower" pleasures/pains. Examples of these would include joint aches, nerve pains, and "butterflies in the stomach," as well as euphoric surges, adrenaline rushes, thirsts, and other urges. Normally, when we think of pleasure and pain, we think of them in this bodily way, associated with the neurophysiological processes of a living animal – like a horse or pig – with an intact nervous system. When Jack Bauer from *24* breaks someone's arm or thumb while trying to get them to talk, or when Samantha Jones faces the prospect of breast cancer, emotionally and physically (*Sex and the City*, "The Ick Factor," season 6), these are further examples of painful feelings associated with the body. So too, when Christian Troy attempts to bring some young lady to the heights of sexual ecstasy, or when you just find a nice fitting pair of shoes, these are examples of pleasurable feelings associated with the body.

Mill distinguishes these lower pleasures of the body from "higher" pleasures and pains, understood as *qualitative experiences associated with a mind*. Examples of these would include the satisfaction of discovering the solution to a complex math problem, the regret of having made an immoral decision that cannot be undone, the joy of knowing one is loved by a friend, the elation experienced by Jack Bauer after he realizes that he has thwarted a terrorist attack, or Samatha Jones's emotional fear of dying from breast cancer. Here, the pleasures and pains are less bodily and more mental, and have names like *joy, contentment, elation, satisfaction, regret,* and *sorrow*.

Now we can see that those moral goods associated with art and music, the unconditional love of family, and raising well-trained children, are higher pleasures. Therefore, utilitarianism does not necessarily encourage a society of people who only pursue their animal urges. Experiencing more and more higher pleasures is also morally good.

But surely, most people will just pursue lower pleasures. Achieving higher pleasures requires quite a bit of education, experience, time, energy – in a word: work. But lower pleasures are easy and immediate. If people adopt a utilitarian ethic, won't they just end up promoting base animal urges? Mill says no.

Mill argues that the higher pleasures are morally better than lower pleasures – that is, they constitute more overall happiness. He makes the now-famous claim that "it is better to be a human dissatisfied than a pig satisfied; better to be Socrates dissatisfied than a fool satisfied" (2002b: 242). His arguments surrounding this claim have to with what we spoke about already, namely, that pleasures of the mind are morally better than pleasures of the body and, hence, pleasures of the mind should be pursued. "And if the fool, or the pig, are of a different opinion, it is because they only know their own side of the question. The other party to the comparison knows both sides" (2002b: 242).

And, in fact, Mill offers a way to test this. He says, just ask anyone who (a) has experienced both higher and lower pleasures and (b) has the capacity to appreciate both higher and lower pleasures. Anyone who meets both conditions will testify that higher pleasures are morally better than lower pleasures. Now, it's not clear that Mill is right about this, but he has at least given us an empirical test. Recently, there has been a resurgence of popular interest in the card game Texas Hold 'Em. Texas Hold 'Em is a much more complicated and mentally trying game than, say, Spades or Crazy Eights, so it might seem that Texas Hold 'Em brings a "higher" form of pleasure. But which do more people who meet conditions (a) and (b) play?

120   *What's Right and Wrong? Ethical Theory*

There are a couple of problems, here. First, how do you know who has the ability to appreciate both higher and lower pleasures? We know plenty of smart, well-educated people who have little interest in the arts. So we'll need a further test for this. Second, many people who play Texas Hold 'Em do so because they stand to gain a lot of money – a lower pleasure. Does engaging in a higher pleasure to achieve a lower pleasure count as morally better than simply pursuing lower pleasures? These are questions the utilitarian must answer before we can substantiate Mill's claim.

Nevertheless, if Mill is correct, then, while the pleasures enjoyed by Christian Troy and Samantha Jones are good, there are much better pleasures available. A responsible utilitarian *should* choose higher, more satisfying pleasures over lower, purely bodily pleasures.

Even though Mill doesn't offer any experimental data, he does suggest some intuitive reasons for thinking his claim is true:

> Few human creatures would consent to be changed into any of the lower animals, for a promise of the fullest allowance of a beast's pleasures; no intelligent human being would consent to be a fool, no instructed person would be an ignoramus, no person of feeling and conscience would be selfish and base. (2002b: 241)

These examples provide reasons for thinking that higher pleasures are better, at least in the long run, than lower pleasures.

Following Jeremy Bentham, Mill offers a kind of "pleasure metric" such that there are better and worse pleasures of the mind, as well as better and worse pleasures of the body. And this pleasure metric is based in, and justified by, the person who has experienced any and all forms of bodily and mental pleasure. Think about it: having had filet mignon, valet parking, and vacationed in Palm Springs or Malibu, who in their right mind would ever go back to burgers, self-parking, and the Jersey Shore (no offense to Bon Jovi fans)? Now, apply this kind of thinking to any and all pleasures of the body and mind. The following represents our rendition of a classification of Millian pleasures:

1. Most valuable

- higher pleasure of the mind: e.g., the love of a friend, philosophical contemplation resulting from reading this book, solving a difficult math problem, pleasures associated with art and music;
- lower pleasure of the mind: e.g., gossip, crude humor, fantasies associated with the lower pleasures of the body;

- higher pleasure of the body: e.g., eating filet mignon, valet parking, vacationing in Palm Springs;
- lower pleasure of the body: e.g., Big Macs, French fries, sex, drunkenness, getting high, sleeping in.

2. *Least valuable.* Another way to think about this has to do with (a) short-term, frivolous pleasures, or pleasures that seem to be pleasurable at first, but turn out to bring pain later, and (b) long-term, genuine pleasures, or pleasures that are truly pleasurable and do not bring pain later. Often, short-term, frivolous pleasures are associated with "lower" feelings of the body, while long-term, genuine pleasures are associated with "higher," qualitative experiences associated with a mind. Utilitarians – as well as several other ethicists – would say that someone should strive for long-term, genuine pleasures and steer clear of short-term, frivolous pleasures, especially if those pleasures turn out to bring pain, which is the exact opposite of what the utilitarian wishes to promote. So, for example, utilitarians would not promote a use-and-abuse, sex-addicted lifestyle like that of Christian Troy or Samantha Jones. After all, when actual people engage in the kinds of sexual encounters these fictional people engage in, the consequences are often painful and far-reaching – a sexually transmitted disease, an unwanted pregnancy, emotional scarring. Therefore, we have at least some reasons for thinking that higher pleasures are more desirable than lower pleasures.

But why is pleasure a moral good?

Even if you are fully convinced at this point that pleasure is good and pain is bad, and that there are multiple kinds of pleasures and pains, you are right to ask why pleasure is a *moral* good and pain a *moral* bad. In *Utilitarianism*, Mill devotes an entire chapter to responding to this worry.

Mill argues that happiness, defined as the increase of pleasure and decrease of pain, is the only thing that humans value as an end in itself. If something is valued in and of itself, and not for any further consequence, it is often thought that that thing has moral worth. Mill explains:

> No reason can be given why the general happiness is desirable, except that each person, so far as he believes it to be attainable, desires his own happiness. This ... being a fact, we have not only all the proof which the case admits of, but all which it is possible to require, that happiness is a good: that each person's happiness is a good to that person, and the general happiness, therefore a good to the aggregate of all persons. (2002b: 270)

Since every person desires his own happiness, the aggregate of persons also seeks pleasure as one of the goals, or "ends," of life. Therefore, happiness is a moral good.

Is pleasure the only moral good?

Of course, the argument just given does not justify adopting utilitarianism as a moral theory. Lots of moral theories allow, at least, that the absence of pain is a moral good. In order to justify adopting utilitarianism, Mill must give evidence for thinking that pleasure is the *only* human end. He considers that some people claim to pursue "virtue" over pleasure (see Episode 7 on virtue ethics): "Now it is palpable that they do desire things which, in common language, are decidedly different from happiness. They desire, for example, virtue, and the absence of vice, no less really than pleasure and the absence of pain" (2002b: 270).

As we will see in the next Episode, the philosopher Aristotle (384/3 BCE – 322 BCE) argues that "happiness" (by which he means a life of virtue) is better than "happiness" (Mill's idea of higher and lower pleasures). But Mill argues that this is not quite right. People do desire virtue, but *only because it constitutes a certain sort of pleasure*:

> Virtue, according to the utilitarian doctrine, is not naturally and originally part of the end, but it is capable of becoming so; and in those who love it disinterestedly[1] it has become so, and is desired and cherished, not as a means to happiness, but as part of the their happiness. (2002b: 271)

According to Mill, virtue, money, and lots of other human motivations that, at first, seem independent of happiness, are really just different forms of happiness.

So, not only is pleasure the primary moral good, and not only are most of our human activities motivated by pleasure, whether higher or lower (even caring for our kids and working at a homeless shelter), but pleasure is the *only* moral good. Therefore, if happiness is an *end in itself*, it is a *moral good*. And if it is plausibly the only end that motivates human action, it is the only moral good and Utilitarianism is the most plausible moral theory.

---

[1] "Disinterested" does not mean the same as "uninterested." Uninterested means "having no particular affection for something." Disinterested means "viewing something objectively, without bias."

Should I be concerned only *with* my own *pleasure?*

At this point, you might be worried that utilitarianism still sounds rather selfish. It seems I should be primarily concerned with promoting my own higher pleasures, regardless of anyone's feelings. Since most would agree that wonton selfishness is immoral, a moral theory that promotes it might sound implausible.

Recall that there are two consequentialist ethical positions: utilitarianism and ethical egoism. The ethical egoist is concerned with bringing about good consequences for himself, but the utilitarian is concerned with bringing about good consequences for all persons affected by some decision.

Despite being a torturer, deceiver, and killer, in the second season of *24* (episode "Day 2: 10pm–11pm") Jack Bauer is willing to give his own life by flying a plane containing a nuclear bomb into the Mojave Desert, away from people and valuable infrastructures. Many would call such an action heroic. Bauer sees the consequence of saving the lives of thousands of people from a nuclear blast as extremely important and valuable, and virtually no one would dispute such a benefit. His action, of course, is a very happy thing for those people saved from the pains associated with a nuclear blast, though not necessarily for Bauer.

Would Mill condone this selflessness? Perhaps surprisingly, yes. Mill says that the world is in such an imperfect state that sometimes the only way to serve the moral goal of happiness is self-sacrifice. He writes: "[S]o long as the world is in that imperfect state, I fully acknowledge that the readiness to make such a sacrifice is the highest virtue that can be found in man" (2002b: 249). Why is self-sacrifice such a virtue? Because increasing happiness is the highest good, even if it is not *your* happiness: "[U]tilitarianism requires him to be as strictly impartial as a disinterested and benevolent spectator" (2002b: 250).

According to utilitarianism, it is not simply the individual's *own* happiness that should always be pursued. That is a consequential view known as ethical egoism. And a good case can be made that Christian Troy from *Nip/Tuck* and Samantha Jones from *Sex and the City* are both ethical egoists, who think that one's own pleasure is the most important thing in life that should be pursued. According to Mill, who is definitely *not* an ethical egoist:

> [T]he happiness which forms the utilitarian standard of what is right in conduct, is not the agent's own happiness, *but that of all concerned*. As between his own happiness and that of others, utilitarianism requires him to be as strictly impartial as a disinterested and benevolent spectator. (2002b: 250; emphasis added)

So, we are not supposed to pursue the most amount of pleasure simply for ourselves, but also for everyone involved.

Why does Mill say this? If I am pursuing my own happiness and my own happiness is moral, who cares what happens to others? The main reason is that, according to utilitarianism, all rational beings are morally equal. Following fellow utilitarian Jeremy Bentham, Mill believes:

> That principle [the Greatest Happiness Principle] is a mere form of words without rational signification, unless one person's happiness, supposed equal in degree (with the proper allowance made for kind), *is counted for exactly as much as another's.* Those conditions being supplied, Bentham's dictum, "everybody to count for one, nobody for more than one," might be written under the Principle of Utility as an explanatory commentary. The equal claim of everybody to happiness in the estimation of the moralist and the legislator, involves an equal claim to all the means of happiness. (2002b: 298–9; emphasis added)

In the grand scheme of things, *overall happiness* is good, not merely your happiness or my happiness. Thus, your happiness counts for no more and no less than mine, the prince's no more and no less than the pauper's, the Harvard professor's no more and no less than the Harvard groundskeeper's. The goal is the most overall happiness, so if I have the option to suffer a little so that a large amount of happiness can be achieved for a large number of people, this is, morally, what I should do.

A handful of objections

Now that Mill has made utilitarianism more palatable, he responds to six further objections. Here, we'll just review two: first, that utilitarianism is a "godless" moral theory, antagonistic to religious belief, and second, that there is rarely enough time to calculate how much happiness one act will produce as compared with another.

Some opponents of utilitarianism argue that a morality that depends on only seeking pleasure and avoiding pain must be antagonistic to religion, since most religions teach self-sacrifice and suffering for a greater good. Mill responds by arguing that not only is utilitarianism not contrary to religion, but it is actually the clearest expression of most religious moralities, though it depends partially on your conception of God. Mill writes: "If it be a true belief that God desires, above all things, the happiness of his creatures, and that this was his purpose in creation, utility is not only not a godless doctrine, but more profoundly religious than any other"

(2002b: 255). The idea is that, if it is plausible to think that God wants us all to be happy, then utilitarianism is perfectly consistent with God's morality. He even says of Jesus Christ: "In the golden rule of Jesus of Nazareth, we read the complete spirit of the ethics of utility. To do as one would be done by, and to love one's neighbor as oneself, constitute the ideal perfection of utilitarian morality" (2002b: 250). Since Jesus suggests that everyone treat everyone else as they themselves would like to be treated, and since everyone wants to be happy, the result would be the most happiness for the most people. Therefore, Jesus was, at heart, a utilitarian.

There are a few worries about the parallel Mill draws between utilitarianism and Christianity. Mill's conditional claim seems true: if God wants us to be happy, then we should be utilitarians. But the first part is controversial on a Christian theology. Jesus tells his disciples that they will be persecuted for his sake (Matthew 5:11; John 15:20–1) and that the ultimate goal of humanity is not pleasure, but relationship with God (Matthew 6:1–4, 10:32–3; Mark 8:34–8; Luke 24:25–6). Similarly, the apostle Paul tells the Thessalonians that their suffering is evidence that they are in God's favor. Paul writes:

> [W]e ourselves boast about you in the churches of God for your steadfastness and faith in all your persecutions and in the afflictions that you are enduring. This is evidence of the righteous judgment of God, that you may be considered worthy of the kingdom of God, for which you are also suffering – since indeed God considers it just to repay with affliction those who afflict you, and to grant relief to you who are afflicted as well as to us. (2 Thessalonians 1:4–7, ESV)

If these passages are indicative of Christianity, then it is not likely that God is concerned exclusively with our happiness.

You might ask, "But what about heaven?" On the Christian story, doesn't God promise eternal happiness to those who follow Jesus? True, but if this is all there is to it (that is, if God has no other purpose for humans), why endure any miserable time on earth? If God simply wanted us to be happy, it seems he could have simply skipped any intervening hardships. Of course, it might be that those sorts of hardships are necessary in order for us to experience higher pleasures. The point, however, is that, while there may be a case to be made for the consistency of utilitarianism with religion, particularly Christianity, it is anything but obvious.

Another objection to utilitarianism has to do with humans' ability to rate the level of happiness a certain action brings, especially when there is little time to make a decision. To compare and contrast the possible happiness

I might obtain from a set of actions might take hours or days. But we are often confronted with decisions we must make immediately. If this is right, then utilitarianism is at least very impractical.

   Mill begins his response to this objection with an analogy: this is like saying it is impossible to conduct our behavior according to Christianity because there is not enough time to read the entire Old and New Testaments before making a decision. Surely, no one would object to Christianity on these grounds. Similarly, you wouldn't expect a sea captain to consult all his maps and charts before every decision he makes. As humans, we have learned what generally contributes to pleasure and what generally contributes to pain, and we're quite efficient at employing this knowledge at a moment's notice. On occasion, there are more difficult decisions that require a good deal more reflection. But this is no different from Christianity or the ship captain. If it is no objection to these, then it is no objection to utilitarianism.

Summary of the summary

Now, given what we have said so far, we can formulate a rough description of utilitarianism:

1. An act is *moral* if it results in *good* consequences, defined as obtaining more higher level pleasures than pains, *for all those affected by the action*, and, hence, one should always strive to bring about as many pleasurable consequences for all those affected as possible.
2. An act is *immoral* if it results in *bad* consequences, defined as obtaining more pains than higher level pleasures, *for all those affected by the action*, and, hence, one should always strive to bring about as few bad consequences for as many are affected as possible.

So, according to utilitarianism, Jack Bauer is acting morally when he flies a plane into the Mojave Desert in order to save the lives of others (*24*, "Day 2: 10pm–11pm"), as is anyone who gives his or her life to save a number of people. When the World Trade Center in New York City was hit by planes on September 11, 2001, many people gave their lives to save complete strangers from the horrible consequences of pain, suffering, and/or death resulting from the collapse of the Twin Towers and other buildings in the area. Again, these actions are morally permissible and possibly obligatory, even according to utilitarianism. On the other hand, if I'm a utilitarian and I need some important information from you – in the words of

Jack Bauer – "You're going to tell me what I want to know, it's just a question of how much you want it to hurt."

CASE STUDY 1: *Battlestar Galactica*, "You Can't Go Home Again," season 1

AVAILABILITY: **Netflix**

Pilot Kara Thrace, AKA "Starbuck," has crash-landed on a foreign planet with a hostile environment. Thrace has only enough oxygen to keep him going for 46 hours. The planet's surface is hostile, not only to life, but also to electronic searching devices as well as visibility even from low-flying ships. Admiral William Adama (Edward James Olmos), with consent from President Laura Roslin (Mary McDonnell), orders all ships to join in the search effort.

Unfortunately, the humans are at war with the Cylons. Though the battle is in a lull, the return of the Cylons is imminent, and diverting war ships to the rescue of one pilot places the whole fleet in danger. What's worse, as pilots attempt low-flying searches, their ships are severely damaged by the planet's atmosphere, further debilitating the humans' ability to fend off the Cylons.

Just before her oxygen runs out, Starbuck finds a crippled Cylon ship. She discovers that the ship itself is part biological organism, part machine. She digs her way through the muck to discover an oxygen hose, which she uses to make the air in the meat-cabin safe to breathe. Though Admiral Adama knows Starbuck has no more oxygen, he continues the search. Opposition to Adama's obstinate refusal to call off the search grows heated, and the president pays a visit to convince the Admiral that the lives of all the remaining humans are at stake.

Admiral Adama finally consents, the search is called off, and the fleet prepares to move to another galaxy, when suddenly a lone Cylon ship approaches. Adama's first reaction is to eliminate the threat. But the Cylon ship's flying is a little better than is typical for their enemy and they soon discover that the pilot is Starbuck, re-emerged from the planet, a little worse for wear, but alive.

Commentary: How much is saving one life worth?

According to Kant, our duties are absolute and irrevocable. It is always wrong to take a human life because human lives are ends in themselves.

Kant also says that if you have a duty, you are obliged to do that duty regardless of the consequences. But there are reasons for thinking this position is too strong. Sometimes consequences seem relevant to our moral decisions. "You Can't Go Home Again," highlights this intuition.

No one doubts that the life of Starbuck is extremely valuable. The question is whether her life is *more* valuable than the lives of all the humans sent out in the fighter ships to look for her. As President Roslin signs the order approving the search, Dr Gaius Baltar (James Callis) respectfully challenges her decision: "You are compromising the security of the entire fleet while we search for one, solitary pilot." Roslin responds: "It is a risk. But those pilots put their lives on the line for us everyday."

Notice that Roslin's response is very Kantian. The idea is that, because each of the pilots risks his or her life for us, we owe it to them – we have a *duty* to them – to risk our lives for each of them. The utilitarian could not offer this argument. It seems that the utilitarian should side against Adama in favor of the thousands over the one. Being alive at least offers the possibility of more happiness than being slaughtered by Cylons. As much as we might like Starbuck, she is just one soldier among many, and part of her job is risk her life for the good of the many. Her loss is lamentable, but not immoral.

Could the utilitarian offer any argument in favor of risking the lives of thousands to search for one pilot? Perhaps. If the happiness of the group increased as a result of the search efforts more than the fear of death, the utilitarian might have a reason to search for Starbuck. For instance, the whole population might love Starbuck in such a way that searching for her gives them a deep sense of pleasure, and this deep sense of pleasure makes the fear of dying less troublesome. But this is seriously stretching the limits of utilitarianism. If the thousands actually die, the few remaining humans will suffer terribly, or there will be no humans left to feel pleasure or pain.

But there is an interesting implication of utilitarianism that might justify Adama's decision. Mill says that the morality of an action depends on its *actual* consequence and not its intended or potential consequence. Mill writes that:

> The utilitarian does recognize in human beings the power of sacrificing their own greatest good for the good of others. It only refuses to admit that the sacrifice is itself a good. A sacrifice which does not increase, or tend to increase, the sum total of happiness, it considers as wasted. (2002b: 249)

In addition, Mill rejects the Kantian idea that a good act depends on the will or intention of the agent (2002b: 251). An agent may have all the good intentions in the world, but make decisions that result in horrendous consequences. Therefore, an action's worth is judged by its outcomes. Since Adama's selfishness and stalling ultimately lead to the crew being reunited with Starbuck and with no lives lost among the thousands of humans, more happiness is ultimately achieved for all. This would seem to justify Adama's actions, even for a utilitarian.

So, where does this leave us? It seems to raise a problem for utilitarianism. Before knowing whether Starbuck will make it, the utilitarian should have been against Adama. After the results are in, the utilitarian should praise Adama. Is this consistent? Thankfully, Mill predicts this worry.

CASE STUDY 2: *The Twilight Zone (Newer)*, "Cradle of Darkness," season 1

AVAILABILITY: **NetFlix**

Andrea Collins (Katherine Heigl) goes back in time to Braunau am Inn, Austria to kill the infant Adolf Hitler. Collins poses as housekeeper Marta Eickelmann, who is supposed to arrive at the Hitlers' house in two days. She offers a plausible story for her early arrival and is put immediately to work. The former housekeeper, Kristina (Jillian Fargey), takes over care of baby Hitler because his mother Klara (Nancy Sivak) is ill. The Hitlers have lost three children and Herr Alois Hitler (James Remar) is overprotective of the infant and allows only Kristina to care for him. He even considers Klara too weak of body and mind to help with the baby.

Collins's first attempt on Adolf's life is thwarted by Klara, who snuck into Adolf's room to watch over him. On her second attempt, Collins is struck with a pang of conscience at having to kill an innocent baby. She consults a priest who tells her that only God can take a life, and she pleads with Klara to take the baby and leave the country, to no avail. After a brief interior monologue from Herr Hitler on "Jews, gypsies, vermin everywhere, corrupting our Aryan nation," Collins becomes steadfast that "something has to be done."

During an important dinner, baby Adolf starts crying. Collins leaves Kristina to tend to the guests while she pretends to check on Adolf. She takes the baby, slips through the window, and creeps through the streets so she won't be seen. When Kristina runs after her, Collins jumps into a river with the baby, sacrificing herself in order to protect 60 million future lives.

Unfortunately, Kristina buys another baby from a gypsy woman and passes it off to both mother and father as baby Adolf. Despite her sacrifice, the narrator tells us, Collins "created the very monster she sought to destroy," because, "History can never be changed. Not even in The Twilight Zone."

Commentary: How much is taking one life worth?

> What if you had a chance to go back in time, to save millions of lives by killing one man? Andrea Collins will soon discover this mission to be more difficult than she ever imagined, as she takes a one-way trip into *The Twilight Zone*. (From, "Cradle of Darkness")

Is it ever morally permissible to take one person's life in order to save the lives of millions? In this episode of *The Twilight Zone*, Andrea Collins goes back in time to try to kill baby Adolf Hitler in the hope that he won't be around to murder millions of innocent people in the Holocaust. It is interesting to note that most of us would not have a problem with killing Hitler *after* he had committed all those horrific crimes against morality. But what about *before*? Is he liable for those deaths even though they haven't happened yet? Even if we know they *will* happen?

It seems the utilitarian is committed to saying both that Hitler is innocent and that he should be killed. A utilitarian might suggest stopping the travesty of the Holocaust by almost any means. The death of one baby is nothing compared to the 60 million lives lost in invasion, combat, firing squads, and concentration camps. In addition, babies are so easy to kill, there would be no psychological torture for him (because he doesn't understand you're trying to kill him) and very little physical pain. The majority of the suffering would belong to the parents, which, compared to the suffering of the other 60 million, seems rather trivial.

What about Collins's crisis of conscience? It seems she has a Kantian moment. There seem good reasons for not holding innocent people responsible for the moral crimes of others. Baby Adolf Hitler has committed none of the crimes of adult Adolf Hitler. It would be like spanking your 7-year-old on New Year's Day because you have extremely good evidence that he will lie to you at some point this year. Surely he is not morally responsible *now* for something he hasn't yet done. Nevertheless, Alois revives Collins' utilitarian intuition. The massacre of millions of innocents must be stopped, even if it means killing an innocent.

The problem with this response is one that plagues utilitarianism. It is no doubt true that killing baby Hitler will have good consequences (forget the actual ending of the episode for a moment). The dictator Adolf Hitler will not exist as we know him. But is it morally permissible to kill an innocent person to bring about a more pleasurable outcome?

Imagine the following case. You are the sheriff of a small, isolated western town in late nineteenth-century America. You discover that someone has been murdered and the town is divided over which of two prominent families to blame. There were no witnesses and there is apparently no evidence to help you solve this case. The town is up in arms and soon people will start shooting one another to avenge this murder. By lucky chance, a drifter has recently arrived in your town, with apparently no home, no family, and no outside connections. Clever sheriff that you are, you decide you can pin the murder on the drifter, let the town hang him, and, in the process, stop numerous deaths and make the whole town happy and content once again. According to utilitarianism, this is exactly what you should do. But surely this is not morally permissible. It may be useful, it may be practical, it may result in very good overall consequences (after subtracting the brief suffering of the drifter), but it doesn't seem *right*. The drifter is obviously innocent. This is a famous counterexample to utilitarianism known as "The Drifter Dilemma" (see Driver 2007).

Now notice, this case is almost identical to the baby Hitler case: kill one innocent person in order to prevent the deaths and suffering of large numbers of people. If you don't think you should pin the murder on the innocent drifter, then you should also refrain from killing baby Hitler. On the other hand, if you think you should kill baby Hitler, you should also pin the murder on the drifter. It is a difficult dilemma that has led many moral philosophers to become deontologists.

Of course, the episode throws in a twist. It presupposes a view called "fatalism," which means that whatever is fated to happen will happen regardless of what human beings do. In "Cradle of Darkness," we are led to believe that Hitler's horrors would have happened regardless of whether Andrea Collins killed Alois Hitler's biological child. If fatalism is true, then a utilitarian need not take a side about what Collins should do. Whatever will happen, will happen, so humans cannot do anything to increase or decrease the amount of happiness in the world. Therefore, it is irrelevant what you *should* or *should not* do.

STUDY QUESTIONS

1. According to Mill's utilitarianism, is it morally permissible to place a whole battalion of soldiers in danger in order to save one soldier?
2. If you are trying to decide what will bring you more pleasure, *how* might you compare the pleasure of kissing someone you're really attracted to with: (a) eating a really good meal? (b) having sex with someone you're only moderately attracted to? or (c) going to see a really good movie with friends? [Notice: the question is not, "Which would you prefer more?" but "On what basis would you decide whether one is more pleasurable than the other?"

3. Before Starbuck runs out of air, are you more sympathetic with Admiral Adama or with Dr Baltar? What about after Starbuck runs out of air? If there is a difference, what do you think accounts for the difference?

4. Imagine that, instead of thousands of lives on the line, only two others are on the line. According to a utilitarian, would it still be morally permissible to call off the search?

5. At the end of the *Battlestar Galactica* episode, Adama's son, Lee Adama (Jamie Bamber), asks what his father would have done if he had crashed on the planet. Admiral Adama responds, "If it had been you, we would never leave." Is this sort of response justifiable on utilitarian grounds?

6. Would a utilitarian condone killing one innocent person to save the lives of many others?

7. Knowing how "Cradle of Darkness" turns out, is there anything else Andrea Collins could have done instead of killing baby Hitler to prevent the Holocaust?

8. Is it ever morally permissible to *punish* someone for an immoral act they have not yet committed?

9. Can you think of any utilitarian reasons for killing baby Hitler but not pinning the murder on the drifter? Can you think of any Kantian reasons?

10. Is "The Drifter Dilemma" similar enough to the Hitler example to cast doubt on the decision to kill baby Hitler? If you think so, list the similarities. If you don't think so, how could you change the Drifter Dilemma so that it would be more like the case of baby Hitler?

ALTERNATIVE CASE STUDIES

1. *Smallville*, "Rabid," season 9
   (Do the ends justify the means for Chloe?)
2. *Lost*, "He's Our You," season 5
   (Is Sayid justified in shooting Ben Linus?)
3. *The Sopranos*, "Second Opinion," season 3
   (Are we good at figuring out what makes us happy?)

EPISODE 7: VIRTUE ETHICS

INTRODUCTION

In the *Family Guy* episode, "The Thin White Line" (season 3), the family dog, Brian, sees a therapist because he is listless and generally unhappy. The therapist tells him that he's too self-centered and should try to think about others for a change. Brian tries by volunteering as a seeing-eye dog and sitting with an old woman in a nursing home, but he doesn't seem to find any more satisfaction in these things than in his daily routine. Accidentally, Joe, Brian's neighbor and a policeman, discovers that Brian has a super-sensitive nose that could be used to locate illegal drugs. Brian takes the job and discovers that helping take criminals off the streets is very satisfying.

What's Good on TV?: Understanding Ethics Through Television, First Edition.
Jamie Carlin Watson and Robert Arp.
© 2011 Jamie Carlin Watson and Robert Arp. Published 2011 by Blackwell Publishing Ltd.

After making his first big bust, he says, "This is great! This is the rush I've been looking for." Unfortunately, Brian sniffs some cocaine along the way and gets hooked. Though he continues to do well at his job, his personal life deteriorates quickly. He begins talking harshly to people he cares about, complaining about his job, and he even brings a hooker home to the family.

One interesting thing about this story is that, though Brian does just what his therapist suggests and everything he does is generally considered morally good – he helps the blind and indigent, and he helps reduce crime – in only one very narrow set of circumstances is he actually satisfied and happy. So, is Brian acting morally? If his actions are consistent with the categorical imperative, and they seem to be, Immanuel Kant would say yes. Despite his discontent, he is doing his duty. If the pleasure his actions bring about is greater than his own painful emotions, and it seems they could, John Stuart Mill would say yes. Brian's happiness is being sacrificed to bring more happiness to more people over a longer period of time.

Nevertheless, there is something unsettling about the answers that Kant and Mill give to the question: "Is Brian acting morally?" They seem to ignore many of the morally relevant features of Brian's actions. In fact, this episode of *Family Guy* might suggest that there is more to being moral than just "doing the right thing."

What more could there be? The philosopher Aristotle (384/3 BCE – 322 BCE) argued that we cannot understand whether a person's actions are good or bad unless we know more about the person, that is, we need to know something of that person's *character*. This approach to morality sounds very different from those we have considered in the past few Episodes. There, we were concerned with questions about what makes an action right or wrong – obligatory, permissible, or impermissible. On this approach, we are directed to ask questions about what makes a *person* good or bad. To see what this might mean, we will look at Aristotle's moral theory, known as "virtue ethics." We will then evaluate the plausibility of this theory in light of television episodes from the BBC series *Foyle's War* and *Star Trek: The Next Generation*.

ARISTOTLE'S THEORY OF VIRTUE

Aristotle, from *Nicomachean Ethics*

As we noted in the "Pilot Episode," the earliest philosophers were concerned with discovering what is "good." They did not restrict their discussions to actions alone, but wanted to understand the good wherever it could be found. Aristotle writes: "Every art and every inquiry, and similarly every action and pursuit, is thought to aim at some good; and for this reason the good has rightly been declared to be that at which all things aim" (*NE* 1094a 1–3). Aristotle then distinguishes two general types of goods: *activities* and *consequences*. If an activity is good for some consequence, the good of the activity is subordinate to the good of the consequence, for the ultimate good of the activity is achieved only if the consequence occurs. In his book of ethics, Aristotle attempts to provide an account of the good at which all activities and consequences aim, that is, "the *ultimate* good."

But the ultimate good of some actions and their consequences may differ from those of a different set. "[The good] seems different in different actions and arts; it is different in medicine, in strategy, and in other arts likewise" (*NE* 1097a, 16–17). The good differs from pursuit to pursuit, and some goods are subordinate to others. And Aristotle admits that these activities are so varied there "could not be a common Idea set over all these goods" (*NE* 1096a, 22–3).

But there must be something was can say about the good, that is, in answer to the question: "What is the good?" Aristotle answers that it is, "Surely that for whose sake everything else is done. In medicine this is health, in strategy victory, in architecture a house, in any other sphere something else … for it is for the sake of this that all men do whatever else they do" (*NE* 1097a, 18–21). The good, then, is *what makes an act worth doing*.

We could ask important questions about the goods of all the various human activities (as Aristotle notes, medicine, strategy, etc.), but they all lead to one central question for the moral philosopher: What is the ultimate good for humans? At what should our lives and pursuits aim? What would make life worth living? Notice that this question is significantly different from that asked by relativists, deontologists, and consequentialists, which is: What *actions* are good (or permissible or obligatory or impermissible)? Philosophers who approach morality as Aristotle suggests argue that there is more to morality than the motivation for, or the consequences of, an action. There is also the *character* of the agent. Though actions are important for Aristotle, his primary concern is with character.

According to Aristotle, someone of bad character might do something that leads to good consequences. Or someone of bad character might commit an act out of pure motives. But in neither case can the actor be said to be a "good person." "[T]he man who does not rejoice in noble actions is not even good; since no one would call a man just who did not enjoy acting justly" (*NE* 1099a, 17–19). In addition, making a right decision on one occasion doesn't make a person moral any more than going to the gym on one occasion makes someone strong, or eating too much at one meal makes someone fat.

As we unfold Aristotle's view, we can begin to see what is unique about Brian's situation in our *Family Guy* episode. Even though his actions are good (according to the other moral theories), something changes about Brian over the course of the episode. At first he is indifferent, then he appreciates the good he is doing, and then he becomes an addict. Brian is only happy when his emotions are in sync with his actions (when he appreciates the good of fighting crime). And his satisfaction is fleeting because his moral character is undeveloped. So, even though his actions are good, *Brian* is not good.

So, what makes humans (or "moral agents," in Brian's case) good? Aristotle argues that it is *the activity of the soul in conformity with virtue in a complete life* (*NE* 1098a, 17–18, 20). This definition raises a number of questions: What does he mean by "virtue"? What would it mean to act "in conformity with" virtue, and why "over a complete life"? And, why believe this account is an accurate account of what it means for a human to be good? In this section, we will address each of these.

What is a *"virtue"*?

To fully understand the concept of a virtue, we need to understand something of Aristotle's view of reality – his metaphysics. Aristotle defends the idea that every contingent thing (things that do not exist by necessity; numbers and a creator deity might be necessary beings, while cows and rocks are contingent) has a goal it is designed to achieve (a "*telos*" in Greek). This goal for each individual entity is determined by the "form" or "type" that entity belongs to. We can think of "forms" or "types" sort of like "biological species." Aristotle was the first biologist, drawing, naming, and categorizing various creatures. We get many of our taxonomic terms (genus, species, kingdom, etc.) from Aristotle's *History of Animals*, *Parts of Animals*, and *Generation of Animals*, so the metaphor is appropriate.

Aristotle argues that two causes determine what an animal will look like. The first is "necessity," by which he seems to mean the physical operation of natural laws, as they apply to the nutritional value of food and the substance out of which an object is made. " [W]e say that food is necessary; because an animal cannot possibly do without it" (*Parts of Animals*, 642a, 7–8). The second is the "final end," by which he means that which determines what the animal is designed to look like. This aspect of an object is not physical. " [A] dead body has exactly the same configuration as a living one; but for all that is not a man" (*Parts of Animals*, 640b, 35–6). Therefore, some non-physical property encourages an object from its potential good (its not-yet-complete form) to its ultimate good (its complete, fully realized form), which Aristotle called its "*entelechy*" or "actuality."

The point is that there seems to be more to reality than merely physical causes. We must also ask about "teleological" causes (from *telos*):

> To say, then, that shape and colour constitute the animal is an inadequate statement, and is much the same as if a woodcarver were to insist that the hand he had cut out was really a hand. ... What, however, I would ask, are the forces by which the hand or the body was fashioned into its shape? The woodcarver will perhaps say, by the axe or the auger; the physiologist, by air and by earth. Of these two answers the artificer's is the better, but it is nevertheless insufficient. For it is not enough for him to say that by the stroke of his tool this part was formed into a concavity, that into a flat surface; but he must state the reasons why he struck his blow in such a way as to effect this, and what his final object was; namely, that the piece of wood should develop eventually into this or that shape. (*Parts of Animals*, 641a, 5–7, 8–13)

So, for example, each animal has an *telos* that directs it toward the predetermined shape of its species. And the *telos* of animals is to thrive and reproduce: "The life of animals, then, may be divided into two acts – procreation and feeding; for on these two acts all their interests and life concentrate. Their food depends chiefly on the substance of which they are severally constituted" (*History of Animals*, 589a, 3–6). The shape of a carved piece of wood or an animal must be attributed, in part, to the *telos* of those objects.

The *telos* of any object is the best, or most complete, version of that object. So, Aristotle argues, to achieve your *telos* is an "excellence" – an object that does this is everything it is intended to be. So, the block of wood that is being carved is better than the uncarved block because it is on its way to becoming what it is meant to be. And the completed carving is better than the block that is being carved because it is what it is supposed to be – it has achieved its excellence.

What, then, is the *telos* of humans? Aristotle explains that it is the thing that is worthy of pursuit for its own sake, and not for any other end. If there are more than one of these things, he says, "the most final of these will be what we are seeking" (*NE*, 1097a, 29–30). He then argues that "happiness" seems to be the one thing that is always desirable for its own sake; it is the "chief good":

> Now such a thing happiness, above all else, is held to be; for this we choose always for itself and never for the sake of something else, but honour, pleasure, reason, and every virtue we choose indeed for themselves (for if nothing resulted from them we should still choose each of them), but we choose them also for the sake of happiness, judging that by means of them we shall be happy. (*NE* 1097a, 37 – 1097b, 5)

So, even though we often include "honor" or "pleasure" among our motivations for some action, and even though these might be desirable in themselves, we typically choose them because they tend to make us happy. The word we translate as "happiness" is the Greek, " *eudaimonia*," probably more clearly interpreted as "the good life." It is important to note that Aristotle distinguishes happiness from pleasure. This prevents us from confusing him with a utilitarian, who would argue that the only morally relevant feature of an action is whether it leads to pleasure or suffering.

Therefore, the "good" for humans, according to Aristotle, is to achieve "happiness," and happiness is something over and above honor, pleasure, and reason. What, then, is happiness? Since happiness is the ultimate good, the *chief* good of humans, we have our answer already: "human good turns out to be activity of soul in accordance with virtue ... in a complete life" (*NE* 1098a, 17–20). Why is *this* the definition of happiness? Because acting according to the virtues leads to happiness:

> For no function of man has so much permanence as virtuous activities ... and of these themselves the most valuable are more durable because those who are happy spend their life most readily and most continuously in these; for this seems to be the reason why we do not forget them. The attribute in question, then, will belong to the happy man, and he will be happy throughout his life. (*NE* 1100b, 11–18)

Living according to the virtues consistently produces happiness, therefore happiness consists in living according to the virtues. But what are the "virtues"?

Virtues are "excellences," either of *intellect* or of *moral character*. Aristotle tells us that the virtues of intellect include "philosophic wisdom," "understanding," and "practical wisdom," and virtues of moral character include "liberality" and "temperance" (*NE* 1103a, 5–6). There are certain character traits that lead to the *telos* more efficiently than others. For example, it is an excellence of intellect to reject fallacious arguments because doing so leads more efficiently to the *telos* of intellect, namely, knowledge. Similarly, it is an excellence of moral character to give to others in need when you are able because doing so leads more efficiently to the *telos* of moral character: happiness/*eudaimonia*.

Therefore, a "good person" is someone who consistently works to achieve happiness (his *telos*) by doing those things that lead most efficiently to happiness (the virtues). Recall our *Family Guy* episode. If Aristotle is right, Brian just hasn't been performing good actions long enough to develop a moral character that will lead him to happiness (remember, his therapist told him he was too self-centered). So, how could Brian encourage the process? To answer that, we need to know more about particular virtues and how they work.

What are some virtues?

How do we know which behaviors are virtues? By watching people. Just as Aristotle learned about animals by observing them and categorizing them according to their biological kinds, so we can watch humans and determine which actions lead most efficiently to happiness. Notice that we used the term "behavior" instead of "action." For moral philosophers since the eighteenth century, morality has been primarily an activity of the mind – a study of how to make principled ethical decisions. For Aristotle, being good requires the whole person – the emotions, intellect, will, and body. This is because the happy person doesn't just make the right decision; he makes the right decision consistently (will) for the right reasons (intellect), appreciates the goodness of the act (moral emotions), and acts on that decision (body).

If happiness is the primary excellence toward which humans are to direct themselves, the most efficient way to achieve it is to perform all actions in the best possible way – that is, to act excellently. To do something excellently is to avoid doing it poorly, which Aristotle calls a "vice." There are two ways to do something poorly. You can do it with too little passion, which is called a "vice of deficiency." Or you can do it with too much passion, which is called a "vice of excess." Doing something well, virtuously, means to achieve the mean between these two excesses. Aristotle calls each virtue the "golden mean" between its vices of deficiency and excess.

What sort of excellences lead to happiness? Aristotle lists dozens, but we'll only discuss two here: courage and honesty. "Courage" is the virtue of acting excellently in the face of danger. If you have too little passion for

Table 7.1

Vice of Deficiency	Virtue	Vice of Excess
Peevishness	Patience	Apathy
Buffoonery	Wit	Crudeness
Flattery	Friendliness	Rudeness
Prudishness	Modesty	Shamelessness
Jealousy	Righteous Indignation	Malice

acting in the face of danger, you may run away or hide, or act out of an inappropriate amount of fear. Even if what you do leads to a good outcome (say, by accident), since you acted poorly in the face of danger, you did not display the virtue of courage. So, the vice of deficiency for courage is "cowardice." Alternatively, if you have too much passion for acting in the face of danger, you may storm into it without taking proper precautions; you may put yourself at too much risk for the task at hand. It does not benefit any army if its troops merely charge to the slaughter without concern for safety or strategy. Again, even if doing so leads to a good outcome, since you acted poorly in the face of danger, you did not display the virtue of courage. So, the vice of excess for courage is "recklessness."

"Honesty" is the virtue of telling the truth. If you have too little passion for the truth, you may lie or twist the truth to serve your own interests, or you may just not tell the whole truth. So, fairly obviously, the vice of deficiency for honesty is "dishonesty." A person can also be overly passionate about the truth. You might relay some bad news to someone, but instead of just telling them the news accurately, you go into details in a way that upsets him or hurts him. Similarly, you might tell the truth arrogantly or boastfully, or tell the truth in the wrong circumstances or in front of the wrong people. Being too honest in any of these ways expresses the vice of excess for honesty, which is "boastfulness" or "overstatement."

In addition to the two classic virtues of courage and honesty, table 7.1 shows a handful of others with their attendant vices.

What does it mean to act "in conformity with virtue," and why "over a complete life"?

As we have noted, to act in conformity with virtue doesn't mean simply acting courageously, or acting honestly. In fact, Aristotle argues that you couldn't *simply* act courageously or honestly. In order for actions that look courageous or honest *to actually be* courageous or honest, your moral emotions must be the motivation for those actions. And for most of us, our moral emotions are not properly developed for years and years. So, we "do the right thing" out of duty or custom or selfishness and, if we do this for long enough, our characters will develop in such a way that our actions will be excellent, which leads to the ultimate good for humans: happiness.

The idea that morality requires practice and discipline is essential to Aristotle's theory of virtue. It's even part of the name of his book: *Nichomachean Ethics.* "Nichomachean" is likely named after Aristotle's son, Nichomachus, to whom either the book was dedicated or by whom it was edited. But the word "ethics" is a Greek word that is derived from the root word "ethos," which means "habit." So to act "in conformity with virtue" is to make it a habit to act virtuously to the best of your ability.

How long does the process of living virtuously take before we become "good" people? For most of us, a lifetime. Very few people become international athletic stars in just a few years. It takes many years of hard work, discipline, and patience to compete among the best athletes. Similarly, very few people become world-renowned scholars in just a few years. It takes years of dedicated reading, writing, and interaction with other scholars before someone can take their place among the best. Should the same be any different for a skill so much more important than athletics and scholarship? To be truly good, Aristotle argues, requires a lifetime of diligently pursuing the virtues.

So, how could Brian, from our *Family Guy* episode, encourage the process of becoming a good dog? According to Aristotle, he just has to keep at it. There may be some pitfalls along the way, but if he continues trying to act courageously, attempting to be temperate, acting as if he were humble, etc., eventually his moral emotions will be trained to motivate these actions on their own.

Why is virtue ethics not a type of deontology or consequentialism?

At this point, it is important to ask why virtue ethics is not simply a version of deontology or consequentialism. Is it a "duty" to seek happiness? Aristotle rejects "pleasure" as the goal of ethics, but this just means he is not a utilitarian consequentialist. Could "happiness" be the morally relevant consequence?

There is one huge difference between virtue ethics and these more contemporary moral theories. Aristotle's theory does not include a decision procedure. Whereas Kant and Mill offer a way to make moral decisions, Aristotle explains the conditions necessary for a good life. To be sure, there are rules that a person must follow. For instance, part of your moral development involves participating in the political process, and you are obligated to obey the laws of the government. Virtue ethicist Alasdair MacIntyre explains: "[I]t is a crucial part of Aristotle's view that certain types of action are absolutely prohibited or enjoined irrespective of circumstances or consequences. Aristotle's view is teleological, but it is not consequentialist" (1984: 150). What does it mean for a theory to be "teleological"? It means the goal you are supposed to achieve is the guide for your actions.

Even though there is a goal everyone is supposed to achieve, Aristotle's view is not deontological either. It is certainly not Kantian. Recall that Kant argues that only an act performed from duty and not motivated by emotion or consequences has moral value. But emotion is essential to Aristotle's view. MacIntyre explains: "To act virtuously is not, as Kant was later to think, to act against inclination; it is to act from inclination formed by the cultivation of the virtues. Moral education is an 'éducation sentimentale' [an emotional education]" (1984: 149).

The deontologist, more broadly, argues that morality is an inherently rational pursuit. The moral value of an action derives from the intrinsic goodness of an agent acting for the *right reasons*. Aristotle doesn't hold that moral agents are intrinsically good; they must become good over a lifetime of acting virtuously. And reasons, for Aristotle, are secondary to emotions, since, if we are not intrinsically good, emotion is our primary motivation. Consider the development of a child into an adult. Only after many years and much training does the child suborn his immediate emotional concerns to rational considerations of long-term goods. And finally, the deontologist argues that each individual is responsible for the morality of his own actions. But for Aristotle, a person's community is partly responsible for her moral development. If the community is nurturing and virtuous, the child will more quickly develop her moral emotions. If the community is indifferent and vicious, it will take much longer and much more effort on the child to develop virtuous emotions. These considerations show that virtue ethics is a moral theory distinct from consequentialism and deontology.

In order to evaluate the plausibility of virtue theory, we turn to a couple of television episodes. The BBC show *Foyle's War* depicts a detective who does the right thing, but, perhaps, not for reasons that Kant or Mill would find satisfactory. If this is intuitively right, we may have a reason for preferring virtue ethics to deontology or consequentialism. On the other hand, *Star Trek: The Next Generation* places a generally virtuous person in a position where he is tempted to do some really bad things. And although it takes a community of virtuous people to bring him around, we may have reason to believe that all the moral education in the universe cannot make up for not having a clear decision procedure.

CASE STUDY 1: *Foyle's War*, "Enemy Fire," set 3

AVAILABILITY: iTunes, NetFlix, YouTube (10-minute clips)

In the brilliant BBC television show *Foyle's War*, Detective Chief Superintendent Christopher Foyle (Michael Kitchen) investigates crimes, usually murders, in Hastings, East Sussex, England in the early years of World War II. In addition to being a well-written murder mystery show, *Foyle's War* also depicts many of the social and political controversies and economic difficulties that Britain faced while fending off Nazi Germany.

In this episode, a man's large country manor home has been requisitioned by the RAF (Royal Air Force) as a hospital for wounded airmen. One of the doctors assigned to the house, Dr Wrenn (Jonathan Slinger), learns that, while he spends long hours at the hospital, his wife is having an affair with an RAF mechanic named Drake (Shaun Dooley).

Detective Foyle's son Andrew (Juilan Ovenden) is a pilot in the RAF and has an argument with Drake, because Drake is lazy and has not fixed a faulty slide on his cockpit window. The slide sticks and could be life-threatening if Andrew needed to eject. As it turns out, one of Andrew's close friends flies the plane next, the slide sticks, and the pilot is badly burned, perhaps never to see again. The strain of flying so many missions and of seeing so many of his friends hurt or killed begins to overwhelm Andrew and he is told to take some leave time.

For much of the episode, Detective Foyle and his associates investigate several instances of sabotage around the manor house/hospital. But soon, Drake turns up dead. Now, Dr Wrenn, because of his wife's affair with Drake, is a suspect, but he has an alibi. And Sergeant Milner (Anthony Howell), Foyle's colleague and a grateful former patient of Wrenn, explains that Wrenn is a good doctor and a good man because he made it so Milner could walk again after an accident early in the war. And Andrew, because of his recent arguments with Drake, is also a suspect, but is suddenly nowhere to be found. While Foyle and Milner attempt to solve the murder, Andrew's Wing Commander Turner (Martin Turner) tells him that Andrew has exceeded his leave time but has not returned.

Turner begins by saying, "I shouldn't be here, Mr Foyle. It goes against every rule in the book." He then explains that many high-ranking officials in the RAF are anxious to punish any soldier they feel exhibits "LMF," "lack of moral fibre." But Turner is more sympathetic, understanding battle fatigue. "These young men . . . we ask so much of them. It's not just the number of ops they fly and the mental strain, it's lack of sleep. It's no wonder they get ill. 'Flying stress'; 'combat fatigue'; 'shell shock,' even. There are many names, there just aren't enough of us prepared to recognize it." Andrew has been gone less than 48 hours, and if Foyle can convince him to come back, he will show some leniency. When Foyle tells Turner that he hasn't seen Andrew, Turner says, "Then there's nothing I can do. He'll be charged with desertion." Foyle asks how long his son has. Turner says, "I can give him till 2 o'clock this afternoon. No longer than that."

Luckily, Foyle discovers a blossoming friendship between his driver Sam (Honeysuckle Weeks) and Andrew. Upon hearing the conversation with Turner, Sam tells Foyle that Andrew has been staying with her. Andrew and his father have a long talk over a pint and Foyle explains that he, Turner, and Sam have, "his best interests at heart, because, uh, we, uh, care about you." Andrew agrees that going back would be in his best interests and consents to letting Sam drive him back to the base. Of course, Foyle had solved the murder long before he knew Andrew was missing.

As it turns out, Dr Wrenn did attack Drake, but not badly enough to kill him. After the attack, Drake was dragged across the yard and was drowned in a fountain by his own brother-in-law. It turns out that Drake had a wife whom he was not only cheating on with Wrenn's wife, but whom he was also physically abusing. The woman's brother, Peter (Richard Huw), finished the job Wrenn started, hoping the blame would fall on Wrenn. Wrenn doesn't know this part of the story and Foyle explains that he could still be charged with common assault or attempted murder. Wrenn pleads that he didn't intend to kill Drake, to which Foyle replies: "Oh, I believe you. I also believe that, uh, I'm in your debt, since it seems I wouldn't have Milner, here, if it, uh, hadn't been for you." Wing Commander Turner offers a similar grace to Andrew. He transfers Andrew to an OTU (Operational Training Unit), where he will teach new pilots.

Commentary: Christopher Foyle on the virtuous life

Detective Foyle could have easily pinned Drake's murder on Dr Wrenn. He knew that Drake was cheating on his wife and abusing her. The brother-in-law, Peter, was doing a good thing by finishing the job that Wrenn started. In addition, it would have been much less complicated to convict Wrenn than to try to prove that Peter was also present at the time Drake was attacked. But Foyle doesn't do this. He not only gives Wrenn a pass on the murder charge, but lets him go completely free, even though he could easily have convicted him for assault or attempted murder.

If Foyle were a utilitarian, he might have chosen the easiest, clearest conviction. The result for the justice system and for the family of the victim would have been the same. What's more, Wrenn didn't know he hadn't killed Drake. At trial, he wouldn't even have denied it. On the other hand, if Foyle were a deontologist, he might have convicted Wrenn of assault or attempted murder. Even though Wrenn didn't kill Drake, he still did something morally wrong – he attacked a man who wasn't attacking him. Wrenn could have divorced his wife or taken out his frustration on her – she was the one who was betraying a trust, not Drake. In addition, if Foyle allows Peter to take the full brunt of the conviction, he is being punished for something he didn't do, namely, the initial assault on Drake.

In contrast to both approaches, Foyle takes certain aspects of Wrenn's character into account. Given what he'd recently learned about wartime stress, Foyle views Wrenn's actions as a weakness brought on by the conditions of his job. Nevertheless, given Wrenn's relationship with Milner and his work at the hospital, Foyle is convinced that Wrenn is, for the most part, worthy of the pardon. Peter, on the other hand, was conniving and deceitful throughout the investigation. Foyle doesn't regard his character with much respect, and therefore, doesn't think it inappropriate to lay the full blame on him. Given Aristotle's emphasis on character, it would seem that Foyle most likely holds a virtue theory of morality.

Similarly, Wing Commander Turner ignores Andrew's unofficial leave even though he doesn't have to and he would be punished if anyone found out. It would have been safer for Turner to turn Andrew in to the RAF police. In addition, since Andrew accepts his guilt, he fully expected to be charged with "desertion" and punished according to the law. Nevertheless, Turner understands that there are certain stresses and temptations that no one can be expected to face successfully. Since Andrew's character was impeccable prior to this incident, Turner considers Andrew worthy of the pardon and even of a promotion.

So, it would seem that the actions of both Christopher Foyle and Wing Commander Turner are more consistent with virtue ethics than with utilitarianism or deontology. Does this mean that these characters are virtuous? According to Aristotle, we'll just have to wait and see.

The virtues of virtue theory

Philosophers who defend virtue ethics over utilitarianism and deontology typically point to two of its central features, noting that they offer a more accurate picture of how humans evaluate moral choices and actions.

1. Virtue theory includes a more realistic account of moral development. One criticism of seventeenth-century moral theories is that they do not accurately reflect the development of a moral agent. Moral reasoning, on these theories, is primarily a rational process and actions are evaluated according to how well they conform to the guidelines of the moral theory. However, moral decisions are rarely made in circumstances where reasoners have time to reflect rationally and unemotionally before acting. Moral decisions, at least, many of the ones that really count, are often made under duress.

Virtue ethics accepts this and, instead of a decision-procedure, offers a method of character-building. If your character has been properly developed, you will not need to reflect rationally or unemotionally before making a decision. You are conditioned to make good decisions. You have spent your life training your emotions and your reason so that when you are under duress, you have a much better chance at making a moral decision.

2. Virtue theory includes a more accurate account of what makes an act morally good. Imagine going to visit a friend who is in hospital after a serious accident. The friend expresses her gratitude that you so selflessly came to check on her. But instead of saying something normal like, "It was no big deal," you say, in good Kantian fashion, "I am simply doing my duty. I have no particular feelings about it, since then I would not be acting *from* duty, but merely *in accord* with it." Would your friend praise your moral excellence? Probably not.

What if, instead, you replied in good utilitarian fashion, "Well, being here reduces the amount of suffering in the world, and I am always morally obligated to do that. If I thought I could relieve more suffering by talking with someone down the hall, that's where I'd be." Again, your friend would probably not feel very comforted in her time of need.

Now imagine you replied, "Well, I was concerned about you and I wanted to make sure you are alright. I am trying to be more compassionate lately, and I've always felt a deep connection with you." This seems a much more natural, much more appropriate account of what makes an act morally good. If deontology and utiltarianism cannot account for this dimension of a moral action, virtue theory may be a more comprehensive moral theory.

CASE STUDY 2: *Star Trek: The Next Generation*, "Hide and Q," season 1

AVAILABILITY: **NetFlix**

Star Trek: The Next Generation is the second incarnation of Gene Roddenberry's famous sci-fi franchise. Captain Jean-Luc Picard (Patrick Stewart) leads a crew of Starfleet officers on the Starship Enterprise as emissaries of the United Federation of Planets in the twenty-fourth century. As with the original *Star Trek*, they "boldly go where no one has gone before."

In this episode, the divine entity "Q" (John de Lancie) has once again taken an interest in humanity. In the first episode of the show, Q tested the limits of Captain Picard's confessed care and respect for other cultures. Now Q turns the test on Picard's first mate, William T. Riker (Jonathan Frakes). It seems the "Q continuum" (the metaphysical entity, of which the recurring character Q is only a small aspect) has a premonition that the human race will eventually advance to the power and intelligence of divine beings that can compete with the powers of the Q. Q explains to Riker, "We discovered ... that you are unusual creatures, in your own limited ways. Ways which in time will not be so limited." Riker explains, in response, that humans have a drive that compels them to grow. Q continues: "Yes, the human compulsion. And, unfortunately for us, it is a power that will grow stronger century after century .... We must know more about this human compulsion ... that we may better understand it."

In order to test their premonition that humans will eventually become something much like gods, the continuum sends Q to test another of humanity's best and brightest. Q offers Riker all the power of the Q continuum. Given this much power, an inferior being would cause immeasurable destruction in the pursuit of his self-interests. At first, as might be expected from an honorable soldier, Riker turns down the offer of unlimited power. But then Q tempts Riker by placing his companions in grave danger. Riker uses his power, but then rejects Q's offer again. To quell his temptation and prove Q wrong, Riker promises Picard that he won't use his newfound powers. However, just knowing he has them, Riker becomes arrogant and presumptuous. He begins acting like a god even though he refuses to demonstrate his power.

Picard scolds Q for his nefarious gift: "It's too great a temptation for us at our stage of development." When Riker confronts Picard about the possibility of using his powers, he addresses him as "Jean-Luc," ignoring the respect attending Picard's rank. Picard shares his worry: "Perhaps we're all remembering the old saying, 'Power corrupts ...'," and Riker finishes the thought, "'... and absolute power corrupts absolutely.'"

Finally, Q puts a challenge to Riker to give his friends a gift of affection. Picard, knowing how his crew would react, permits the farce. Riker gives Wesley Crusher (Wil Wheaton) his wish of being 10 years older, a grown man. He attempts to give Data (Brent Spiner) emotion, but he refuses. Data explains: "I've never wanted to compound one illusion with another. It might be real to Q, perhaps even you, sir. But it would never be so to me. Was it not one of the Captain's favorite authors who said, 'To thine own self be true.'" He gives Geordi (LaVar Burton) his eyesight back. But Geordi asks to go back to the way he was before. "The price is a little too high for me and, I don't like who I'd have to thank." Afterward, even Wesley reneges on the deal: "Sir, it's too soon for this. ... I just want to get there on my own."

Feeling shame at not being able to use his powers wisely, Riker turns to Picard and says, "How did you know, sir? I feel like such an idiot." To which, Picard responds, "Quite so, well you should." When Q's offer is officially and finally rejected, the continuum recognizes that Q has failed, so they strip away Riker's power and drag Q back to the continuum.

Commentary: Is Riker a hero of virtue or duty?

This episode recalls a classic myth called, "The Ring of Gyges," found in Plato's famous philosophical book, *Republic*. In that myth, the ancestor of Gyges is, as far as anyone can tell, a perfectly normal, moral person, working as a shepherd for the ruler of Lydia. But upon finding a ring that turns him invisible (but not intangible), he follows the messengers of the king into the palace, seduces the queen, kills the king, and becomes ruler of the kingdom. Socrates suggests:

> Let's suppose, then, that there were two such rings, one worn by a just and the other by an unjust person. Now, no one, it seems, would be so incorruptible that he would stay on the path of justice or stay away from other people's property, when he could take whatever he wanted from the marketplace with impunity, go into people's houses and have sex with anyone he wished, kill or release from prison anyone he wished, and do all the other things that would make him like a god among humans. (*Republic*, Book II, 360b–c)

Socrates is arguing that all the character development you can imagine is useless when faced with a moral decision for which there is no accountability. The "virtuous" man will act no better than the vicious.

In this episode of *Star Trek: The Next Generation*, Q is testing the hypothesis that humans will someday become godlike by putting Riker to a test similar to the one Gyges' ancestor was given. With limitless power, humans will act no better than savages. If he is right, then humans will not likely advance enough to be like the Q continuum.

If you know the show, you know that Riker has one of the most consistently moral characters of the cast. He regularly exhibits great virtue and discernment in difficult circumstances. Nevertheless, with the gift of unlimited power, Riker exhibits all the worries of the Ring of Gyges myth. Even though he only uses his powers to do what he thinks is good, he still becomes arrogant and learns that, ultimately, he doesn't know what is best. If humans cannot develop moral characters that will lead them to act morally when no one is watching, or when they can get away with some immoral act they want to do, it is not a successful moral theory. In addition, it would seem that, despite Riker's solidly built character, we can still clearly evaluate some of his actions as vicious, or, at least, non-virtuous. But, by what standard are we using to evaluate his actions? Virtue theory suggests that individual acts are not good or bad, but individual characters are. Surely, Riker has one of the best characters on board the *Starship Enterprise*. But, clearly, he begins down a very bad path.

This episode is interesting in that it highlights both good and bad aspects of virtue ethics. Because of Riker's moral character, he is at least trying to do morally good things with his powers. This suggests that virtue ethics has a somewhat accurate account of our moral development. And when he begins down the path to immorality, his closest friends are able to step in and show him the error of his ways. This suggests that virtue ethics has a somewhat accurate account of the role of community in character-building.

The vices of virtue theory

Despite the virtues of virtue ethics, there are several serious criticisms of it.

1. It is not clear that it has anything to do with morality. Notice that Aristotle's virtue ethics begins from an assumption about the way things are. Humans are designed in such a way that their *telos* is happiness. This is your goal as a human, and the goal you are supposed to achieve serves as the guide for your actions throughout life. But why should you try to achieve that goal? Why is happiness a "morally good" goal? This suggests that Aristotle is guilty of the naturalistic fallacy (see the "Pilot Episode"): you *are* this sort of being (a being with the *telos* happiness); therefore, this is how you *should* act (you should act virtuously so you can achieve happiness).

Even if he is right that we are naturally inclined toward happiness, this does not entail a moral obligation to pursue happiness. We might be naturally inclined to pedophilia or vanilla ice cream or rape or sex, but none of this entails a *moral obligation* to pursue these things. They might be good, they might be bad, but we have to ask moral questions about our *telos*. Aristotle simply assumes that we have a moral obligation to achieve our *telos*, and this seems fallacious.

Interestingly, if someone wanted to defend virtue ethics by supplying a moral motivation, it seems she would have to reformulate it as a version of deontology or consequentialism. For instance, if "happiness" is intrinsically good, it would seem that humans have a *moral duty* to achieve it, in which case, virtue ethics simply becomes a version of deontology. On the other hand, if "happiness" is defined as a morally good consequence of our actions, then virtue ethics simply becomes a version of consequentialism. If there are no moral motivations, then virtue ethics is not concerned with morality in any meaningful sense.

2. It is not action-based, so cannot help with decision-making.   Since virtue ethics is concerned primarily with character-building, it cannot serve as a decision-procedure. The actions suggested by Aristotle are typically those associated with one's community, social or legal norms, as well as the virtues. Through these, Aristotle argues, a person is conditioned by the values of his society, and thereby comes to act according to them.

But Aristotle rejects the idea of considering an "action" immoral unless it is a specific cultural code, like breaking the law. If the law were to permit lying to your mother, then a single act of lying to your mother doesn't necessarily make you a liar – your character may be such that it is an unfortunate and momentary setback in your moral development. This may seem intuitive when it comes to lying. But what about murder or rape? Should we just let one or two of those slip by because a person's character, on the whole, is consistent with the virtues? This seems strange. But because living virtuously is tied essentially to the development of your moral emotions, no one can instruct you, in a particular moment, how to act. You will act on the basis of those emotions. If they are well developed you will probably make a good decision; if they are not well developed, you probably won't. Nevertheless, it seems strange, in terms of virtue ethics, to hold you morally responsible for any particular action.

Because of this problem, many moral philosophers suggest supplementing a deontological or utilitarian theory of morality with a virtue ethics account of moral development. This seems to quell many of the worries with both types of theory. Interestingly, this is not contradictory, as it would be if we tried to reconcile deontology with utilitarianism. The latter theories offer competing accounts of what makes an act right or wrong and say little about moral development. Virtue ethics, on the other hand, says little about right and wrong actions, and focuses almost exclusively on moral development. Therefore, it is plausible that virtue ethics is compatible with some versions of deontology and consequentialism.

STUDY QUESTIONS

1. Why is virtue theory not simply a version of consequentialism?
2. How should Detective Foyle have treated Doctor Wrenn if he (Foyle) were a deontologist?
3. According to Aristotle, a person's community plays an important in helping him or her develop a virtuous character. How does the community of the characters in the *Foyle's War* episode influence some of their more important decisions?
4. Andrew's commanding officer, Wing Commander Turner, gives him an opportunity to return to service without court martial. As it is portrayed in the episode, is this decision best described as motivated by duty, consequences, or virtues? Explain.
5. Is Detective Foyle's decision to let Doctor Wrenn go better explained by the fact that he knows Andrew's commander just showed Andrew some leniency or by Foyle's commitment to the virtues? According to Aristotle, does it matter?
6. What makes a virtuous act virtuous?
7. Punishment: A primary difficulty with a virtue theory of ethics is that it suggests little for how to respond to someone who commits truly vicious acts. What should we do with Q (if we could, of course)?
8. Does Riker do what is virtuous or what will bring the most pleasure or his duty?
9. Why might virtue ethics not be a theory of "morality" at all?
10. Since Data is a machine, and thus cannot experience emotions (moral or otherwise), what sort of considerations might motivate his rejecting Riker's offer?

ALTERNATIVE CASE STUDIES

1. *Star Trek: Voyager*, "Death Wish," season 2
   (Who exhibits virtue, Janeway or Q?)
2. *The Twilight Zone* (Original), "The Masks," season 5
   (How have your past actions shaped your character?)
3. *Smallville*, "Lexmas," season 5
   (Can your family determine your moral character?)

SERIES III
BUT WHAT'S RIGHT WHEN . . . ?
PRACTICAL ETHICS

EPISODE 8: ENVIRONMENTAL ETHICS

INTRODUCTION

In the show *Community*, Dean Craig Pelton (Jim Rash), always wanting to keep Greendale Community College hip and politically correct, institutes "Green Week" to reflect the school's ongoing interest in being "Earth smart" ("Envirodale," season 1). In honor of Green Week, he attempts to rename the school, "Envirodale." In a twist of irony, a not-too-bright student points out, "Look, we're already called '*Green*dale.'" Embarrassed, Dean Pelton whispers to the student in charge of printing new posters, "We need to re-do these." Although the student explains that she has already

---

What's Good on TV?: Understanding Ethics Through Television, First Edition.
Jamie Carlin Watson and Robert Arp.
© 2011 Jamie Carlin Watson and Robert Arp. Published 2011 by Blackwell Publishing Ltd.

printed 5,000, Pelton responds, angrily, "Well, print 5,000 more! I'm trying to save the planet here!"

The irony, of course, is that while Dean Pelton claims to be sensitive to the planet's needs, he is wasting 5,000 large sheets of paper just to protect his image. But does it really matter that's he's wasting all that paper? Maybe environmentalism is just a social fad – a way for people to get involved in their community and deepen their relationships by working for a common cause. Today it is the environment, tomorrow it will be the penguins in Antarctica, the next day it will be scrapbooking. But it's also possible that there is more to it. To determine which is the case, we must answer some moral questions.

Do we have any moral obligations to the environment we inhabit? If not, why not? If so, what establishes them? It seems uncontroversial that there are at least practical reasons that would prevent anyone from advocating wonton destruction of the biological and chemical life on planet Earth. If for no other type of reason, we need most of it in order to survive. Therefore, we can begin this discussion recognizing that, at least practically, there are good reasons to preserve much of nature, both chemical and biological, as we now find it. Nevertheless, the questions we are most interested in are whether there are *moral* reasons to preserve nature, and, if so, how these moral reasons restrict our actions.

Practically, we could not survive without our environment. But is *our* survival a moral issue? Is there something valuable about humans that would make it wrong to eliminate us? Or is nature valuable in and of itself? Perhaps it is more valuable than any particular human or group of humans. There are two very general types of argument that defend the claim that we have moral responsibilities to nature.

The first is that nature is valuable in and of itself, that is, it has its value "intrinsically" (see Episode 5). Even if it were not valuable for anything or anyone, it is valuable. It does not derive its value from anywhere else. This view is called "biocentric," or "life-centered" (from the Greek words "bio," meaning "life," and "kentrikos," meaning "concentrated"). If this view is correct, we have an obligation to preserve nature because it is valuable irrespective of what it offers us.

The second is that nature is only valuable *for something* other than itself, that is, it has its value "extrinsically" (see Episode 5). It is not valuable in and of itself, but insofar as it is good *for something else*, and, most often, the argument is that it is good *for human beings*. Therefore, its moral value derives from the value that morally valuable beings give it. This view is called "anthrocentric," or "human-centered" (from the Greek words "anthropos," meaning "human," and "kentrikos," meaning, "at the center"). If this view is correct, we have an obligation to preserve those aspects of nature that are valuable to us as human beings. Any preservation beyond this is permissible, but not obligatory.

We will look at each of these views in a bit more detail, then discuss William Baxter's paper, "People or Penguins," in which he argues that the motivation for biocentric approaches is undermined by rational considerations about the nature of moral value and practical considerations about how environmental legislation works. Finally, we will evaluate the plausibility of these arguments in light of television episodes from *Northern Exposure* and *Family Guy*.

TWO APPROACHES TO ENVIRONMENTAL ETHICS

Nature is intrinsically valuable

Biocentric approaches to environmental ethics often argue that life is intrinsically valuable, regardless of whether it is conscious or can feel pain, or whether it has any particular biological or chemical make-up. If it is alive, it is valuable. If this is correct, then it is immoral to "use" nature in ways that are inconsistent with its moral interests. This is, however, difficult, since humans require plants and chemicals in order to survive. But that is not the point; it may be necessary for our survival and yet immoral. But we are a part of nature – we are alive – so our survival is at least as important as the survival of the next plant. Therefore, biocentric philosophers defend "biological egalitarianism," which means that all living organisms deserve the same moral consideration.

Proponents of this view, often called the "Deep Ecology Movement," argue that anthrocentric approaches – sometimes characterized as the "Shallow Ecology Movement" (Naess 1973) – lose sight of humans as part of the biological community, and thus tend to perceive themselves as having some sort of moral superiority over non-human flora and fauna. They argue, in contrast to this view, that, since humans are merely products of their environment, there is no non-arbitrary way to distinguish the moral value of humans from the moral value of other living things. Therefore, if humans are valuable, so is nature.

One motivation for this perspective comes from cultures that hold nature to be divine in some sense. Pantheists believe that God is everything and in everything, and that therefore everything must be treated with divine reverence. A prominent strain of Buddhism, known as "Theravada Buddhism," derives its respect for nature from ancient beliefs about nature as the home of divine beings: "Therefore among the Buddhists there is a reverential attitude towards specially long-standing gigantic trees. They are called vanaspati in Pali, meaning 'lords of the forests'" (De Silva 1987: 256). Because of this reverence, practicing Theravadins must reject weapons of any kind, attempt to not deprive any being of its life, and "abstain from trading in meat" (1987: 258). And Theravadin monks are obligated to obey even stricter rules, refusing to act in ways that might even unintentionally harm a living creature.

But, unless you hold a pantheistic or Buddhist view of reality, this motivation will not be very compelling to you. In addition, Buddhists offer very few arguments that their perspective on reality is true, so it is difficult to evaluate the plausibility of its claims. And finally, it is not clear that, because everything is divine, it deserves moral respect (see Episode 3). Therefore, you will probably want to know whether there are other reasons to adopt a biocentric approach to the environment. Paul W. Taylor (2008) offers one argument along quite different lines. He defines a "life-centered ethic" as the view that "we have prima facie moral obligations that are owed to wild plants and animals themselves as members of the Earth's biotic community" (2008: 374). According to Taylor, all living things have a "well-being" that "is something to be realized *as an end in itself*" (2008: 374; italics in original). What does this "well-being" consist in? Taylor says it means that the organism, "without reference to any other entity ... can be benefitted or harmed" (2008: 375). Rocks cannot be benefitted or harmed by breaking them apart. But plants and animals, on the other hand, have states toward which they tend: growing, sprouting, seeding, reproducing, producing fruit, etc. All these states can be encouraged or discouraged by our actions. This capacity for benefit or harm establishes the organism as intrinsically valuable. Therefore, according to Taylor, to discourage these states is immoral.

What reasons does Taylor give for this view? It is primarily that, since we are a part of Earth's biotic community, there is no reason to think we have any moral superiority over the natural world. We can reformulate the details of Taylor's argument as follows:

1. All living things share a common relationship to the Earth.
2. All living things are interconnected.
3. We understand the world better when we see things from all perspectives.
4. Objectively, humans are not superior to animals.

5. Therefore, however valuable humans are, living things share that degree of value.

In defense of premises (1) and (2), Taylor points out that humans are only one small part of a large biological system, which is not only interconnected in many ways, but which also produced us. Physical and biological laws apply to each member of this system equally, and we all face the same challenges of survival and reproduction. In support of premise (3), Taylor notes that we see this interconnectedness all the clearer when we step outside the anthrocentric perspective and take a more biological perspective. This new perspective can lead to a deep affection for nature. "One may become fascinated by it and even experience some involvement with its good and bad fortunes..." (2008: 382). In defense of (4), Taylor notes that humans are hardly superior to animals in their capacities. Although humans have a keen intellect, physically they are rather weak and vulnerable: "There is the speed of a cheetah, the vision of an eagle, the agility of a monkey. Why should not these be taken as signs of *their* superiority over humans" (2008: 383; italics in original). From these premises, Taylor concludes that we cannot draw a sharp distinction between our moral value and that of the rest of nature.

Is Taylor's argument conclusive? Those who defend an anthrocentric approach are not convinced. First, Taylor's argument would seem to extend moral value to viruses, hazardous bacteria, and mosquitoes. If Taylor's view prohibits humans from killing cows, it seems it would also prevent them from killing deadly bacteria. But surely this is not consistent with how the life cycle works. Much of nature is at fundamental odds with itself: lions kill wildebeest; foxes kill rabbits; bears kill fish. If this is the natural cycle of the biotic system, why can't humans kill cows and deadly bacteria?

Second, it is not clear that any of Taylor's premises establish *moral* value for humans or non-human nature; therefore, a primary moral question has been ignored. Next, we will discuss this objection in detail. And then, in the section that follows, we will discuss William Baxter's version of this objection and consider an anthrocentric alternative.

Nature is extrinsically valuable

Anthrocentric (also called "anthro*po*centric") approaches to environmental ethics often point out that there is no "moral" state of nature independent of human considerations. For instance, is it "wrong" for the lion to kill the wildebeest, or for the fox to eat the rabbit? Surely not. Similarly, would it be a great moral "good" for natural selection to produce a species of intelligent, self-reflecting agents? It seems strange to say so. Therefore, moral considerations can only be conceived from the perspective of beings capable of recognizing and acting on moral reasons.

So, what things are valuable? From this perspective, only those things that we value have value. Why is it wrong for you to steal my car or hurt my neighbor's dog? Because I value my car, and my neighbor values his dog. Why is it permissible to eat cows? Because we value eating beef.

Does this mean we can use the environment however we want? Anthro-centrists say no. Our existence depends on our environment being a certain way: we cannot live without clear air, clean water, food plants, etc. In addition, we value more than just the minimum amount of clean air, water, and food plants. We like tranquil streams, bird-watching, scenic vistas, etc. Therefore, if we value ourselves, it is morally necessary that we preserve at least a basic minimum level of natural resources, and it is in our best interests to preserve a great deal more.

Does this mean that we will eliminate *all* pollution? Absolutely not, but anthrocentrists ask why it should be a goal. To achieve that goal would mean the destruction of the human species. It is precisely because we are part of Earth's biotic community that living here affects it – living impacts the environment. But our living here, we think, is a good thing – and we're the only ones who can even ask the question, so we're the only relevant source of moral concern.

SILLY ENVIRONMENTALISTS, NATURE IS FOR PEOPLE

William Baxter, "People or Penguins"

William Baxter argues that, if it comes down to making a decision between protecting people or penguins, we should always choose people. Baxter defends an anthrocentric approach to environmental ethics, and argues that not only is it the only place to start; it is the most efficient way to resolve ethical disputes over how we affect the environment.

He acknowledges that the only way to resolve ethical disputes is to argue in such a way that appeals to as many people as possible. Therefore, Baxter begins with a principle he thinks almost everyone in the United States can agree to: "[E]very person should be free to do whatever he wishes in contexts where his actions do not interfere with the interests of other human beings" (2008: 370). Baxter calls this the "spheres of freedom criterion" – a view that already existed in an earlier form. It forms the core of the political view known as "classical liberalism," which is defended most ably by John Locke, John Stuart Mill, Thomas Jefferson, and Robert Nozick.

Classical liberalism is the view that individual liberty takes precedence over the interests of the political state, its leaders, and any groups of its citizens. This view stands in stark contrast to political philosophies that take the whole collection of citizens as the primary subject of moral interest (often associated with socialism). Classical liberalism is expressed today in more limited forms, for example contemporary liberalism (often defended by political parties such as the Democratic Party in the US, and the Labour Party in the UK) and contemporary conservatism (often defended by political parties such as the Republican Party in the US, and the Conservative (or Tory) Party in the UK).

Both the "right" and the "left" in modern democratic governments claim to be part of the classical liberal tradition to some degree. So, Baxter's idea is that, if you buy classical liberalism (and, if you're living in a democratic society, chances are that you do), he can offer a practical solution to moral questions about the environment. With this starting point, he argues that the only plausible approach to resolving environmental disputes is anthropocentric: "Damage to penguins, or sugar pines, or geological marvels is, without more, simply irrelevant" (2008: 371).

Baxter considers that some people might call this approach "selfish" or elitist. He responds by conceding: "It is undeniably selfish. Nevertheless I think it is the only tenable starting place for analysis" (2008: 371). He then offers six reasons for thinking anthropocentrism is the only defensible starting place:

1. "*... no other position corresponds to the way most people really think and act.*" Most people are not extreme environmentalists. Therefore, if you want to offer an argument that will help the environment, you should appeal to the interests of the majority. Most people are anthropocentric, therefore, anthropocentric arguments are more plausible than any alternative.

2. "*... this attitude does not portend any massive destruction of nonhuman flora and fauna.*" Since people depend heavily on natural resources, many ecosystems and therefore, plant and animal life, will be preserved.

3. "*... what is good for humans is, in many respects, good for penguins and pine trees.*" Humans will protect their own air and water. And much of the air and water that will be protected has the benefit of supplying water and air to animals. Baxter writes, "humans are, in these respects, surrogates for plant and animal life" (2008: 371).

4. "*... I do not know how we could administer any other system.*" Our decisions are made privately (the decisions we make as individuals) or collectively (the decisions we make as a state or government). Collectively,

there must be some foundation on which base to our collective decisions, and the value of the individual seems the most plausible. Baxter explains: "[M]y basic premise does not rule out private altruism to competing life-forms. It does rule out, however, Mr. Jones' inclination to feed Mr. Smith to [a] bear" (2008: 371).

5. *"... if polar bears or pine trees or penguins, like men, are to be regarded as ends rather than means ... someone must tell me how much each one counts."* Since plants and animals cannot engage us in informed moral debate, it is left to us to consider their moral interests. Privately, we can choose to eat and act almost however we choose. But publically, we can only consider public interests. And only rational beings can present the interests of non-rational beings. In fact, we already do this with children and the mentally handicapped.

6. *"Questions of ought are unique to the human mind and world – they are meaningless as applied to a nonhuman situation."* Here Baxter explains that "normative" considerations can only bind and be binding for creatures that can consider moral reasons. "Was it 'right' or 'wrong' for the earth's crust to heave in contortion and create mountains and seas? Was it 'right' for the first amphibian to crawl up out of the primordial ooze?" (2008: 372). If moral obligations are unique to humans, then we are a unique and, according to Baxter, primary source of moral concern.

CASE STUDY 1: *Northern Exposure,* "Zarya," season 6

AVAILABILITY: **Netflix**

Northern Exposure is about a big city doctor, Joel Fleischman (Rob Morrow), who is spending the first four years of his medical career in the rugged, rural, and rather culturally backwards community of Cicely, Alaska in fulfillment of a contract with the state of Alaska, which financed his medical school. Though Cicely leaves much to be desired in the way of technology and amenities, Fleischman discovers that the residents have big hearts and a clear understanding of human nature.

This episode takes us back to the early days of Cicely, as Dr Fleishman's Inuit assistant Marilyn Whirlwind (Elaine Miles) tries to remember a story her grandfather told her about the time Russian Communist leader Vladimir Lenin met the presumed-dead Anastasia Romanov there to discuss the relationship between the new Communist government and the family of the former monarchy. (As interesting as this would be, we can find no evidence that Lenin ever visited Alaska.)

For the flashbacks, the normal cast takes on the characters of old Cicely. Former astronaut and millionaire Maurice Minnifield (Barry Corbin) is now former outlaw and "influential civic leader" Mace Mobrey. Chris Danforth Stevens (John Corbett) is now the waffling preacher and spiritual seeker Kit. Mace, wanting to compete in the business world (much like Maurice), has an idea for a vehicle that doesn't need roads, so that people will be better able to settle the rugged tundra of Alaska. Kit, perplexed over the relationship between good and evil, agrees to put aside his spiritual musings and help Mace build his vehicle.

The vehicle turns out to be a half-track (two normal front wheels and tank tracks in the back), though this isn't mentioned in the show. Mace and Kit build it and get it running, but the breaks do not work well. The machine scares the former Grand Duchess Anastasia, who is out riding bicycles with Marilyn's grandfather. Anastasia crashes into her Inuit guide and they are late to the meeting with Lenin, forever sealing the fate of her people.

Kit crashes the half-track, and he and Mace head back to the bar to regroup. Mace is still eager, wanting to fix the braking system, but Kit is dismayed with the technology. He finds the material realm too harsh and decides to return to preaching.

Commentary: Kit's inconvenient truth

The key scene in this episode comes near the end. After Kit and Mace have crashed the half-track, Mace is considering how to fix the braking system. But Kit is wrestling with a deep "conceptual" dilemma. He tells Mace: "Did you notice the birds? They quit singin' when we cranked 'er up. The squirrels lit out. It's like nature herself cringes at this thing – the noise, the smoke. It's – it's out of harmony with the universe."

Mace gets angry at this and reminds Kit of his promise not to talk about "spiritual" things anymore. So, Kit changes his objection to considerations Mace might find more appealing:

Okay, look at it in practical terms. You get enough of these fossil fuel engines kickin' up CO_2, which when you think about it could bond with water up in the atmosphere, trap in solar radiation. Stay with me, here. It's not inconceivable, you could actually raise the temperature of the planet.

Mace just says: "Are you sayin' you live in a greenhouse? Ha ha! You are outta your mind!" Kit shrugs off the criticism, and says, "Eh, maybe so. I'm headin' back to the spiritual world where I ain't gonna mess up the scrub pine."

Of course, it is intentionally absurd that Kit would just imagine such an accurate depiction of global warming off-handedly. But as a social and moral commentary, this scene is ripe with implications. Kit's first objection to the new technology sounds very biocentric. He seems to assume that nature has a personality deserving of moral consideration: "It's like nature herself cringes . . . . It's out of harmony with the universe." He seems to be implying that the universe deserves at least some moral consideration independently of humans.

Might this be correct? Sure. If someone could offer an argument showing that nature is intrinsically valuable, the conclusion that this machine is immoral might (with a few connecting premises) follow. Unfortunately, we have little reason to believe nature is valuable independently of human considerations. Buddhists do not offer reasons for thinking that nature is divine or that a divine reality is a morally valuable one. And Paul Taylor's argument seems open to counterexamples like mosquitoes and deadly bacteria. Someone might appeal to the Judeo-Christian view that God created nature and values it independently of humans (derived, perhaps, from the verses in Genesis, chapter 1, where the narrator repeats the phrase: "and God saw that it was good." But even if this is true, it does not answer the question whether nature is good because God values it or because God created it as fitting for humans – arguably the hallmark of creation. Therefore, we are better served to move on to Kit's second response to Mace.

Kit's second objection is much more anthrocentric. If we produce enough CO_2, we might actually raise the temperature of the planet. The first thing to note about this claim is that it is empirical. This is not a moral claim, but a claim about the natural world. This sort of claim can be checked using scientific instruments. Whether we can actually raise the temperature of the Earth by producing more and more CO_2 is a non-moral issue. Therefore, there are three non-moral questions we need to ask of climatologists: (1) Is the Earth's temperature rising? (If not, the whole "global warming" issue is no longer viable.) (2) If the temperature is rising, are humans contributing to the increase in temperature (or could they at least help decrease it)? (If not, then our focus should be on adaptation, not lowering our CO_2 emissions.) (3) Can we stop contributing to, or reduce, the increase? (If the temperature is rising, and regardless of whether we are contributing, if we cannot stop contributing, or reduce the effects, then we should still focus on how to adapt to the changes.) We won't attempt to answer these questions here, but they are a good place to start if you are interested in this debate.

The second question we need to ask is whether it is a bad thing for humans if the temperature of the planet rises. We have at least some reason to believe the average temperature has risen about one degree over the past 40 years. What if this is right? Is it such a big deal? We also have reasons to believe that average temperatures cycle between very low (during the last five ice ages) and very high (a period like we're in right now). But, if the increase continues indefinitely, the ice caps could melt, raising the sea levels, forcing hundreds of millions of people into smaller and smaller geographic areas. Economically, this would be devastating. Clean water would become more difficult to find, overpopulated areas would have an overabundance of unemployed people, homelessness would grow exponentially, there would be too few hospitals and prisons, so crime and disease would increase. And since most of the world lives in a coastal area, most of the world would suffer to some degree. We conclude that, in fact, this would be bad for humans.

Alright, so how does Kit's musings on global warming inform our discussion of environmental ethics? *If* the Earth's temperature is continuously rising (i.e., global warming is true), *if* we are contributing to it, *if* we can change it, and *if* it is a bad thing for humans, then, according to the anthrocentric approach, we *should* do what we can to reduce the negative effects. If global warming is true, but either we are not contributing to it or we cannot do anything about it, we should still act, but quite differently. We should learn what it would take to adapt to these changing conditions, and do that. As you investigate these issues further, it is important to keep in mind that most of the questions associated with environmental ethics require a large amount of non-moral information – for instance, data from climatologists and weather historians.

CASE STUDY 2: *Family Guy*, "It Takes a Village Idiot, and I Married One," season 5

AVAILABILITY: NetFlix, iTunes, www.watchfamilyguy.tv/episodes

Family Guy is an animated satire of twenty-first-century US culture. Unlike *The Simpsons* and *South Park*, which take on social issues one episode at a time, *Family Guy* embeds a number of unrelated satirical clips into the broader plot of each episode. Sometimes these broader plots have a social theme, and sometimes they do not. The extreme crudeness of the show forces us to reflect on our own sense of social and moral norms.

This episode pits Lois Griffin against Mayor Adam West (really the voice of Adam West of the 1960s *Batman* TV show) over the destruction of Lake Quahog by Quahog Oil Refinery. Quahog Oil has been dumping waste into the lake and when the Griffin family goes swimming, they lose all their hair. Lois begins campaigning to become mayor on a platform of cleaning up the lake and helping the community. Unfortunately, the town's citizens only respond positively to rhetoric and political jargon, especially the words, "Nine Eleven" and "terrorists."

For the sake of the community, Lois employs this rhetoric, wins handily, and leads a successful effort to clean up Lake Quahog. After the clean-up though, there is money left over after, so Lois decides to dip into the fund to buy herself a new purse costing $600. As her popularity grows, so does her desire for the finer things. She agrees to take a bribe from Quahog Oil for a $4,300 fur coat in exchange for letting them dump some waste into the lake – the same lake she just cleaned up. Ironically, the public is indifferent and supports the new deal just as they had supported the clean-up. Lois soon realizes the error of her ways and resigns as mayor, leaving the town, once again, in the hands of Adam West.

Commentary: "What kind of world is this where you can't even trust the oil companies anymore?"

Even from an anthrocentric perspective, industrial pollution of recreation areas is a bad thing. Forested ecosystems with large watersheds filter pollutants out of the air, soil, and rainwater. In addition, these areas provide pleasant places to spend our recreation time. Lois confronts Mayor Adam West about the pollution, saying, "I mean, you couldn't possibly have sanctioned that kind of blatant industrial pollution, could you?" West, indifferent to the lake's plight, says, "Yeah, I told them it was fine. ... And in return, I get free oil for my hair."

Lois is outraged and vows to run against West in the next mayoral election. But she soon discovers that the citizens of Quahog are indifferent to any serious political and moral discussion. At the mayoral debate, she caters to their fears and reminds them of September 11 over and over until she is declared the winner. She wins the election and prepares to clean up the lake. But when she proposes a tax increase to pay for the clean-up, she is booed. So, once again, she caters to their fears and explains that, "We have intelligence that Hitler is plotting with the Legion of Doom to assassinate

Jesus, using the lake as a base," and that, "Darth Vader tried to buy yellow cake uranium from unwed teenage mothers!" The crowd murmurs in awe and fear, and someone asks, "How much money before I can feel safe again?" Lois throws out $100,000 as an estimate and the crowd showers her with money.

There are at least two important moral questions to ask here. First, what role do we allow politicians and the media to play in how we answer moral questions? We might let them tell us what to believe about certain moral claims. If we do, we risk becoming like the citizens of Quahog, forming a judgment based on media hype, and then encouraging other politicians to feed us more of the same. If we are politicians, we are in an even more difficult position. Many people are like the citizens of Quahog. Therefore, we can either argue on what we find to be compelling rational and moral grounds, and thereby lose the election, or we can cater to their fears, lying to accomplish what we perceive to be good, but for bad reasons. Lois chooses to lie in order to accomplish what she considers to be morally obligatory. But what if she was wrong? People must know her actual reasons in order respond effectively.

Second, once we've gotten past the political rhetoric and resolved the moral question, how should we act? Let's assume the antrocentric view is roughly correct, and that, in this case, human interests outweigh the interests of Quahog Oil Refinery. This means that the oil refinery is doing something immoral and is perhaps blameworthy for it. Now, what should anyone do about it? With the moral question settled, it is important to ask what it is reasonable to do about that conclusion. In the episode, Lois runs for mayor and leads an effort to clean up the lake. Are we willing to take such a time-consuming, labor-intensive stand for our moral beliefs? What if Lois learned that Lake Quahog couldn't be cleaned up, or couldn't be cleaned up in one lifetime? How should she have acted, then? Would it be permissible to go ahead with the clean-up to show her political followers that she at least tries to keep her promises? Or would it be more prudent to take different steps, perhaps steps that would prevent the same or further destruction in the future? These are difficult questions to answer, but they are essential to the practice of ethics. Once you've engaged in casuistry – that is, you've made your list of rights and wrongs (see the "Pilot Episode"), or have at least identified some rough moral principles – your actions can be evaluated in terms of how consistently you act on those actions and principles.

What reasons might Quahog Oil have for disregarding Lake Quahog? They might simply be immoral people, as the episode portrays. Are all companies this way? We're optimistic that they are not. Nevertheless, it is easy to turn a blind eye the further you are from the actual impact of your actions. In 2010, one of the worst oil spills in history occurred in the Gulf of Mexico. BP owned the drill site and was responsible for its operation, and thus for the spill. In an irresponsible statement, BP's CEO Tony Hayward said: "We're sorry. We're sorry for the massive disruption it's caused their lives.... There's no one who wants this over more than I do. I'd like my life back." We can't say whether Hayward is an immoral person, but his distance from the spill has made its huge environmental and economic damages seem morally equivalent to the inconvenience it has caused him as the CEO of a company. Surely, these are not comparable moral ills. Perhaps if Hayward had taken our ethics class, he would have had the tools needed to see the difference.

STUDY QUESTIONS

1. What sort of moral considerations can be inferred from Kit and Mace's conversation (*Northern Exposure*)? Are these considerations biocentric or anthrocentric?

2. What sort of evidence would it take to convince you that global warming is true? How might you find this evidence?

3. According to William Baxter, what standard should we use to determine whether we've affected the environment too much?

4. What reasons do we have for thinking nature is intrinsically valuable? Are you convinced by any of these reasons? How do your answers affect how you treat nature?

5. Much of the media on global warming suggests ways to reduce our carbon emissions (reduce factory farming, use fluorescent bulbs, unplug appliances, drive cleaner cars, etc.). If global warming is true but humans are not causing it or contributing to it, how should we react, instead? Write a brief public service announcement advising people how to prepare for the increase in temperature.

6. Would Lois have been as successful at raising money for clean-up of Lake Quahog if she had argued from a biocentric perspective? Why or why not? How is this question relevant to Baxter's argument?

7. The citizens of Quahog were easily persuaded by talk of September 11 and terrorists. What worries does this create for Baxter's suggested solution to environmental problems?

8. How have you been influenced by the media's portrayal of a moral issue? How have you responded?

9. At the end of the episode, Lois leaves the town in the hands of Mayor West. One can infer that Quahog Oil will resume dumping in the lake. How does Lois's resignation reflect on her moral beliefs?
10. Find three sources of evidence about water pollution in your area. How does your water compare with nearby cities'? Who are the major contributors to water pollution in your area? What, if anything, is being done to lower this pollution?

ALTERNATIVE CASE STUDIES

1. *The Simpsons*, "Two Cars in Every Garage and Three Eyes on Every Fish," season 2
   (What duties do corporations have to the environment?)
2. *Captain Planet*, "A Hero for Earth," season 1
   (Is environmental ethics just "New Age" spirituality?)
3. *My Name is Earl*, "Robbed a Stoner Blind," season 2
   (Given the evidence Earl has, does he behave rationally?)

EPISODE 9: ANIMAL WELFARE

INTRODUCTION

Perhaps you've seen the SPCA (Society for the Prevention of Cruelty to Animals) commercials that show abused animals while the Sarah McLachlan song "Angel" plays. Many of us are horrified by these commercials, and some of us even turn to another channel so we don't have to be exposed to images that make us so uncomfortable. What is the point of these commercials? It is not to convince you to adopt

What's Good on TV?: Understanding Ethics Through Television, First Edition.
Jamie Carlin Watson and Robert Arp.
© 2011 Jamie Carlin Watson and Robert Arp. Published 2011 by Blackwell Publishing Ltd.

a pet; they use other commercials for that. The abused animal commercials attempt to convince you that it is wrong to harm animals and that you should give money to the SPCA so they can help relieve the suffering of abused animals.

Do you feel badly when you see pictures of abused animals? Many of us do. It would be difficult to be indifferent toward a neighbor who smashes puppies' paws with a hammer. It would be hard to watch someone light a live bunny on fire. Yet, most of us have no problem eating animals that have had their throats slit, their bodies boiled (sometimes still alive) so their feathers will fall off, or their heads chopped off. What is the difference between these cases and the puppy-paw smasher or the bunny arsonist? Are dogs more valuable than cows? Do bunnies have more moral value than chickens? These apparently inconsistent emotions cry out for an explanation. And part of that explanation requires us to settle some moral questions about decisions that involve animals. Is it *wrong* to harm animals? If not, why not? If so, why? In order to answer these questions clearly, it will be helpful to first remove some common distractions.

TWO DEAD ENDS

Appeals to emotion

The main goal of the SPCA commercials is to make you feel bad for the animals. If you feel bad enough, you'll be motivated to give money to allay any guilt that might come from sitting idly by while animals are abused. To be sure, you may feel bad for animals and your feeling bad may be justified on rational grounds. But is emotion by itself a legitimate moral motivation? It is not. In fact, arguments that appeal to your emotion commit a fallacy called *argumentum ad misericordium*, "appeal to pity."

To see why this type of argument is fallacious, consider how emotions might work in an argument. Presumably they would serve as evidence, much like our sense experiences. I believe that a cup is red because it *seems* red to me – I see it as red. Similarly, I might believe that an action is permissible if it seems good to me – I *feel* it as good. Now think about how many times you've felt something and been wrong – when you thought your boyfriend/girlfriend was cheating but wasn't; when you thought someone was accusing you of something but wasn't; when you felt like you would win a game, but didn't; when you felt like it was sure to snow but it didn't; when you were afraid of someone because they were different (a different color, spoke a different language) but were really harmless; etc. Now think of all the times your eyes have played tricks on you – when you were in dim lighting, when something was very far away, etc. There are lots of times when your eyes are unreliable. But there are dozens and dozens of times when your emotions are unreliable. They don't seem to be connected with reality at all. They are more like wishful thinking than evidence. So, emotions are terribly unreliable as evidence. This is what makes arguments that appeal to emotion fallacious.

But emotions are powerful. They are so powerful, in fact, that, in scientific experiments, researchers have lab assistants to collect data and disguise the experimental and control groups so researchers won't be affected by their wishes and desires that the data come out a certain way (this is what is known as "confirmation bias"). Therefore, when you are evaluating the moral status of an action, make sure you are doing all you can to keep your emotions out of it.

Appeal to inappropriate authority

If the appeal to emotion alone doesn't get you, the SPCA marketers have a back-up. They include the well-known and well-liked celebrity Sarah McLachlan. McLachlan is an expert at writing songs that resonate with human nature. She has a keen knack for communicating powerful emotion. Is she also an expert on the moral treatment of animals? That is not as obvious.

It would be different if the ad were for a drug and the spokesperson were the relevant sort of doctor (as in ads for the heart medicine Lipitor, which include the doctor that invented the artificial heart as a spokesperson). In that case, the ad would include an *appropriate* authority. But in cases where celebrities are employed to try to convince you to vote or to recycle or to stop animal abuse, their celebrity status is not contributing any support to the conclusion. It is an irrelevant feature of the SPCA commercials.

Since it is particularly relevant to this Episode, notice that much of PETA's (People for the Ethical Treatment of Animals) marketing campaign depends on celebrity endorsements. On their website you will find videos from Pamela Anderson, Joachim Phoenix, Eva Mendez, Alicia Silverstone, Perez Hilton, and dozens of others. But be careful: that these people are celebrities adds *no support whatever* to the conclusions that PETA wants you to draw. So, how might the SPCA and PETA better defend their views? To answer that question, we turn to moral philosophy.

THREE APPROACHES TO ANIMAL WELFARE

With these dead ends out of the way, we can now begin to ask what our moral theories have to say about how we should treat animals. Before we get to specific arguments, it will be helpful to lay out the general strategy of most arguments about animal welfare and identify some starting assumptions.

All arguments surrounding animal welfare typically begin with the assumption (a) that all humans are morally valuable. This value typically entails that there are things we cannot do to other humans, including harming them unnecessarily, killing them without just cause, and eating them. Philosophers then (b) offer moral reasons that explain *why* it is wrong to do these things to humans, and these reasons are often utilitarian (see Episode 6) or deontological (see Episode 5). Finally, philosophers then argue that (c) whatever establishes this unique moral value for humans also/or does not also extend to animals.

When you read the literature on animal ethics, you will notice that some arguments talk about animal "rights" and some simply talk about "welfare." "Rights" are difficult to define and defend even for humans, so some philosophers have dropped the term when it comes to animals. Others argue that if there is some act it would be immoral to do to you, then you have a "right" not to be treated that way. For purposes of this Episode, we will write in terms of animal "welfare" except when an argument addresses a specific right, for instance the "right to life."

We'll begin by explaining two popular arguments in favor of animal rights from competing moral positions. We'll then evaluate the plausibility of these arguments in light of Mary Anne Warren's paper, "Difficulties with the Strong Rights Position." Finally, we'll see how these arguments are presented on screen through *Bones* and *House, M.D.*

The utilitarian argument for animal welfare

Most people agree that suffering is a morally relevant feature of an action. It is wrong to treat humans in certain ways because certain things hurt them unnecessarily. For instance, it is considered to be generally wrong to break someone's arm. Why might this be generally wrong? One reason might be that the arm belongs to someone else, and that person did not authorize you to break her arm. This could explain why breaking someone's arm is wrong if ownership establishes moral boundaries. A deontologist might be perfectly content with this explanation, since, if individuals are intrinsically valuable, then others are obligated to treat them as such, in which case breaking something that belongs to them would be immoral.

A utilitarian, however, would say that breaking someone's arm is generally wrong because it produces more pain than pleasure. If breaking someone's arm would produce lots of happiness for lots of people, then it is morally permissible.

And it is not just *my* pain that's morally relevant. I would consider it wrong if someone caused *you* unnecessary pain, as well. There seems to be something morally bad about pain and morally good about pleasure. We think it is wrong to hurt others just as we think it is wrong for them to hurt us. If this is right, then how can anyone resist the conclusion that it is wrong to cause animals unnecessary suffering?

If *what makes it wrong* to do certain things to humans is that it *hurts*, and if animals feel pain just like humans, then it is wrong to do certain things to animals. Thus, the classic utilitarian argument for animal welfare is some version of the following argument:

1. Pain is morally bad.
2. Actions that cause humans pain are generally wrong.
3. Animals also feel pain.

---

4. Therefore, it is generally wrong to act in a way that causes animals pain.

How might someone respond to this argument? We will consider four objections, and then move on to the deontological argument for animal welfare.

Objection 1: Animals don't feel pain.   If animals do not feel pain, then premise (3) is false and the conclusion doesn't follow. But we can't trade places with animals, so how can we know if they experience pain the way we do? To answer this question, it will help to ask how we know whether other *humans* are in pain. I can't get inside your skin. You may use expressions like "Ouch!" and "That hurts!" and grab at the appendage you say is in "pain," but I can't be sure that you are experiencing what I experience when I use those expressions and perform those actions. Nevertheless, these *pain behaviors* are *good evidence* that you are experiencing what I am experiencing. We could even go a step further and compare your brain waves with mine when, say, we've each had a concrete block dropped on a foot. But do we really need that extra evidence? Isn't your pain behavior sufficient for me to infer that you're in pain?

If pain behavior is sufficient for concluding that a person is in pain, it should also be sufficient for concluding that animals feel pain. Animals exhibit many of the same pain behaviors that humans do: they whimper, scream, move away from the source of the pain, attend the wound (by licking or rubbing), limp, etc. Therefore, it seems absurd to think that at least most animals do not feel pain.

There are, however, some exceptions. What about shrimp? Or oysters? These animals exhibit some pain behaviors, but very few. Scientists were relatively united a few years back in claiming that only vertebrates – creatures with advanced nervous systems – can feel pain. But the fact that lobsters are cooked by being boiled (or even grilled) alive led some researchers to begin studying whether crustaceans feel pain. The results? Unfortunately, mixed. In 2007, one study claimed to show that prawns feel pain. When acetic acid was applied to the antennae of 144 prawns, "[i]mmediately, the creatures began grooming and rubbing the affected area, while leaving untouched ones alone" (Sample 2007). The scientist who conducted the study commented that this behavior is "consistent with an interpretation of pain experience" (Barras 2007).

Is this pain behavior sufficient for concluding that lobsters and shrimp feel pain? It is certainly difficult to say. Some single-celled organisms move away from toxic chemicals, but it is not clear that they do so because they are in pain. A human-type nervous system may be required for substantive claims about pain. But Sample (2007) argues: "Using the same analogy, one could argue that crabs do not have vision because they lack the visual centres of humans." Nevertheless, objection 1 fails for most of the animals we keep as pets and consume as food.

Objection 2: Human pain is more morally significant than animal pain. Even if most animals feel pain, it may still be that human pain is more morally significant than animal pain. If this is the case, then animals would not deserve the same moral respect that other humans expect. On what grounds might we distinguish the significance of the pains of animals from those of humans?

According to the standard picture, humans and other animal species evolved together and from the same original genetic material. We developed roughly the same sorts of mechanisms for experiencing pain, though, to be sure, in varying degrees of complexity and sensitivity. So, it is not clear that the experience of pain in animals is drastically different from that in humans.

In addition, even if some being had a completely different biological make-up from that of humans, that being could not experience pain, phenomenologically, the same way we do. And if that is the case, and if it is the phenomenology of pain that matters, then it seems we have no reason to draw a moral distinction between this being's pain and ours.

Objection 3: This argument leads to absurd consequences, such as allowing animals to vote. It might be that an argument protecting animals from pain might lead to all sorts of absurd consequences. It may establish all the same rights that humans have, including the right to vote, the right run for public office, the right to equal opportunity housing, government assistance in the form of a welfare check, unemployment, etc. If this were true, it would constitute a counterexample to the utilitarian argument for animal welfare.

However, it is not clear that these implications follow from the argument above. In fact, it is not clear that the above argument even establishes a right to life. All the above argument establishes is that it is wrong to harm an animal. As long as no pain comes to an animal, it might be the case that we can treat it however we wish. Peter Singer argues that this is not quite the case, but that equal moral respect for animals does not entail equal treatment of animals. He explains:

> Many feminists hold that women have the right to an abortion on request. It does not follow that since these same people are campaigning for equality between men and women they must support the right of men to have abortions too. Since a man cannot have an abortion, it is meaningless to talk of his right to have one. Since a pig can't vote, it is meaningless to talk of its right to vote. There is no reason why either Women's Liberation or Animal Liberation should get involved in such nonsense. (2008: 412)

Singer argues that it would be nonsense to think the utilitarian argument entails that animals have the right to welfare or to run for office. A pig does not have the faculties required for appreciating, or having an interest in, those benefits. However, given its capacity for pain, a pig does have some moral interests. If equal moral respect (Singer calls it "equal moral consideration") does not imply or entail equal treatment, the conclusion still follows and this objection is misguided.

Objection 4: There are significant moral considerations other than pain and pleasure. If pain and suffering are not the *only* morally significant features of an action, then the conclusion that animals must be treated with the same moral respect as humans might not follow. For instance, imagine a small boy has a broken arm that is healing in such a way that will significantly restrict his movement if something is not done. Even if the pain of re-breaking the arm is morally significant, the boy's freedom of movement might outweigh the moral significance of the pain.

This might be true, but such an objection is aimed not at the argument for animal welfare, but at the utilitarian theory of morality that justifies it.

This may be a consideration that leads you to adopt a deontological or virtue theory over utilitarianism, but it is not directly relevant to the animal welfare argument. To know whether animal welfare is justified on accounts other than utilitarianism, we must evaluate those arguments. But, assuming utilitarianism for the sake of argument, this objection is irrelevant.

Notice, now, that utilitarians are able to justify the claim that animal abuse is immoral on the grounds that causing unnecessary suffering is immoral, and they don't even need pictures of sad animals or a Sarah McLaughlin song.

The deontological argument for animal welfare: the "strong rights" view

Most contemporary deontologists agree with utilitarians that suffering is a morally relevant feature of an action. (Recall that deontologists, like Kant, argue that what makes an act right or wrong depends on an actor's duties, which can be derived using reason alone.) But for deontologists, pain is certainly not the only morally relevant feature of an action. For instance, if I am forced to choose between lying to my mother and dropping a brick on your foot, I should probably choose to drop the brick. Similarly, if I must choose between allowing your broken arm to heal improperly or re-breaking it so it will heal properly, I should probably re-break it. Nevertheless, suffering *is* a moral consideration. If I am giving you a vaccine, it is morally better to make the injection as painless as possible than it would be to make it as pain *ful* as possible. Therefore, contemporary deontologists might say: we have a *prima facie* duty to reduce suffering where we can.

How does this recognition that suffering is morally relevant fit into the deontological defense of animal welfare? Some deontologists argue that it leads to the same conclusion as the utilitarian argument. Tom Regan makes such an argument. He argues that animals have a number of rights that humans have a duty to respect, including the rights to not be abused, used in experiments, and eaten. Regan argues that these rights are established for animals by the same moral facts that establish them for humans. What are these moral facts? Regan argues that all mature mammals, including humans, are "experiencing subjects of a life," which means "a conscious creature having an individual welfare that has importance to us whatever our usefulness to others" (2008: 426). Since animals are relevantly similar to humans in this respect, and since humans are widely regarded as inherently (intrinsically) valuable, Regan concludes that animals must also be treated as having inherent value.

We can reformulate Regan's argument as follows:

1. All mature mammals are "experiencing subjects of a life."
2. Experiencing subjects of a life are inherently valuable.
3. Things that are inherently valuable deserve moral respect.
4. Therefore, all mature mammals deserve moral respect.

Premise (3) seems uncontroversial. If something has value in and of itself, then it would seem to deserve appropriate moral consideration. The difficulty comes with offering a reason for thinking animals are inherently valuable. Regan's idea seems to be that having a welfare (we can be helped or harmed) of which we are aware constitutes the grounds of human moral rights. This connection between "having a welfare" and "deserving moral respect" is expressed as premise (2). Our consciousness of our own welfare explains (a) why we are *inherently* morally valuable (because my value of myself is not dependent on what anyone else can use me for), and (b) why we and mature mammals like us are morally distinct from rocks, trees, plankton, and mollusks (because, while these have a welfare, they are not conscious of it).

Recall from Episode 5 that this is very similar to Kant's idea of what constitutes intrinsic value. Kant argued that what constitutes a good will is a being that can recognize and act on moral reasons. This good will is the foundation on which all Kant's duties can be derived. Unfortunately, contemporary Kantians find this emphasis on rationality overly restrictive, not allowing us to say that infants, children, and the mentally handicapped are intrinsically valuable. Regan's concept of "subjects of a life" addresses this worry. As long as you are conscious of your own welfare, you are inherently valuable.

If this is convincing, then the rest of Regan's argument follows. If you have a welfare you are conscious of, then you meet the conditions for being a subject of a life. If you meet the conditions for being a subject of a life, then you are inherently valuable. If you are inherently valuable, then there are things we cannot do to you. And, finally, mature mammals have a welfare they are conscious of.

There are, however, a few difficulties with Regan's argument. For example, how is the moral status of mammals related to what we generally call "rights"? In response, Regan is rather vague. Since he considers his argument the best explanation for why humans have value, he is content to conclude that animals have whatever rights we are willing to grant humans. He writes: "It surpasses all other theories in the degree to which it illuminates and explains the foundation of our duties to one another – the domain of human morality" (2008: 426). But this seems a bit too strong. We allow that humans have many political rights (e.g., the right to run for public office, to vote, etc.) to humans apparently on the same grounds that we allow that they have rights to life and liberty. Yet the former should clearly exclude non-humans.

In our suggested reading section below, we will look at an additional problem for Regan's argument. For now, notice that his argument would be a bit harder to sell in an SPCA commercial. While it is easy to point to suffering as a moral reason for supporting the SPCA, it is more difficult to portray "experiencing subjects of a life" and "inherent value" in a 30-second television slot. So, even if the SPCA were more sympathetic to Regan's reasons, with respect to marketing strategy, they may be better off presenting a utilitarian argument.

Deontological: "weak rights"

Mary Anne Warren argues that Regan's conclusion that the capacity to recognize our own welfare establishes "rights" for both humans and animals is too strong. Though this capacity may have some implications for how humans and animals should be treated, they are not sufficient to establish any substantive concept of "rights."

Warren argues that, at best, Regan's argument should lead us to mitigate any harm we might cause animals by not participating in practices that inflict unnecessary or unreasonable suffering on them. She calls these moral prohibitions "weak rights." In the following section, we will discuss Warren's response to Regan and her argument that animals deserve some degree of moral consideration, though not as much as adult humans.

ANIMALS ARE MORALLY VALUABLE, BUT NOT AS VALUABLE AS ADULT HUMANS

Mary Anne Warren, "Difficulties with the Strong Rights Position"

Like Tom Regan, Mary Anne Warren offers deontological reasons for thinking that humans have moral rights. But unlike Regan, Warren argues that humans' inherent value derives from their ability to "listen to reason":

[I]t is not just because we are subjects-of-a-life that we are both able and morally compelled to recognize one another as beings with equal basic moral rights. It is also because we are able to 'listen to reason' in order to settle our conflicts and cooperate in shared projects. This capacity, unlike the others, may require something like human language. (2008a: 432)

If it is our language and capacity for reason that establishes moral rights, then the conclusion of Regan's argument changes drastically. Premise (2) of Regan's argument, given above, is false: animals do not have the capacity to reason, and so do not have the same rights that humans do. Warren quotes another moral philosopher, Bonnie Steinbock, in support of this conclusion: "[I]f rats invade our houses . . . we cannot reason with them, hoping to persuade them of the injustice they do us. We can only attempt to get rid of them" (2008a: 432).

Why does she think premise (2) of Regan's argument is false? Primarily, she argues, it is because Regan's concept "inherent value" is too mysterious to do the work that he argues it does:

> It is not dependent upon the value which either the inherently valuable individual or anyone else may place upon that individual's life or experiences. It is not (necessarily) a function of sentience or any other mental capacity, because, Regan says, some entities which are not sentient (e.g., trees, rivers, or rocks) may, nevertheless, have inherent value. (2008a: 430)

According to Warren, Regan's concept of "inherent value" cannot be derived from the value that individuals give to other individuals (extrinsic value – see Episode 5), and it cannot be derived from conscious states. What establishes it? Warren says Regan doesn't tell us. "Inherent value appears as a mysterious non-natural property which we must take on faith" (2008a: 430).

Regan does a bit better at clarifying what he means in his more recent book, *Defending Animal Rights*. There, he explains that:

> Like us, they possess a variety of sensory, cognitive, conative, and volitional capacities. They see and hear, believe and desire, remember and anticipate, and plan and intend. Moreover, as is true in our case, what happens to them matter to them. Physical pleasure and pain – these they share with us. But they also share fear and contentment, anger and loneliness, frustration and satisfaction, and cunning and imprudence; these and a host of other psychological states and dispositions collectively help define the mental lives and relative well-being of those humans and animals who (in my terminology) are "subjects of a life." (2001: 43)

This is certainly a more positive account of what *might* establish an animal's inherent value. It is not a function of sentience or any particular mental capacity, but a function of a "host of. . . psychological states." Nevertheless, it still doesn't connect the descriptive concept of "subjects of a life" with the normative concept of "inherent value." And this effectively closes off inherent value for any non-sentient being. Warren concludes: "In short, the concept of inherent value seems to create at least as many problems as it solves" (2008a: 430).

Warren clearly doesn't think Regan's argument works, but what will she replace it with? Why does she think humans' capacity for rationality is the morally relevant condition for having moral rights? She explains:

> Why is rationality morally relevant? It does not make us "better" than other animals or more "perfect." It does not even automatically make us more intelligent. (Bad reasoning reduces our effective intelligence rather than increasing it.) But it is morally relevant insofar as it provides greater possibilities for cooperation and for the nonviolent resolution of problems. It also makes us more dangerous than non-rational beings can ever be. (2008a: 432)

Rationality is relevant, then, according to Warren, because it is the capacity by which we make moral decisions. We decide how cooperative or destructive we will be, and we recognize the moral features of each of these actions. This capacity to understand moral concerns and act on them establishes that we are morally unique. (Recall that Kant said something similar: see Episode 5.)

If Warren is right, then mature adult humans have full moral rights. Interestingly, it also follows that anything with a lesser degrees of cognitive ability has fewer moral rights. The worry here is that human fetuses, infants, small children, and mentally handicapped people do not share the same moral status. Warren responds that this is inconclusive, since "there are powerful practical and emotional reasons for protecting non-rational human beings, reasons which are absent in the case of most non-human animals" (2008: 433). But do these "practical and emotional reasons" amount to moral consideration? It is not clear. Plus, Warren draws a peculiar analogy between children and pets: "We don't normally care for animals in the same way [that we care for children and the mentally handicapped], and when we do – e.g., in the case of much-loved pets – we may regard them as having special rights by virtue of their relationship to us" (2008a: 433). This implication is perfectly consistent with her view, but it requires that we regard children and mentally handicapped people as having rights *only when* they are in relationships with people who care about them.

It seems, then, after considering both utilitarian and deontological arguments for animal welfare, that we are faced with an interesting dilemma. Either accept that all animals (human and non-human) deserve equal moral consideration, which may require that we become vegetarian, or accept that human fetuses, infants, children, and mentally handicapped people are no more morally valuable than the family pet. Let's see if we can get some help with this decision from *Bones* and *House, M.D.*

CASE STUDY 1: *Bones*, "Finger in the Nest," season 4

AVAILABILITY: NetFlix, iTunes

Bones is a show about an FBI forensics team that investigates unusual murders. The main characters, Agent Seely Booth (David Boreanaz) and forensic anthropologist Dr Temperance Brennan (Emily Deschanel) (nicknamed "Bones" by Booth), approach crime from diametrically opposed perspectives. Booth focuses on psychological tendencies and motives, and Bones focuses strictly on the empirical data. But, as any good crime drama proves, these approaches work best when combined.

In this episode, Booth and Bones investigate the murder of a well-liked veterinarian. They quickly learn that the victim was killed by a dog used in illegal dogfighting. Their investigation leads them to a barn on a rural property owned by one of the vet's clients, Don Timmons (Dean Norris). As it turns out, the barn is the venue used for the illegal dogfighting. Timmons denies knowing any of what happens in the barn – he says he rents it to someone, the Humbert Company. A mold made from the victim's wounds confirms that one of the dogs they found chained up in Timmons' barn is the dog that killed the vet.

The team learns that the dog once had a computer ID tag that has now been removed. Though the tag leads them nowhere, the stitching on the dog's neck is distinctive. They explain that surgical stitches are like signatures – each surgeon has his own. In this case, it turns out that the tutor hired by Timmons to help his son through high school is in medical school and runs a dogfighting operation to pay for school. The vet found the operation and was taking pictures to send to the police, but the tutor saw him and released the dog that subsequently killed him.

Commentary: Fighting like dogs

Dogfighting is an increasingly popular gambling sport in which two dogs, generally pit bull terriers, are placed in a ring to fight until one of them can no longer move, and, often, until one of them dies. Dogfighting is a felony in all 50 US states, as stipulated in the Federal Animal Welfare Act. Why? Dogfighting violates the Act's provisions with respect to the care and treatment of animals. Why was the Act passed? Most likely, because people generally agree that suffering is a morally relevant feature of an act and dogfighting causes an extreme amount of suffering.

This episode of *Bones* raises two moral questions. First, can animals be morally responsible for their actions? And second, how does the answer to the first question bear on the question of how we should treat animals? When Booth and Bones explain to Don Timmons that his veterinarian has been killed by a dogfighting dog, he asks, "Seth was murdered by a dog?" Bones responds abruptly: "The *murderer* was a human being. The murder *weapon* was a dog." Bones is drawing a distinction between the mental state of the dog and the dog's actions. Is this distinction plausible?

If someone said, "He was killed with a 9 mm pistol," it would seem odd to ask, "He was murdered by a pistol?" This is because the term "murder" has moral implications. Someone can be killed without being murdered. Murder is a killing coupled with a certain state of mind, usually malice. Can a dog actually be "malicious"? Obviously a pistol has no malice – it has no mental states. But what about a robot? If we designed a robot to do exactly what we tell it to do, then, again, it would seem strange to say that a robot "murdered" someone. We would still blame the programmer, because even if the robot has mental states, "malice" isn't one of them, since its motivation comes solely from its programming.

Now, dogs are somewhere between robots and humans with respect to their mental capacities. They are not merely passive like a pistol, and it seems they have at least some mental states. But they certainly do not have the full range of mental states that mature humans do. We also know that, if dogs kill without being trained to do so, it is usually because of fear or hunger. It is not clear what it would mean for a dog to harbor ill will against someone, and then form an intention to kill that person, and then carry it out. Therefore, it seems Bones's distinction is roughly accurate. At the end of the episode, Bones plans to adopt the killer dog, but Booth tells her he's been put to sleep. "He was put down. I'm sorry. You know, he killed somebody and they had to put him down." Bones responds, sadly, "It wasn't his fault. People made him do what he did." If a dog kills someone on command, it is because someone else trained the dog to do so. Therefore, the blame falls to the person and not the dog.

Interestingly, the same seems true of a mentally handicapped person or a child. If a mentally handicapped person or a small child started firing a gun into a crowd, we would not morally blame him or her for this action. We may have to take drastic steps to protect people, either shooting the person with the gun or, if we are able to arrest him, we may have to remove him from society. But moral blame does not accurately apply in these cases.

Let's assume that Bones's distinction is roughly correct: dogs are not morally responsible for their actions. How does this bear on the question of whether animals have rights? If having a certain type of cognitive capacity is the basic condition for having intrinsic moral value, then it bears directly on the question. Interestingly, both utilitarians and deontologists agree that a particular type of cognitive capacity is the basic condition, though they disagree about which one. Most utilitarians argue that it is the capacity for pain and pleasure. Most deontologists argue that it is the capacity to consider moral reasons (however, Regan is a deontologist and doesn't agree). But the fact that we regard animals' actions differently from how we view those of humans may suggest a distinction in the type of moral value those beings have. But we should be careful in accepting such a distinction, since this would also imply that children and the mentally handicapped have a different type of moral value from that of mature humans.

CASE STUDY 2: *House, M.D.*, "Babies and Bathwater," season 1

AVAILABILITY: NetFlix, iTunes

House, M.D. is a show about how a brilliant, but incredibly rude and self-righteous, physician, Dr Gregory House (Hugh Laurie), and his team of research physicians diagnose and treat strange and rare medical problems. The writers of the show attempt, rather successfully, to outdo each previous episode by combining ever-stranger diseases with ever-stranger moral dilemmas.

In this season 1 episode, a pregnant woman is brought into the hospital after having passed out while driving. After several failed diagnoses, the team discovers the woman has small cell lung cancer, a particularly aggressive form of cancer. There is no doubt that she will die from this disease, the only question is how quickly the doctors can start her treatment so they can prolong her life as long as possible. Since the woman is 28 weeks pregnant, she has to decide whether to have a C-section and start treatment immediately (which would give the baby about an 80 percent chance of survival), or to wait a week or two before having the C-section and then start treatment (upping the baby's chance of survival to around 90 percent, but significantly decreasing the time she has left to live). A complication arises and emergency surgery is necessary. The husband is forced to decide between losing both the mother and the baby or just the mother. He chooses to give the baby a chance to survive.

In the midst of all of this, a young couple brings in an underweight baby with pneumonia. House accuses them, in a roundabout fashion, of child abuse. They explain that they've had the baby on a vegan diet since it stopped breast-feeding. House scoffs and puts the baby on an IV drip until the pneumonia clears up. He runs additional tests and discovers that the baby has a thyroid problem, and that it wasn't the diet after all.

Commentary: Dr House on being vegan

In this episode, a couple comes into the hospital with a sick baby. House diagnoses the baby with pneumonia, but says that's only its second worst problem. The baby's weight has dropped from the 25th percentile to the 3rd percentile in just one month. House says, "I'm not a baby expert, but I'm pretty sure they're not supposed to shrink." The couple explains that they changed the baby's diet after it stopped breast-feeding, feeding it an all raw food, vegan diet.

The term "vegan" describes a diet slightly more restrictive than "vegetarian." Whereas a vegetarian does not eat meat, a vegan does not eat meat or use animal products, including cheese, eggs, milk, butter, leather, or wool. Vegan diets are especially worrisome for infants because babies need fats for healthy brain development and for physical size. The only safe way for an infant younger than one year old to get this much fat is through whole milk – either the mother's or another animal's. Even vegan diets allow for whole animal milk for infants under the age of one.

Dr House editorializes, patronizingly: "Raw food. If only our ancestors had mastered the secret of fire." Then he explains, "Babies need fats, protein, calories. Less important: sprouts and hemp. Starving babies is bad . . . and illegal in many cultures." Clearly the parents face a dilemma. They feel a particular moral obligation to eat a certain way. Yet their baby requires certain nutrients that cannot be obtained from this diet. Therefore, this scene raises an important moral question: What if our moral obligations to animal welfare come into conflict with our moral obligation to our own welfare or the welfare of our children?

Clearly, if a mother cannot breast-feed, her only option is to use the products of other animals. When our moral obligations come into conflict, we have a prime opportunity to see just how good our moral reasons are. We should first ask why anyone would choose to be a vegan and not simply a vegetarian.

Milking a cow and taking eggs from a chicken does not harm those animals. So why else might someone refuse to eat them? Unfortunately, in many places, milk production supports the veal industry. The veal industry is one of the cruelest, legally permissible animal industries. Veal is prized for being lean and tender. But calves that are allowed to wander openly develop muscle that changes the flavor of the meat. Because of this, veal calves are tied down by their necks and confined in crates to restrict their movement. They are often fed diets that keep them anemic, so their meat remains a light white color, which brings more money at market. Similarly, in many places, four or five full-grown chickens are confined to "battery cages" with a floor space of only $18'' \times 20''$. In this confinement, chickens cannot spread their wings, their feet are damaged by the wire cages, they cannot dust bathe as they would in a field, and the stress causes them to fight. To avoid lots of carnage from the chicken fights, farmers often sear off their beaks with a hot iron. Vegans take the connection between their food and these conditions very seriously. They do not want to promote this degree of suffering, so they refuse to participate in the process.

This raises another interesting moral question: Does purchasing food produced in a way that causes suffering constitute participating in causing that suffering? If you believe in a capitalist version of classical liberalism (see the Episode 8), it seems you should say *yes*. A capitalist argues that, in a free market, the economy reflects the values of a society. Why does one product sell better than a similar product? Because the first product does more of what people *want* than the second one does. Why do people buy more regular vegetables than organic vegetables? Because they value the immediate cost of the vegetable over the probability that it is covered with harmful pesticides. Now, what about chicken? Why buy eggs from the grocery store instead of the local farmer? Because grocery eggs are cheaper. But more chickens are harmed because the grocery store buys from factory farms that abuse their chickens. When people do not value chickens more than the eggs they produce, they continue to buy the grocery store eggs. This constitutes participation.

Let's say we believe in capitalism and are concerned with animal welfare. Where does this leave the mother of a 4-month-old infant? If suffering is morally relevant for all animals that can suffer, she must choose between the suffering of her infant and the suffering of the animals involved in milk production. She might be able to find a local farmer who does not sell his dairy cows to the veal industry, but if she is any large city, that is unlikely.

Nevertheless, a deontologist could claim that she has a *special obligation* to her child that she does not have to any other animals – even the human infants of other mothers. Surely, it is not immoral to choose to protect your child over a stranger (it may be a moral good to sacrifice for another, but it is certainly not an obligation). You have duties to your offspring that you do not have to any other creature.

Could a utilitarian introduce a similar distinction? It is not clear that a utilitarian could adequately resolve this dilemma. Surely the factory conditions that would provide milk to a large city would introduce a measure of suffering to animals that would outweigh one person's pain over losing a child. It would be strange to hold a moral theory that implies that vegans who cannot breast-feed must refrain from having children. Perhaps a utilitarian could argue that the measure of the vegan mother's participation in animal suffering (the amount of suffering she is responsible for by supporting the industry) is outweighed by the pleasure her child brings her. This may work, but it is far from clear that this is satisfactory, or that anyone could calculate pleasure and suffering accurately in these scenarios.

STUDY QUESTIONS

1. What implications do Mary Anne Warren's argument for animal welfare have for dogfighting?
2. If most people generally think that suffering is a morally relevant feature of an action, why do you think some people are able to watch and support dogfighting as a sport? How could you convince someone who fights dogs that it is immoral?
3. If someone trained a grizzly bear to attack and kill people, who would be morally blameworthy for the deaths, the trainer or the bear? Why?
4. Come up with your own case in which someone is responsible for an act (they physically committed the act) but not morally responsible (they are not blameworthy or praiseworthy). How does this distinction apply to dogfighting?
5. For years, large dogs were trained as guard dogs to protect important people or property. Is there a moral difference between training a dog to kill to protect someone and training a dog to kill another dog for sport? Explain your answer.
6. Dr House eventually learns that the baby's weight loss is due to a thyroid condition. Does this undermine his earlier criticisms of the couple's choice to feed the baby a vegan diet? Why or why not?
7. Suppose that the baby's low weight was due to the vegan diet. Would the parents be guilty of child abuse, as portrayed in the episode? Explain your answer.

8. Do you agree with capitalists that purchasing goods is a way to express your moral values? Why or why not? If someone doesn't agree, would it be morally permissible to purchase chicken from a chicken farmer who tortures his chickens before he slaughters them?

9. Is there any evidence to corroborate our claims about factory farming? Find three different sources of evidence about the conditions in which food animals like cows, chickens, and pigs are typically raised. What does your moral theory tell you about the moral permissibility of these conditions?

10. Does talk about moral "value" translate cleanly into talk about moral "rights"? Why or why not?

ALTERNATIVE CASE STUDIES

1. *CSI*, "Lying Down with Dogs," season 8
   (What impact might the images of dogfighting in this episode have on the animal welfare debate? Should they have this effect?)

2. *South Park*, "Fun with Veal," season 6
   (Is "eco-terrorism" – breaking the law in attempt to preserve a natural object or environment – morally justified if the cause is morally justified?)

3. *The Simpsons*, "Apocalypse Cow," season 19
   (How should facts about meat production affect the ethical discussion about animal welfare?)

EPISODE 10: ABORTION

INTRODUCTION

In 1964, the soap opera *Another World* became the first television show to address the issue of abortion. The character Tom Baxter (Nicholas Pryor) convinces his girlfriend Patricia "Pat" Matthews (Susan Trustman) to have an abortion. In 1964, the procedure was still illegal. The first decision to have a legal abortion portrayed on TV was on the show *Maude* in 1972, a

What's Good on TV?: Understanding Ethics Through Television, First Edition.
Jamie Carlin Watson and Robert Arp.
© 2011 Jamie Carlin Watson and Robert Arp. Published 2011 by Blackwell Publishing Ltd.

year before the decision made by the Supreme Court in *Roe v. Wade*. But *Maude* takes place in New York, where abortion was legal at the time. The first decision to have a legal abortion post-*Roe v. Wade* was portrayed on the soap *All My Children* in 1973. Susan Lucci's character, Erica Kane, decides to have an abortion because she didn't want to gain weight and compromise her modeling career.

Some common questions that these television characters consider before making the decision to abort include: *Am I ready for the responsibility of a baby? Will a baby interfere too much with my life? Will I be a good parent?* Are these the relevant questions for determining the moral permissibility of abortion? In this Episode, we'll take a look.

Abortion is one of the most controversial topics in ethics, and for good reason. If some people who argue that abortion is morally impermissible are right, then many abortions are probably murder. On the other hand, if those who argue that abortion is morally permissible are right, then any laws prohibiting abortion would probably violate women's civil rights. So, how do we wade through this tangle of emotion that is the abortion debate? We will start by identifying an assumption that almost everyone agrees on, explaining a few key terms, and then defusing a few dead ends. This will give us a solid foundation for the rest of the debate.

ONE COMMON ASSUMPTION

As with the animal welfare debate, all parties in the abortion debate agree that *mature human beings are morally valuable and that it is wrong, in most circumstances, for one human being to kill another.* It may not be wrong in every circumstance – for example, if someone is trying to kill you, it may be morally permissible to kill that person in self-defense. It may even be permissible to kill someone who is morally innocent. For instance, if a severely mentally handicapped person starts firing a gun into a crowd and there is no other way to stop her, it may be permissible to kill that person to save the lives of others, even though she is not morally responsible for her actions. Nevertheless, in most cases, it seems that innocent mature humans have a right to life that it is impermissible to violate by killing them.

With this assumption in hand, philosophers attempt to explain what makes it wrong to kill mature humans, and then argue one of two ways. Some argue that whatever considerations make it wrong (in most cases) to kill humans also make it wrong (in most cases) to kill fetuses; therefore, most abortions are impermissible. Alternatively, one might argue that whatever considerations make it wrong (in most cases) to kill humans do not apply to fetuses; therefore, most abortions are permissible. From these conclusions, additional moral considerations are offered to address hard cases, including those where the mother's life is in danger, the pregnancy is a result rape or incest, and the pregnancy is the result of a failure of birth control. However complicated the arguments get, it is important to remember that we can always return to this shared assumption and retrace our steps.

There are a few terms that it will be handy to be familiar with in this Episode. The organism in the womb that is the subject of this debate is referred to by a number of different medical terms throughout its development. At the moment a sperm enters an egg, the organism is called a "zygote." After the chromosomes separate (about 24 hours later), cell division begins. Between days seven and twelve, the organism reaches the eight-cell stage, after which "twinning" (the potential for the organisms to become twins or triplets) is no longer possible (it is no longer "totipotent"). When the organism has eight cells, it is called a "blastocyst." Around week two, when the blastocyst implants in the uterine wall, it becomes an "embryo." At eight weeks, the organism is called a "fetus." It remains a fetus until birth at around forty weeks. The term "baby" is medically inappropriate for an unborn organism; it is not technically a baby until birth and is an emotionally loaded term than can bias the debate. Many moral philosophers use the term "fetus" referring to the organism at any point of development. Technically, "fetus" (which means "young unborn" in Latin) only applies after the eighth week of pregnancy. We will use the term "organism" to refer to the organism at any point in development and "fetus" when we are talking about the organism after the eighth week of development.

SIX FALLACIES TO AVOID

There are various argument strategies that can lead to irrational biases in the abortion debate. These biases are unfortunate because they often lead to roadblocks in the discussion where genuine progress might be made. We will try to defuse six fallacies that commonly creep into the arguments for or against the moral permissibility of abortion.

Fallacy 1: The pro-life/pro-choice false dilemma

It is helpful for participants in this debate to recognize that the terms "pro-choice" and "pro-life" are *political* terms, not *moral* terms. Many who identify themselves politically as "pro-life" also argue that abortion is permissible in rare cases – for instance, when pregnancy results from incest or where the mother's life is in danger. Similarly, many people who identify themselves politically as "pro-choice" also argue that abortion is impermissible in some cases. For instance, some argue that abortion should not be used as a method of birth control, or that abortions of convenience are immoral.

A false dilemma is an argument that uncharitably attempts to restrict the choices to two when there may be a third or fourth or fifth option available. For example, imagine the following argument: you're either a liberal or a conservative, and you're not a liberal, therefore you must be conservative. The problem is that there are positions other than liberal and conservative – such as moderate, libertarian, socialist, etc.

The pro-life/pro-choice false dilemma is based on the assumption in an argument that the two political positions imply two, and only two, mutually exclusive moral positions: either you're against all abortions or you're for any abortion at any time. For instance, someone might argue: you're either pro-choice or pro-life; given that you think some abortions are impermissible, you must be pro-life. This argument is a false dilemma because someone might be against some abortions, but still vote pro-choice. They may simply defend a law that restricts certain types of abortion, for instance, late-term abortions or abortions of convenience. Note that this fallacy can be committed by anyone in the debate. The argument might just as easily go like this: you're either pro-choice or pro-life; given that you think some abortions are permissible, you must be pro-choice.

To be sure, there are genuine dilemmas. Any argument in which a conclusion is drawn from two and only two mutually exclusive, neither of which is favorable, is a genuine dilemma. For instance, imagine you discover that your long-time roommate just cheated on his girlfriend, who is also your best friend. You will either find a way to let her know, or you won't. If you tell her, you will lose his friendship (and rent!). If you don't, then you risk hurting her and losing her friendship. In this case, there seem to be only two options, neither of which is favorable. The pro-life/pro-choice dilemma, however, is a false one – there are more than two positions with respect to the moral permissibility of abortion.

In the 1964 episode of *Another World*, characters Baxter and Matthews disregard the legal norm against abortion (the pro-life legislation) because they feel there is no moral norm against it. Because the political terms "pro-life" and "pro-choice" do not reflect mutually exclusive moral positions, they are too imprecise to inform our discussion. Therefore, we will speak of abortion as being permissible or impermissible in particular cases and then try to identify principled reasons for these distinctions.

Fallacy 2: The potentiality argument

Some people argue that abortion is impermissible (or permissible) because the organism is potentially a person (or not potentially a person) with rights. Interestingly, almost everyone agrees that, at some point, an organism (all conditions being normal) will become a person with a right to life. In addition, almost everyone agrees that, at some point, the organism is not a person with a right to life. The hard question to answer is *when exactly* the fertilized egg becomes a being with a right to life.

Some argue that it is at the moment of "conception." Others argue that it is at the moment the fetus emerges from the womb as a baby (around 40 weeks). Still others argue that it is when the fetus becomes viable (can live outside the womb; between 22 and 28 weeks). Still others argue that it is when the fetus becomes capable of feeling pain (around 20 weeks). And still others argue that it is when the baby develops the capacity for self-reflection (between 18 and 24 months after birth).

Whatever the point actually is, before this point, it does not have the same moral status as after it reaches that point. That it is potentially a person with rights does not transfer to this organism the rights of a person. Rob is potentially president of the United States (though a lot less potentially than he would like to believe). Nevertheless, he does not receive the protection of the Secret Service just because he is *potentially* president. Jamie is potentially a Supreme Court justice, but as of now he does not have the authority to decide important legal cases. Similarly, because an organism is potentially a person, it does not have the rights that come with personhood.

Interestingly, this fallacy can be committed by anyone in the debate. Many advocates for the permissibility of abortion cite the number of "spontaneous abortions" and miscarriages that occur (cases where the

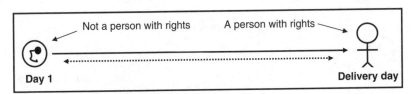

Figure 10.1 When do rights begin?

body naturally disposes of the organism), and conclude that intentionally ending a pregnancy is not immoral since that pregnancy has a high chance of failing anyway. The argument commits the potentiality fallacy because it implies that since the organism is not likely to become a person with rights, it is not immoral to dispose of it.

Fallacy 3: The "look at the pictures" argument

Some organizations attempt to convince others of the impermissibility of abortion by printing brochures with pictures of aborted fetuses. The idea is supposed to be that seeing pictures of little humans burned and ripped apart will convince you that abortion is immoral. There are two problems with this line of reasoning.

First, just because something looks human doesn't mean that it is, or that it has moral value. For instance, a sculptor could mould little statues that look like aborted fetuses. But these would have no more moral value than the clay they were made from. Similarly, something can have moral value that looks nothing like a human. Some of the organizations that offer these pictures claim that an organism is a person with rights from the moment of fertilization. But during the first few weeks of development, the organism looks nothing like a human. It may have moral value, but look only like a blob of tissue. So, the fact that aborted fetuses look human has nothing to do with whether they are morally valuable. This means that pictures are irrelevant to the moral permissibility of abortion.

Second, the argument commits the fallacy of appeal to emotion, which we have already discussed. The purpose of the pictures is to make you feel disgust or sadness over the loss of human life. But, as we know, emotions are not a reliable source of moral evidence, and some human life is not morally valuable – for instance, humans who have forfeited their right to life by attacking you.

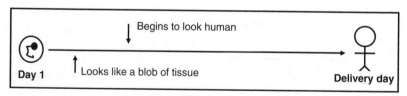

Figure 10.2 Look at the pictures.

Fallacy 4: The "it's my body" argument

You may have seen a bumper sticker or T-shirt that says, "Keep Your Laws Off My Body." The reference here is to an argument for the permissibility of abortion. Some people argue that abortion is always morally permissible because the fetus is a part of a woman's body, over which she has complete rights.

Unfortunately, this argument is question-begging (see the "Pilot Episode," fallacy 3, *petitio principii*). Almost everyone agrees that a woman's body is hers to do as she pleases with. But this argument assumes without argument that anything inside a woman's body has no rights independent of her body. But if we knew this, the abortion debate would be settled; we would already know that the fetus is not a person with independent rights. But this is the very conclusion we need an argument for. If a fetus is not a person with rights, then the fetus most certainly belongs to the woman's body, sort of like hair, fingernails, and skin; she can dispose of it, pierce it, tattoo it, or remodel it however she wishes. But if a fetus *is* a person with rights, then there are certain things she cannot do to it.

This point is clearer when we consider that children belong to their mothers in a way that few things belong to a person. Mothers are often granted more rights than fathers in family court. Nevertheless, we do not allow a mother to do whatever she wants with her child – she cannot kill it, molest it, abuse it, etc. Therefore, if it turns out that a fetus has at least the moral status of a small child, it is not, strictly speaking, "your body" to do with as you please.

Might there be reasons for thinking that a fetus is nothing more than a part of a woman's body? Sure. But we cannot assume that these reasons exist or are sufficient until someone presents them in an argument.

Fallacy 5: The "let nature take its course" argument

Some people argue that pregnancy is a natural process that, once begun, should be allowed to take its course. To stop the process, they argue, is tantamount to playing God. Unfortunately, it is difficult to hold this position consistently. Diseases and natural disasters are also natural processes, but we do not presume that we shouldn't do what we can to either stop them or mitigate the damage they cause. If a pregnancy becomes dangerous or having a child would increase the potential for serious harm, either to the baby or the mother, it is not clear from nature alone whether we should do anything.

In addition, this argument commits the naturalistic fallacy (see the "Pilot Episode," fallacy 6). Just because circumstances *are* a certain way doesn't mean they *should* be that way. Just because a tyrannical ruler does abuse his citizens doesn't mean he or she should abuse them. Just because I have a life-threatening disease doesn't mean I should have it or that I am obligated to keep it if there is a cure available. Without further moral considerations, nature cannot tell us whether abortion is permissible.

Fallacy 6: The consequences of legally prohibiting abortion are too high

It is undeniable that, prior to the legalization of abortion, many women still terminated their pregnancies and that some of these procedures were unsafe and unsanitary. The side effects of these procedures could be traumatizing or debilitating. In addition, the legalization of abortion led to many positive social consequences. Consider the following passage from economist Steven Levitt and journalist Stephen Dubner from their popular 2005 book, *Freakonomics*:

> To be sure, the legalization of abortion in the United States has myriad consequences. Infanticide fell dramatically. So did shotgun marriages, as well as the number of babies put up for adoption.... Conceptions rose by nearly 30 percent, but births actually fell by 6 percent, indicating that many women were using abortion as a method of birth control, a crude and drastic sort of insurance policy.
>
> Perhaps the most drastic effect of legalized abortion, however, and one that would take years to reveal itself, was its impact on crime. In the early 1990s, just as the first cohort of children born after Roe v. Wade was hitting its late teen years ... the rate of crime began to fall. (2005: 139)

Levitt and Dubner go on to offer a detailed account of the reasons for believing lower crimes rates are a result of permitting abortion and not merely a statistical correlation.

Legal abortions are far better regulated and take place in sanitary facilities by licensed physicians. The negative consequences of illegal abortions and the positive consequences of permitting them lead some to argue that any legal prohibitions on abortion would be morally worse than the current laws.

Unfortunately, this argument is question-begging. It assumes we already know that the negative consequences of illegal abortions are morally worse than killing the organism involved in a pregnancy. We have not yet established whether abortion is a moral atrocity. Mary Anne Warren, an ardent defender of abortion rights, argues that this argument is not sufficient to establish its conclusion because it assumes without proof that the organism is not a person with a right to life. She writes, "[T]he fact that restricting access to abortion has tragic side effects does not, in itself, show that the restrictions are unjustified, since murder is wrong regardless of the consequences of prohibiting it" (2008b: 184).

The idea is that, *if* abortion is *not* a moral atrocity, then we *should* implement policy permitting it, because of the negative consequences of prohibiting it. On the other hand, *if* abortion *is* a moral atrocity, then even though the consequences of prohibiting it may be bad, even tragic, we *should not* legally permit it. If the latter is true, we would be sanctioning one person's immoral act in order to prevent someone else's immoral act. We would never argue that we should not make theft illegal because we learn that permitting theft leads to lower violent crime. Theft should be illegal, and we should, additionally, address any crimes that ensue because of that legislation. Therefore, this argument assumes what it needs to prove, that the negative consequences of illegal abortions is more morally significant than the killing of the organisms involved in pregnancy.

With these six fallacies out of the way, we can now consider four classic arguments in the abortion debate. Judith Jarvis Thomson argues that abortion is permissible in cases where a woman is not responsible for the pregnancy. Mary Anne Warren argues that abortion is always permissible because fetuses do not meet the conditions for having moral rights, which, she argues, is the same as meeting the conditions for "personhood." And finally, Don Marquis argues, contrary to Warren, that killing adult humans is wrong not because we are persons, but because killing us deprives us of a future that is valuable to us. And since the organisms of pregnancy have futures like ours, it is also, in most cases, immoral to kill them.

JUDITH JARVIS THOMSON AND THE VIOLINIST ARGUMENT

In an article originally published in 1971, Judith Thomson begins her argument for the permissibility of abortion by acknowledging that, while she does not think a fetus is a person from the moment of conception, she cannot provide compelling reasons for thinking that it is not. So, for the sake of argument, she accepts that, at any point during pregnancy, a fetus is a person with full human rights, including the right to life. Nevertheless, she argues, even if this is true, there are times when abortion is morally permissible. We will present Thomson's argument slightly out of order for the sake of clarity.

One position on abortion is that a woman is never, under any circumstances, morally permitted to have an abortion. Thomson calls this the "extreme position." She argues that the extreme position is implausible because, even if the fetus is a person with a right to life, a woman still has a right to self-defense if the fetus places her life in danger. To support this claim, she asks us to imagine being trapped in a small house with a rapidly growing child: "[Y]ou are already up against the wall of the house and in a few minutes you'll be crushed to death; if nothing is done to stop him from growing he'll be hurt, but in the end he'll simply burst open the house and walk out a free man" (2008: 176).

Thomson thinks that surely you have a right to defend yourself, even though the child is not capable of any malice or a morally responsible intent to kill you. This case parallels our earlier case, where a severely mentally handicapped person is firing a gun into a crowd. If you're in that crowd and you have a gun, and the only way to save your life is to take his, then surely, killing him is simply a matter of self-defense – even though the person is not capable of malice or a morally responsible intent to kill. These cases are supposed to guide your intuitions in those instances where a mother's life is in danger because of her pregnancy, and the only way to save her life is to take the fetus. If this is right, then the extreme view is not right, and there is at least one case where it is morally permissible to take the life of an innocent person.

Are there any other cases? Thomson argues that it is also permissible to have an abortion in cases of rape. To show this, she asks you to imagine a famous violinist who has a fatal kidney disease. You happen to have the only blood type that can cure the violinist of this illness, but it will take nine months of having your kidneys attached to his for the treatment to work. If he doesn't get the treatment, he will quickly die. Imagine now that you wake up one morning with your kidneys attached to the unconscious violinist. Against your will and the violinist's, the Society of Music Lovers has kidnapped both you and the violinist and plugged his kidneys into yours. This case is very similar to a case of pregnancy due to rape. Against your will and that of the organism, someone forcibly attached your bodily organs to, on Thomson's assumption, a being with a right to life, and it's only for nine months. The question, in both cases, is whether you have the right to unplug yourself, thereby killing the innocent person.

Thomson concludes that there can be no doubt that you have the right to unplug yourself. As an individual with sovereign rights over your own body, no one has the right to use your body against your will, regardless of their right to life, or their malice, or their morally responsible intent to do so. She acknowledges that it would be a great good, a very nice thing, if you agree to remain connected to the violinist or the organism. But you are under no moral obligation to do so. Therefore, this is another case where, because the woman does not consent to someone else using her body, abortion is morally permissible.

There is an additional case where Thomson argues that abortion is permissible even if an organism has a right to life. Imagine a woman does all she can to prevent a pregnancy – she uses the best contraceptives available and even only has sex when she thinks she is least likely to be ovulating. If some accident happens, and the woman gets pregnant, Thomson argues that, because the woman has taken all the necessary precautions, the pregnancy is against her will and abortion is morally permissible. "If the room is stuffy, and I therefore open a window to air it, and a burglar climbs in, it would be absurd to say, 'Ah, now he can stay, she's given him a right to the use of her house – for she is partly responsible for his presence there, having voluntarily done what enable him to get in, in full knowledge that there are such things as burglars'" (2008: 179). Thomson then asks us to imagine that microscopic organisms called "people-seeds," which have all the rights that mature humans have, drift through the air at random. And because "[y]ou don't want children ... you fix up your windows with fine mesh screens, the very best you can buy" (2008: 179). Nevertheless, every now and then, one of the screens is defective and a people-seed drifts in and takes root in your carpet. In this case, the people-seeds represent the organism of pregnancy, and the screens represent contraception. But, she argues, it is absurd to think it is immoral to remove the people-seed from your house after doing all you can to prevent it. Therefore, it is absurd to think abortion is immoral in cases where you've used contraception.

If Thomson is right, then even if an organism has a right to life, some cases of abortion are permissible. Are there any reasons to doubt Thomson's conclusions? There is at least one reason to doubt the last of her conclusions – that contraception obviates the woman's responsibility for carrying the organism to full term. Imagine you want to play Texas Hold 'Em poker and you want to win lots of money, but you don't want to lose a lot of money. So, you study the game carefully, learn to count cards, learn to calculate pot odds and card odds, and, by playing online for free, you become the best of the best. Now you decide to go to Las Vegas and win money in a high stakes Texas Hold 'Em tournament. Despite all your preparation and prevention measures, you lose all your money. Can you then go to the tournament committee and prove to them all the protective measures you took and demand your money back? Surely not. You played the game and, due to pure luck, you lost. The same seems to go with pregnancy. The only surefire way to prevent pregnancy is to abstain from sex. However, if you play the game, you might lose – and it seems *you* are responsible for any losses.

What about the case of opening the window and the burglar sneaking in? Even in this case, you have a right to remove him, but not at the expense of his life. Since the burglar is not innocent, you have a right to expel him, but surely killing him would be a punishment disproportionate to the crime. In addition, the people-seed and the organism are innocent. Mary Anne Warren writes: "Mere ownership does not give me the right to kill innocent people whom I find on my property, and indeed I am apt to be held responsible if such people injure themselves while on my property" (2008b: 184). Therefore, there seem to be reasons for doubting Thomson's third case. Can you think of any reason for doubting the violinist case?

MARY ANNE WARREN AND THE SPACE EXPLORER

Mary Anne Warren does not think Thomson's argument covers enough cases. Warren argues that abortion is never a matter of a woman's responsibility for the pregnancy, and all abortions are morally permissible. She begins by arguing that Thomson concedes too much in accepting that an organism is a person from the moment of fertilization. This entails, even granting all the conclusions we noted above, that a woman who simply forgets to take her birth control pill one day is morally responsible for a pregnancy that ensues. Thomson thinks this is absurd and suggests that there is a non-arbitrary way to determine when an organism becomes a person with rights. If she can establish that an organism is in no reasonable sense a person, then abortions are always permissible.

To help us determine whether an organism is a person with rights, Warren asks us to consider the following case:

> Imagine a space traveler who lands on an unknown planet and encounters a race of beings utterly unlike any he has ever seen or heard of. If he wants to be sure of behaving morally toward these beings, he has to somehow decide whether they are people, and hence have full moral rights, or whether they are the sort of thing which he need not feel guilty about treating as, for example, a source of food. (2008b: 188–9)

How could the traveler make such a decision? Warren suggests that he look for certain indicators of personhood. We consider the features of creatures we know to be unique to persons, and then we determine whether these beings have any of them. If these beings have none of the indicators of personhood, then it is morally permissible to not regard them as persons, and morally permissible to regard them as food or fuel.

What traits seem unique to persons? Warren suggests that there are at least five: (1) consciousness, and perhaps sentience (the capacity to experience pain); (2) the capacity to reason; (3) self-motivated activity; (4) the capacity to communicate (even if only with one another); and (5) the presence of self-concepts (self-awareness or self-reflection). A being may not need all or any particular one of these to be a person, but these seem to be the general indicators. If this is right, then any being that has absolutely none of these cannot, reasonably, be considered a person. Moreover, the organism of pregnancy has none of these. Therefore, abortion is always permissible.

If Warren is right, then Thomson's arguments are simply unnecessary. There is no good moral reason to prohibit an abortion, because the organism of a pregnancy, even a fetus of 39 weeks, is no more a person with rights than a single-celled amoeba.

Are there reasons to doubt Warren's conclusion? One might worry that, in her space traveler case, she simply conflates the moral conditions for personhood with the epistemic conditions for recognizing the moral conditions for personhood. An organism can have a right to life even if no one knows it, or could know it. If it does, it would be wrong to kill it, even if no one could be held morally responsible for doing so (recall from the "Pilot Episode" that "ought implies can," so that if someone could not know whether an organism has a right to life, he is under no obligation to not kill it). This distinction does not make a difference for the space traveler, who can only be concerned with the evidence before him, but it does make a difference for the moral philosopher who is concerned to discover the actual necessary and sufficient conditions for personhood. Therefore, Warren's conclusion about the space traveler case is justified only if we already have reasons for believing that the five criteria for personhood are, either individually or collectively, necessary conditions for personhood.

One might also worry that, given the current state of medical science, Warren's conclusion is much more restricted than she originally conceived. We know that fetuses exhibit pain-avoidance behavior as early as 22 weeks. Warren remains agnostic as to whether sentience is a sufficient condition for personhood. However, if it is, then abortions are impermissible after 22 weeks of development. Therefore, even if her conclusion is conclusive for any time before the organism becomes sentient, it is question-begging for any time afterwards – that is, until it is determined whether sentience is sufficient for personhood.

ABORTION IS WRONG FOR THE SAME REASON THAT KILLING ADULTS IS WRONG

Don Marquis, "Why Abortion is Immoral"

Don Marquis offers the most well-respected and widely accepted non-religious argument against abortion. In an article first published in 1989, Marquis argues that the conditions that make it wrong to kill adult humans applies also to fetuses, and that these conditions are irrelevant to whether the organism or the adult meets the conditions for "personhood."

What makes it wrong to kill us – mature human adults? Marquis suggests that it is the loss of a valuable future. He argues that this explains why, when a young person dies, we say things like, "She had so much to live for," and "He had so much potential." Similarly, it explains why terminal AIDS and cancer patients recognize that death is a very bad thing for them – death deprives them of the goods they might otherwise experience. This also explains why we regard murder as one of the worse crimes – "it deprives the victim of more than perhaps any other crime" (2008: 208).

What sort of goods does death deprive us of? Marquis argues that it is "all those activities, projects, experiences, and enjoyments which would have otherwise constituted my future personal life" (2008: 196). They are our "future conscious goods." This explains why immediate death is no more of a loss than death after a 30-year coma. The wrongfulness of death is not a matter of living human DNA, but of the *conscious* goods a person has the potential to experience, the goods that make life now worth living. This also explains why it is wrong to kill a coma patient. Even if a person does not have the capacity to understand or appreciate her future conscious goods, if those goods are what constitute a meaningful life to that person, and there remains the possibility of experiencing them, it is wrong to kill that person. This also explains why it is wrong to kill infants, children, and the mentally handicapped – the beings have future conscious goods even though they cannot fully appreciate them.

To sum up, according to Marquis, what makes it wrong to kill us is that we have *now* future conscious goods that make life worth living *now*, and killing would deprive us of these goods; we need not be conscious of those goods in order for them to make our lives valuable. If this is right, then it turns out that the organisms of pregnancy also have these goods (perhaps even more of them, since they presumably have more goods ahead of them than we, as adults, do), and therefore, it is wrong to kill them. This would explain why we regard it as a great moral harm for a mother to smoke or drink heavily while she is pregnant – because she is decreasing the number of conscious goods that the organism can experience in its future life. It also explains why we regard the killing of a pregnant woman as a double, and not merely a single, homicide – someone has deprived two beings of their valuable futures.

To be sure, the same exceptions that Thomson identifies may apply even if Marquis is right. Marquis says that he is not concerned, in this argument, with extreme cases, but simply with the general question of the permissibility of abortion. In general, he concludes, abortion is morally impermissible. How do we reconcile this conclusion with Warren's argument? We have to conclude that, if Marquis is right, Warren is wrong, and vice versa. Their conclusions are mutually exclusive; that is, they cannot both be true. Therefore, you must consider who offers the most plausible account of the wrongness of killing.

Are there any reasons to doubt Marquis's conclusion? We will consider case studies from the final season of *Law & Order* and the 1970s sitcom *Maude*, and evaluate whether the considerations offered in these shows suggest any reasons to choose Warren's account over Marquis's, or any reasons to doubt Marquis's conclusion.

CASE STUDY 1: *Law & Order*, "Dignity," season 20

AVAILABILITY: NetFlix, iTunes

In the final season of *Law & Order*, the writers explore, once again, the question of the legal permissibility of abortion. After an abortion doctor is shot in the middle of a church service, detectives Bernard (Anthony Anderson) and Lupo (Jeremy Sisto) find themselves questioning suspects in the midst of a heated political, religious, and moral debate. The issue even pits the detectives against one another. When Bernard's questioning reveals his anti-abortion leanings, Lupo tells him, "You wanna forget the abortion debate? You should need a permit to have kids." To which Bernard responds, "In your world, a kid hardly has a chance to be born."

Bernard and Lupo follow a lead from a caller to the abortion clinic where the doctor worked, to his pregnant girlfriend, to her disgruntled father, to a pro-life demonstrator who accosted the father outside the clinic. The demonstrator, Wayne Grogan (P. J. Sosko), admits that he shot the doctor, but offers a justification defense. His attorney argues that Grogan killed the doctor because the doctor was going to kill a 28-week-old viable fetus that would have a normal life span except for a disease that will leave the resulting child with a dangerously delicate skin (the smallest wound would be life-threatening). The doctor decided the child would have no meaningful quality of life and agreed to perform an abortion. Grogan's attorney argues that Grogan was merely acting to defend a person's life. A judge, rejecting precedent, allows the justification defense to go to trial.

With the country leaning pro-life, the DA and crew have to prove that Grogan determined to kill the doctor before he found out about the 28-week fetus. In the end, Executive ADA Mike Cutter (Linus Roache) is able to convince the jury that, even if the abortion doctor acted immorally, so did Wayne Grogan, and that Grogan must be held accountable for his actions.

Commentary: Rape and third trimester abortions

The key discussion in this episode takes place early on. Lupo tells Bernard, "If you think forcing an 11-year-old rape victim to have an abortion is okay, then you and I have nothing to talk about." Bernard comes back with, "You got it backwards, man. The horrible thing is the rape, not the bringing of a life into a world."

What are we to make of this exchange? On one hand, it is easy to sympathize with Lupo. It seems horrible for an 11-year-old girl, who does not have the cognitive and biological maturity to make her own life decisions, to have to try to raise a child. On the other hand, Bernard is right that the crime is the rape – neither the 11-year-old nor the organism of the pregnancy is morally responsible for their relationship to one another. It seems wrong to punish the organism for the crime of a third party. Unfortunately, the detectives do not reach a mutual understanding.

Lupo dodges this response by saying: "All I know is that an unwanted child already has two strikes against it." To this, Bernard offers a potentiality argument: "That unwanted child could change the world, cure cancer, be president!" Lupo turns it back on him, saying: "Yeah, or put his finger on the button and blow up the world." As we saw earlier, the potentiality argument is fallacious for everyone in the debate; a potential something does not necessarily share all the same rights of an actual something.

After this, Bernard explains how he was born two months premature because his mother threw herself down the stairs to try to kill the fetus. He is attempting to show Lupo that a 7-month-old fetus is just as much a baby as a 9-month-old newborn, and that some good can come from unwanted pregnancies. Lupo just shrugs and says: "So I almost had another partner."

So, how do we resolve the question of the moral permissibility of abortion in rape cases? Judith Thomson offers one way. Even if the organism is a person with rights, that person has no right to use your body against your will even if that person hasn't done so of his own accord. It is no different from killing a morally innocent mentally handicapped person who has kidnapped you. Another way might be to admit that the real tragedy is over, and that you and the organism now share that experience, and accept that you now have the chance to build that tragedy into something beautiful. Would resolving the issue this way mean you have a moral obligation to keep the fetus? Probably not. And still a third way would be to regard the organism as Warren does, as a being with no independent moral status until it achieves a certain set of mental capabilities.

Despite its apparently pro-life leanings, this episode includes several substantial reasons for the moral permissibility of abortion in extreme cases. When Detectives Bernard and Lupo first question a nurse at the abortion clinic, she explains that many third-trimester abortions are medical necessities: "Our patients had prenatal diagnoses of genetic disorders . . . fetuses developing without organs. Most of our patients wanted a baby. The others are girls, 10, 11, rape and incest victims. I am proud to work here." While rape and incest remain controversial cases, many moral philosophers conclude that some medical disorders impair development so severely as to undermine any actual or potential personhood the organism might develop. For instance, if a fetus's vital organs do not develop, then even if there is a heartbeat, the fetus is not like a person with rights (according to our arguments above) and will not live to become a person with rights.

A strangely inconsistent scene is when ADA Rubirosa (Alana De La Garza) finds out that one of the nurses from the abortion clinic quit when an abortion of an anencephalic fetus went wrong and the fetus was born alive, but, on the mother's wishes, the doctor killed the baby. Rubirosa had earlier expressed her sympathy with the abortion doctor, but now becomes incensed that DA Jack McCoy (Sam Waterston) doesn't want this mentioned during the trial. "We have to report it to the Bronx DA. . . . Dr Benning killed a human being."

The problem here is that most moral philosophers agree that an anencephalic fetus does not meet any of the typical criteria offered for having a right to life or being a person: its neural system has not and will not develop, so it cannot experience pain; it can never achieve consciousness; it will die within the first one to two weeks of being born having never experienced anything at all. And we have already established that mere geography (being in the womb or out of the womb) doesn't make a moral difference to whether a being has a right to life. Therefore, if all this is right, then Rubirosa is wrong; the doctor did not kill a human being, but merely undeveloped human tissue that will never develop into anything like a person with rights. This is just one more reason why moral philosophy is so important even in political debates and lawmaking.

CASE STUDY 2 : *Maude*, "Maude's Dilemma – Parts 1 and 2," season 1

AVAILABILITY: YouTube

The television show *Maude* was a spin-off of the famous show *All in the Family*, and ran from 1972 to 1978. It is about Maude Findlay, a politically liberal woman who lives with her fourth husband, divorced daughter, and 8-year-old grandson in Tuckahoe, NY, and how she threads delicate political and moral issues with her liberal daughter and their conservative friends.

In this pair of episodes, Maude (Bea Arthur), who is 47, accidentally gets pregnant. Though she and her 49-year-old husband Walter (Bill Macy) do not want a child, they are emotionally torn over whether to keep it. Maude's daughter Carol (Adrienne Barbeau) reminds her that she doesn't have to fret so much, because abortion (though they don't say the word right away) is now legal in New York State.

Maude, Carol, and Walter discuss the pros and cons of having a child at their age. "We're too old," Maude explains. "It's not going to be any fun having a 2-year-old who can beat you up the stairs." Carol tells her: "There is no earthly reason for you to go through with this at your age." After much deliberation, and an ensuing comedy of errors, Maude and Walter decide to have an abortion. But do they decide for the right reasons?

Commentary: Is abortion merely a matter of convenience?

Maude's daughter, Carol, is the foremost proponent of women's libera-tion. She complains that there is a presumption that the responsibility for not getting pregnant is the man's duty, but women bear the consequences when men forget. She says, "It's so unfair. They can put a man on the moon, but women are using the same birth control methods," but she's cut off by the family's friend, Dr Harmon (Conrad Bain). When Harmon suggests that vasectomy is a legitimate option, Maude notes that Walter talks about it but never follows through. Carol then asks: "When are men going to take some responsibility for birth control? . . . The way things are going, if even older people like my mother and Walter start behaving like rabbits, well we're all going to end up living like sardines."

The implication of Carol's complaint is that, if women do not start taking advantage of new birth control methods, the world will become over-populated. And Carol seems to consider abortion simply another type of birth control. She tells her mother: "We're free. We finally have the right to decide what to do with our own bodies. . . . And it's as simple as going to the dentist. . . . When you were young, 'abortion' was a dirty word; it's not anymore."

Is Carol right? Is abortion nothing more than another form of birth control? Perhaps, but she hasn't given us sufficient reason for thinking so. She says that women are free to do what they want with their own bodies. And this is absolutely true. The problem is that we do not yet know whether the organism of Maude's pregnancy is merely a part of her body or an independent person with a right to life. Therefore, Carol's advice to her mother is the question-begging "It's My Body" fallacy.

Does Maude offer any better reasons? At the end of Part 2, she and Walter belt out a stream of reasons why she should abort. Walter says, "Maude, I think it would be wrong to have a child at our age. . . . We would make terrible parents." Maude agrees: "Impatient, irascible." Walter says, "It's just not our time." Maude says, "I don't think it would be fair to anybody." And at the very end of Part 2, Maude asks Walter if she's doing the right thing. He explains: "For you, Maude, for me, and the privacy of our own lives, you're doing the right thing." Are any of these reasons sufficient on their own to justify the permissibility of abortion? It would seem not.

All of these reasons already presuppose the organism is not a person with rights. If it were already established that the organism has no rights, then abortion would be permissible regardless of any of these reasons. On the other hand, if the organism is a person with rights, none of these reasons is sufficient to override that right. It is not morally permissible to take someone's life simply because they are inconvenient to you or because you don't feel like a good parent or friend or teacher or caregiver. If someone with rights is your responsibility, then you have an obligation to be a good parent, friend, teacher, and caregiver regardless of whether you want to or feel that it would be an inconvenience to try. Therefore, as culturally important as these episodes of *Maude* are, the reasons they offer do not inform the question of whether abortion is morally permissible.

STUDY QUESTIONS

1. Why should the legal system be involved in the abortion debate?
2. In one scene from the *Law & Order* episode, Executive ADA Cutter explains that many of the genetic and birth defects that existed when *Roe v. Wade* was decided are now curable. How should this affect abortion legislation? Answer using one of the three positions above (Thomson, Warren, or Marquis).
3. According to Marquis, an organism of pregnancy has as much of a right to life as you because it has a valuable future like yours. Does Marquis's argument apply to an anencephalic fetus? Why or why not?
4. What would Mary Anne Warren tell Rubirosa when she becomes indignant that an abortion doctor would kill an anencephalic infant?
5. After Bernard tells Lupo that he was almost aborted, Lupo says, "So I might have had another partner." How is this supposed to be relevant to Bernard's example? How might you help make Lupo's response stronger?
6. Imagine that abortions are, except in extreme circumstances, morally impermissible. Does the threat of overpopulation count as an extreme circumstance that renders abortion permissible? Why or why not.
7. In these episodes, the possibility of giving the baby up for adoption is never mentioned. How would this option bear on the debate?
8. In the *Maude* episode describer above, Carol gives a version of the "It's My Body" fallacy. If she asked you how she could make her argument stronger, what might you tell her?
9. Do the conditions into which a baby is born affect the moral permissibility of abortion? If Maude and Walter had decided to have the baby, they would have been elderly by the time the child graduated college. There are other families that would abuse, neglect, or starve a child out of selfishness, drug abuse, or extreme poverty. Assuming a fetus has a right to life, do any of these considerations override that right? Assuming a fetus does not have a right to life, how might these considerations affect whether abortion is morally permissible?
10. At the end of Part 2, Maude says, "I don't think [keeping the baby] would be fair to anybody," given that they would be bad parents. Explain why this claim might be irrelevant to the abortion debate.

ALTERNATIVE CASE STUDIES

1. *House, M.D.*, "Babies and Bathwater," season 1
   (Is it morally permissible for a woman to sacrifice herself to save her unborn fetus?)
2. *Scrubs*, "My Best Friend's Baby and My Baby's Baby," season 6
   (Is human life only valuable when *I* value it?)
3. *Law & Order: SVU*, "Undercover," season 9
   (Might being a rape baby make detective Benson less sympathetic to abortion in rape cases?)

EPISODE 11: HOMOSEXUALITY

INTRODUCTION

In the 1980s television show *Cheers*, one of Sam Malone's (Ted Danson) old Red Sox teammates, Tom Kenderson (Alan Autry), writes an autobiography about his days with Sox and reveals, for the first time publically, that he's gay ("The Boys in the Bar," season 1). After some soul-searching (and some

What's Good on TV?: Understanding Ethics Through Television, First Edition.
Jamie Carlin Watson and Robert Arp.
© 2011 Jamie Carlin Watson and Robert Arp. Published 2011 by Blackwell Publishing Ltd.

prodding from Diane (Shelley Long)), Sam supports Kenderson publically. The regulars start worrying that Cheers will turn into a gay bar. Norm (George Wendt) says, "Alright, you've heard of Vito's Pub?" Sam says, "Yeah, it's a gay bar." Norm explains: "It didn't used to be. It used to be a great bar. I hung out there myself. . . . One night Vito lets a gay group hold a meeting in the back room. 'Gays for the . . . metric system' or something . . . . Next thing you know, Vito's Pub becomes (effeminately) *Vito's Pub.*"

Diane tries to defuse the worries by telling them that the bar regularly entertains homosexual clientele. Norm doesn't believe it because he hasn't "seen a gay guy in here in ages." Diane says, "Oh, I see. You can spot a gay person?" To which Norm says, confidently, "Yep." But to prove a point that homosexuals are not a group to be feared or ostracized, Diane reveals that, in fact, there are two gay gentlemen in the bar at that very moment, and she refuses tell them which two. When two customers comment on Sam's picture with Kenderson and order *light* beers, the group gets wary. They give Sam an ultimatum: kick the gay guys out or they will find another bar. And Sam is sympathetic: "If I lose my regulars, I lose my bar. And if single women stop coming in here, I have no reason to live!" This clearly isn't a strong moral argument – it is a practical argument, at best. But it is clear that there is some question over whether homosexuality is a "good" or "morally permissible" lifestyle. Even many of those who say "To each his own" harbor deep uncertainty about the moral permissibility of homo-sexual acts. Is homosexuality immoral, like pedophilia or rape? Or it is merely one among several "life choices" that people are free to make with respect to their sexuality?

Homosexuality is merely one aspect of the broader moral issue of race and gender ethics, but it is important because: (i) a large portion of the population is still undecided as to whether homosexuality is morally permissible, even though many are sympathetic to the claims that women and people of other cultural backgrounds are moral equals, and (ii) addressing the question of homosexuality directly helps us see precisely the types of arguments we *should not* present on either side of any issue in the larger race and gender debate.

It is undeniable that, for most of human history, homosexuality has been considered an illegitimate lifestyle. This is not to say it wasn't widely practiced in many cultures or that these practices were considered morally impermissible. They were, however, *practices*, momentary indulgences; rarely were they *lifestyles*. And most of these were confined to the socially elite, and were not popular among commoners. The ancient Greek poet Sappho writes of many infatuations between women, but it is clear that she mostly only describes particular encounters, and not long-term committed relationships, and it is not clear whether any or all of these "romantic" encounters were sexual. In Plato's dialogue, *Phaedrus*, Socrates acknowledges and condones the fact that some men enjoy one another intimately, but admonishes grown men against seeking such pleasure from young boys, because boys are too young to responsibly enter into sexual relationships. In his book *Laws*, Plato's "Athenian" character says, "homosexual intercourse and lesbianism seem to be unnatural crimes of the first rank, and are committed because men and women cannot control their desire for pleasure" (636c). Historically, then, as a lifestyle, homosexuality has not been widely accepted, while homosexual encounters were considered normal and, in some cases, laudatory.

How do these historical notes bear on the debate? To be sure, they certainly do *not* help us decide the debate. It has also been true, in most cultures, that women were regarded as less morally valuable than men and that slavery was regarded not only as normal, but as a social good. Of course, now we regard these claims as false: we regard the mistreatment of women and the enslavement of other human beings as immoral. To use history as a guide to morality is to commit the fallacy of appeal to the people (see the "Pilot Episode," fallacy number 1). But history is significant since it raises the moral question. Because people regarded homosexual lifestyles as illegitimate, we can legitimately ask whether they are correct.

Sexual relationships in general involve special moral considerations that do not face other types of relationship. In general, moral philosophers roughly agree that, in order for sex to be morally permissible:

- it must be consensual (rape is off limits);
- rational beings who engage in it must be competent to consent (you shouldn't have sex with coma patients or children);
- since it is likely to produce children, rational beings accept a moral responsibility for the life and well-being of the progeny of a sexual act (no one should make parental decisions for you);
- since sex can spread diseases and since people have a general moral obligation to mitigate harm, there are moral obligations that concern honesty in sexual relationships; and
- sexual relationships, for some people, entail further obligations (for instance, a monogamous relationship) that must be agreed on to be binding.

Even if you don't buy all these special conditions, you must face the fact that most people do and that they offer reasons for thinking you should do so too. Therefore, in many cases, the burden is primarily on you to show why they do not apply in your case or why they are simply not legitimate obligations.

Okay, so, morally speaking, sex is tricky business. But why is *homosexual* sex characterized so negatively? Intuitively, it does not seem bad, as rape or cheating on a significant other do. To many, it doesn't *seem* morally *bad* at all. In fact, it may seem that homosexuality is so prevalent in contemporary culture and so well accepted, that there could be no intelligent moral argument against it.

Nevertheless, we cannot fall for the appeal to the people fallacy, and we cannot assume a claim is true before we test it. Therefore, in order to determine whether homosexuality is morally permissible or impermissible, you must (a) show that the moral considerations for or against it, if there are any, are not sufficient to establish its permissibility or impermissibility, and (b) offer positive reasons for thinking it is a morally permissible/impermissible practice (e.g., it engenders certain virtues, it leads to greater moral goods, it is a basic good, it produces more good than harm, or, alternatively, that it engenders certain vices, leads to fewer moral goods, violates a basic moral good, or produces more harm than good).

ARGUMENTS AGAINST THE PERMISSIBILITY OF HOMOSEXUALITY

Are there good reasons for thinking that homosexuality is immoral? Some have argued that it is "unnatural," that is, it violates some moral "order of nature" (Jaffa 1994). But there are clear counterexamples to this. Animals are part of the natural order and they commit homosexual acts. Cars and computers are unnatural (it would be odd to find one wandering a forest, anyway), yet we don't consider it immoral to continue building or owning them.

Others have argued that sex is intended for procreation and gay couples can't have biological children; therefore, homosexuality is immoral. But first, even if this were true, it would also imply that sex between a sterile couple or an elderly couple is also immoral. This is not obviously true and would require a great deal of evidence. And second, it is not obvious that this is the *only* function of sex. Anyone making this claim would have to provide additional reasons for believing that the *only* function of sex is procreation, and that no other goods or virtues override the good of procreation.

Some have even argued that if everyone became gay (or a gay "gene" was selected for, species wide), the whole human race would cease to exist. But, first, it is not clear that people can be rationally *convinced* to be gay. If homosexuality (or whatever aspect of it is objectionable) is a psychological, biological, or emotional state (and not a rational one), then arguing against it would be futile. Second, if homosexuality is a genotype, then its survival or elimination is not subject to anyone's actions against it. And finally, what's so special about the human race that, morally, it *should* be preserved? Perhaps it is a natural progression of evolution that humans are eliminated from the planet – deer and chickens might even be happier without us. *That* humans might cease to exist does not constitute a sufficient moral reason for preserving humans.

Norman Geisler offers four additional reasons for thinking homosexuality is immoral. We will look briefly at two of them. First, he argues that no society accords homosexual sex moral status equivalent to that of heterosexual sex:

> Those that have accorded a place for homosexuals have done so only for a limited class and for a limited time. Although some American Indian tribes gave it a place, all in all the place was not a desirable one. The Mohaves, for example, interchanged the word for homosexual with the word for coward. (1989: 272)

Geisler is pointing out something similar to what we noted at the beginning of this Episode – almost no society has ever condoned homosexuality as a lifestyle – and then concludes that it must be immoral. But as we noted above, this argument commits the fallacy of "appeal to the people." Even if Geisler is right that *every* society condemned homosexuality as immoral (which is far from clear), the fact that a lot of people believed something is not reason for thinking that belief is true. Most societies have also believed that women and animals are morally inferior. Does this mean they are? Clearly not.

What is the difference between our use of this information and Geisler's? Whereas Geisler uses it as evidence in support of the claim that homosexuality is immoral, we use it as a phenomenon that needs an explanation. *That* people have always believed something cries out for an explanation, not necessarily praise or blame. So, whereas Geisler's argument looks like this:

1.   Most people groups have regarded homosexuality as immoral.

2.   Therefore, it is likely that homosexuality is immoral.

Our approach is better constructed like this:

3.   ?

1.   Most people groups have regarded homosexuality as immoral.

And then we ask: What claim (3) best explains (1)? And does (3) – whatever it turns out to be – rationally justify the claim *that* homosexuality is immoral?

The first is fallacious, the second is not.

Geisler's second argument is that homosexuality is a health threat. "There is no question that [AIDS] is spread by homosexual practices. Neither is there any doubt that it is spread from homosexuals to such non-homosexuals as hemophiliacs, users of common needles, medical workers, wives of bisexuals, and others" (1989: 272–3). To be sure, if an act is an obvious threat to health and well-being, it is plausible that there is a moral reason to oppose it. But this is not always the case – for instance, many medical procedures are dangerous (e.g., C-sections, ventricle bypasses) and some are actually detrimental to your health (e.g., chemotherapy, radiation). In these cases, other moral considerations often outweigh the harms involved. On the other hand, letting children purchase firearms and letting drunken people drive are cases where the threat to health and well-being outweighs considerations in favor of those acts.

Are homosexual practices of the latter sort? If they are more dangerous than the practices of heterosexuals, then the answer is yes. Harvard professor Harvey Mansfield (1993) argues that sexual desire "is too strong to be controlled by reason or natural law derived from reason. It can only be controlled by a force of comparable power, and that is shame." Mansfield goes on to argue that if shamefulness is legalized, there would no longer be grounds for prohibiting other shameful acts. Homosexuality is an "open challenge to society's sense of shame, as the gays recognize quite well."

But, given Geisler's examples, homosexual practices are not obviously *more* dangerous than their heterosexual counterparts, even with respect to shame. AIDS is also spread among heterosexuals, from heterosexuals to homosexuals, and through non-sexual behavior, such as sharing needles. Given the threat to health and well-being, perhaps there is a moral prescription against random sex with strangers and sharing drug needles, but it is not obvious that homosexual sex acts *by themselves* are more dangerous than heterosexual sex acts. Therefore, there seem to be no intuitive or empirical reasons for thinking that homosexuality is immoral.

The most prominent line of argument against the morality of homosexual behavior is motivated by religious considerations. Some argue that God has designed mankind for certain sorts of relationships; for example, covenantal relationships, contractual relationships, and intimate relationships. Just as God restricts contractual and covenantal relationships to beings with rational capacities (you can't make a morally binding contract with a goat), he has restricted intimate relationships to people of opposite genders. At least six biblical texts explicitly prohibit homosexual acts: Genesis 19:1–26; Leviticus 18:22; Romans 1:21–32; 1 Corinthians 6:9; 1 Timothy 1:8–10; and Jude 7–8. In addition, all passages that refer to marriage either imply or state explicitly that this relationship is between a man and a woman. Furthermore, Christian tradition, running through 2,000 years of Orthodox, Catholic, and Protestant teachings, interpret these passages as conclusive against the moral permissibility of homosexuality. Religious opponents of homosexuality argue that these passages are not intended as "discriminatory" or "restricting freedoms," but merely express how God designed human relationships and that God views this design in moral terms.

There are several ways to challenge this argument:

- challenge the veracity of biblical texts (did God really inspire the Bible?);
- challenge the accuracy of the interpretation of the texts that prohibit homosexual relationships (are they culturally conditioned like the passages on slavery? or are the passages as clearly about homosexuality as it first appears?);
- challenge some of the concepts, like "male" and "female" (is gender a by-product of our cultural prejudices?); or
- challenge the 2,000-year tradition that interprets these passages as prohibiting homosexuality.

We certainly do not have the room to address these here, but it is important to note that if none of these challenges is successful and if a case for biblical authority can be made, then *regardless of our personal feelings about religion or religious morality*, we are *rationally* obliged to take the argument seriously, and perhaps accept the conclusion. Similarly, if any of these challenges is successful, religious opponents of homosexuality are rationally obliged to take the objections seriously.

ARGUMENTS FOR THE PERMISSIBILITY OF HOMOSEXUALITY

How can we determine whether homosexuality is morally permissible or impermissible? We should resist the temptation to fall back on the principle: "If there are no good arguments against it, it is therefore permissible." This is a fallacious principle, known as an "argument from ignorance." Just because there are no good reasons to believe something, it doesn't mean it is false. And vice versa: just because there are no good reasons to disbelieve something, it doesn't mean it is true. In the absence of reasons for the permissibility of action, we are rationally obliged to suspend judgment.

So, we must ask, aside from arguments *against* the moral permissibility of homosexuality, are there any good arguments *in favor* of it? Some have argued that homosexuality is genetic. If homosexuality is a genetic disposition that a person cannot change or control, how can anyone argue that it is immoral? This is an important argument because it relies on one of our reasoning principles: "ought implies can" (see the "Pilot Episode"). You cannot be morally obligated to do something you physically or logically cannot do. For instance, it could not be a moral obligation that you stop a speeding train with your body, since, physically, you cannot do so. If homosexuality is a genetic disposition like hair or skin color, no one could be morally obligated to refrain from it (this is also an important reason why regarding people with different skin color as being less or more morally valuable is irrational). Unfortunately for proponents of this argument, we just don't have any relevant genetic evidence that homosexuality is a function of a gene or set of genes (at the moment, anyway) (for an easy-to-follow introduction to the research, see: "The Real Story on Gay Genes," http://discovermagazine.com/2007/jun/born-gay).

However, this is not the end of the argument. Just because researchers cannot find a specific gene or set of genes that determines homosexuality, this doesn't mean homosexuality is not biological. There is no scientific evidence of a gene for heterosexuality, either, or for liking ice cream or for liking '67 Camaros or for preferring the taste of orange to the taste of lemon. This does not mean these preferences are not biological. Therefore, it might be possible to revive this argument: if the preference of a man for a woman is broadly biological (and vice versa), it makes perfect sense that the preference of a man for another man or a woman for another woman is broadly biological. Then, again assuming that ought implies can, we are led to the conclusion that homosexuality cannot be morally impermissible.

But, it turns out, this argument won't do, either. We cannot infer that because someone has a biological disposition toward an action, that action is morally permissible. It is also very likely that kleptomania (the psychological disorder that leads to compulsive theft) and pedophilia (the desire for sex with children) are also broadly biological. Should we then conclude, on the same grounds as those offered for homosexuality, that these acts are morally permissible? Surely this doesn't follow. We consider pedophilia immoral on independent grounds and *in spite of* biological dispositions. A man may be sexually oriented toward children, but we ask him (order him, on pain of punishment) to refrain from engaging in that act. In cases of kleptomania, pedophilia, aggression, obesity, alcoholism, drug addiction, etc., we make a distinction between a person's *biological disposition* and her *free moral will*. If we didn't believe people could act independently of their dispositions, we wouldn't consider it a *virtue* to do the right thing even when you don't *want* to. Even the Roman Catholic Church, often lampooned for its views on sexuality, acknowledges that homosexuality is a "tendency," and homosexuals should be treated with "respect, compassion, and sensitivity." The Church also acknowledges the distinction between a disposition and a free will:

> Homosexual persons are called to chastity. By the virtues of self-mastery that teach them inner freedom, at times by the support of disinterested friendship, by prayer and sacramental grace, they can and should gradually and resolutely approach Christian perfection. (Catechism of the Catholic Church, 2nd edition, 2359)

Therefore, if you want to defend the moral permissibility of homosexuality, you will need to look somewhere other than biology.

Another prominent argument for the moral permissibility of homosexuality appeals to culture and history. Despite the apparent fact that homosexuality was rarely regarded as a legitimate lifestyle, it was, nevertheless, widely practiced and widely accepted, especially among ancient Greek leaders. From its moral permissibility as a practice, it is a short step to its moral permissibility as a lifestyle. It might be contended that there were a number of cultural obstacles to its acceptance as a lifestyle. Perhaps a particular view of leadership or religious beliefs, or the superstitions of the common people, prevented homosexuality from public acceptance, though, despite these obstacles, the informed populous knew better.

This argument certainly has some force. It is quite possible that social and religious prejudices prevent certain lifestyles from becoming vogue. Consider polygamy, specifically "polygyny," a man having more than one wife. Many cultures have practiced polygyny publically, and even in the Old Testament a number of kings had many wives without any condemnation from God or the Levitical priests. Nevertheless, many other cultures regard polygyny as taboo or immoral or inappropriate. And, oddly, in polygynous cultures, only rich and powerful *men* are permitted more than one spouse. Commoners could not get away with it. And women could not have more than one husband (known as, "polyandry"). So perhaps there is a case to be made that the moral permissibility of many sexual practices is simply arbitrary, and merely a product of cultural bias.

There are, however, two reasons for thinking this argument is not sufficient to establish the moral permissibility of homosexuality. First, even if the above evidence constitutes evidence that *many* sexual taboos are products of cultural bias, it is not clear that homosexuality belongs in that category, any more than it is clear that pedophilia does. We need independent reasons for thinking that aversion to homosexuality is cultural.

Second, even if our cultural perceptions change and everyone begins to view homosexuality as morally permissible, this does not mean that everyone is correct. This argument seems to commit the fallacy of "appeal to the people" in the same way that Geisler's argument for the opposite conclusion did. Just because everyone believes a claim ("the earth is flat," "the sun travels around the earth") doesn't make that claim true. We might discover that most high school students think it is morally permissible to cheat on their ACT exams if they could get away with it. Nevertheless, if there is a moral duty not to cheat, these students are simply mistaken. Though homosexuality was widely accepted among ancient cultures and is accepted among many contemporary cultures, and even if most aversion to it is simply cultural, to conclude from this that it is morally permissible is to commit the fallacy of appeal to the people.

Perhaps the most compelling argument for the permissibility of homosexuality is an appeal to virtue. If certain types of heterosexual relationships are considered good because of the virtues they engender, and if the same virtues engendered by certain types of heterosexual relationships can be achieved through certain types of homosexual relationships, then certain types of homosexual relationships are morally permissible. It would seem that what is prized in heterosexual relationships, especially committed, monogamous heterosexual relationships, is their tendency to foster deep levels of care, trust, friendship, and patience. Interestingly, many homosexuals in committed relationships claim that they experience the same virtues.

In summary, we have seen that it is difficult to construct conclusive arguments for the permissibility or impermissibility of homosexuality, though there are a few virtues in its favor. Where does this leave us? If there are no good arguments against the permissibility of homosexuality, and a few virtues in favor of it, then it would seem that the burden is on opponents of homosexuality to offer considerations that would outweigh these virtues.

There are, nonetheless, respectable philosophers who still argue that homosexuality is impermissible. After considering some additional concerns, we will look at an exchange between two legal philosophers on this issue. As with any emotional moral issue, the principles of charity and caution (see the introduction) are warranted, and a good deal of frustration will be avoided if we treat one another with respect and as rational equals.

ADDITIONAL CONCERNS

Note well that a discussion about the *morality* of homosexual behavior is very different from a question about whether a country should *legally* allow homosexuals to marry. Most governments legally permit all sorts of immoral actions (e.g., lying to your mother, hurting someone's feelings, playing with someone's emotions, etc.). We can judge these behaviors to be immoral without lobbying to make them illegal. In fact, most of us think they *are* immoral and argue on additional moral grounds that they *should not* be illegal. So, our discussion so far has not been about whether homosexuality should be legal, in marriage or otherwise, but whether it is morally permissible. Of course, if it turns out to be morally permissible, or that there is no argument sufficient to justify its immorality, this constitutes a reason (practical considerations permitting) to permit it legally.

It is also important to note that, even if there is a good argument that *hetero*sexual sex is morally permissible, not *all* heterosexual acts are therefore justified (e.g., rape, incest, pedophilia). This is why, earlier, we noted that only certain types of heterosexual relationships are prized for engendering a set of virtues. Similarly with homosexual acts: If we discover that homosexuality is generally permissible, this doesn't automatically justify wonton sexual behavior or homosexual rape.

In order to delve just a bit deeper into the debate, we will consider arguments from three highly intelligent, well-respected thinkers who disagree on the morality of homosexuality. We will do this through an exchange between Stephen Macedo and legal philosophers Robert George and Gerard Bradley.

NEW NATURAL LAW THEORY AND THE MORALITY OF HOMOSEXUALITY

Stephen Macedo, "Homosexuality and the Conservative Mind"; Robert George and Bradley Gerard, "Marriage and the Liberal Imagination"

At the time of writing, Stephen Macedo is Laurance S. Rockefeller Professor of Politics at the University Center for Human Values at Princeton University; Robert P. George is McCormick Professor of Jurisprudence, also at Princeton; and Gerard V. Bradley is a professor of law at Notre Dame University. George and Bradley, along with philosophers John Finnis, Germain Grisez, and others, defend a view called the "new natural law" theory of morality. George argues on natural law grounds that homosexuality is immoral. Macedo (1995) raises some objections to George and Bradley's (1995) argument.

Natural law theory is a deontological moral theory adapted from Aristotle's virtue ethics by Thomas Aquinas. The view generally distinguishes two categories of moral claims: those that are knowable by the natural light of reason, without any supernatural assistance, called the "natural law," and those that are knowable only by revelation from God, that is "divine law." According to natural law theorists, there are certain moral prescriptions that can be derived from our intuitions about the way nature is supposed to work. For instance, claims like "good should be pursued rather than evil," "love your neighbor," and "always return to a person what belongs to him" seem true to most people when they really consider the nature of morality. *New* natural law theorists extend these moral considerations into the political realm, arguing that natural law considerations also justify the rights to life, freedom of thought and expression, and the rule of law.

George and Bradley (1995) argue that the natural law position entails that marriage is, "a two-in-one-flesh communion" (i.e., not merely a legal contract) consummated by sexual acts of the reproductive type (even if incapable of children), and that this communion is "a basic human good" that cannot be achieved by any other act generally, or any other sex act in particular, including oral and homosexual sex acts. To use sex acts or other acts that stimulate the same physical responses merely as a route to fulfill other goals (e.g., for pleasure, to express emotions, or children) is to treat your body as an instrument, which damages your personal integrity. Therefore, even couples who are legally married could perform immoral sexual acts. But, since homosexuals physically cannot engage in "sexual acts of the reproductive type," a genuine union of the marital type is not available to them.

Stephen Macedo is sympathetic with many of the natural law theorists' views. For example, he agrees with Finnis, George, and Bradley that stable relationships, characterized by marriage and children, provide the opportunity for greater human goods than flippant sexual activity or childless marriages. However, he argues that whatever goods are morally available to those in childless marriages are also available to stable homosexual couples. Similarly, whatever prohibitions apply to flippant, dangerous, homosexual acts also apply to flippant, dangerous, heterosexual acts.

Macedo argues that the sexual goods of a marriage are the virtues the act engenders:

> What is the point of sex in an infertile marriage? Not procreation; the partners (let us assume) know that they are infertile. If they have sex, it is for pleasure and to express their love, or friendship, or some other shared good. It will be for precisely the same reasons that committed, loving gay couples have sex. Why are these good reasons for sterile or elderly married couples but not for gay and lesbian couples? If, on the other hand, sex detracts from the real goods shared by homosexual couples, and indeed undermines their friendship, this should also be the case for infertile heterosexual couples. Sterile couples' experience of sexual intimacy should be as "private and incommunicable" as that of gays. (1995: 278)

The virtues of a sexual relationship include pleasure, the expression of love, and the deepening of friendship. These are available to the couple irrespective of whether they can have children. Therefore, Macedo argues, there seems no good reason to think gay couples cannot experience them.

George and Bradley object that Macedo's argument "presupposes the truth of the very proposition we deny," namely that, "the point and value of sex can only be instrumental." George and Bradley argue that the goods of a sexual relationship are non-consequential in nature:

> It is our position ... that the reasons Macedo identifies are not adequate reasons for spouses – fertile or infertile – to engage in sexual relations. Nor is procreation an adequate reason for fertile spouses to have sex. We reject the proposition that sex can legitimately be instrumentalized, that is, treated as a mere means to any extrinsic end, including procreation. Any such instrumentalization, we believe, damages the basic human good of integrity. Again, the intrinsic point of sex in any marriage, fertile or not, is, in our view, the basic good of marriage itself, considered as a two-in-one-flesh communion of persons that is consummated and actualized by acts of the reproductive type. Such acts alone among sexual acts can be truly unitive, and thus marital; and marital acts, thus understood, have their intelligibility and value intrinsically, and not merely by virtue of their capacity to facilitate the realization of other goods. (1995: 305; notes have been omitted)

They explain that sex acts committed for the purpose of achieving some instrumental or consequential good undermine what they call the "unitive" nature of sex, which is also how they define the consummation of a marriage.

What reasons do George and Bradley give in support of their view? They argue that the basic good of marriage is an intrinsic good and that intrinsic goods cannot be conclusively demonstrated. Nevertheless, such a basic good can be "grasped in noninferential acts of understanding":

> Such acts require imaginative reflection on data provided by inclination and experience, as well as knowledge of empirical patterns, which underlie possibilities of action and achievement. The practical insight that marriage, for example, has its own intelligible point, and that marriage as a one-flesh communion of persons is consummated and actualized in the reproductive-type acts of spouses, cannot be attained by someone who has no idea of what these terms mean; nor can it be attained, except with strenuous efforts of imagination, by people who, due to personal or cultural circumstances, have little acquaintance with actual marriages thus understood. (1995: 307)

Many virtue ethicists argue that if someone has not had the appropriate moral education, she will not be able to clearly perceive the goodness of virtuous acts or clearly recognize the virtuous decision when faced with a moral decision. George and Bradley argue similarly about intrinsic value. If someone has no experience of a genuine "unitive" marriage, then it will be difficult for that person to not regard sexual intercourse as merely instrumental.

Nevertheless, George and Bradley argue that not recognizing this can lead to moral harm. In good Kantian fashion, they claim that using a person merely as a means – that is, as an instrument of your pleasure or friendship or children – is to treat them immorally. Doing so damages "the integrity of the acting person as a dynamic unity of body, mind, and spirit." "To treat one's own body, or the body of another, as a pleasure-inducing machine, for example, or as a mere instrument of procreation, is to alienate one part of the self, namely, one's consciously experiencing (and desiring) self, from another, namely, one's bodily self" (1995: 314). Such alienation denies the intrinsic value of what Kant calls the "good will," and thereby violates the categorical imperative.

Macedo argues that the new natural law theorists defend an arbitrary double standard when they argue that sexual intercourse by sterile couples (who know they are sterile) and the elderly is morally permissible, but homosexual sexual intercourse is impermissible. He says that this distinction is drawn on arbitrary grounds:

> Sexual activity is itself part of the good of marriage, so long as sexual acts are open to new life, and subordinate to "marital love": we must not choose

against the good of new life, and we must ensure that what predominates in our sexual relations is "loving cooperation in one-flesh communion." (1995: 278–9)

It is important to note that George and Bradley's position also entails that contraception is immoral. Since they are Roman Catholics, they are content with this implication, but it is certainly controversial among non-Catholics. Nevertheless, if they are right about the nature of sexual unions, then this implication follows and we are rationally obligated to accept it. Macedo, however, argues that they are wrong because the goods available to a sterile heterosexual couple are not in any obvious way morally better than those available to a homosexual couple.

First, Macedo argues, it is not clear in what sense sterile heterosexual couples (who believe themselves to be so) can be "open to new life." This doesn't seem more possible for the sterile heterosexual couple than for the committed homosexual couple. "One would think that the crucial distinction between valuable and valueless sex in a sterile marriage is the partners' openness to goods that they can share, not to goods that they cannot share" (1995: 279). Second, once we identify the goods attainable to elderly and sterile couples – "impulses to love, affection, mutual devotion, a self-giving desire to please the other, and so on" – "committed homosexual partners seem to fall into the same camp" (1995: 279). If the primary goods available to a committed but sterile heterosexual couple are also available to a committed homosexual couple, there seem no sufficient rational or moral reasons to regard the latter as immoral, while condoning the former.

Macedo considers several ways new natural law theorists might resolve this dispute, but none of these that would be acceptable to them. For instance, they might highlight the goods available to sterile heterosexual couples, but then note that these can be achieved non-sexually and thus prohibit sex as immoral for these couples as well. It doesn't seem, however, that George and Bradley would consent to this solution.

If nothing else, this debate highlights how competent scholars can debate an issue that is otherwise emotional and contentious. In what follows, we will consider, through an episode of *Law & Order*, the argument that "homophobia" (the fear of homosexuals) is merely a biological phenomenon that cannot be helped, and therefore, that homosexuality is not a moral question, but simply a question of our biological tendencies. We will then consider, through an episode of *Family Guy*, the argument that, irrespective of the moral permissibility of homosexuality, gay marriage should be legally permissible.

CASE STUDY 1: *Law & Order*, "Manhood," season 3

AVAILABILITY: **NetFlix, iTunes**

In this episode of the crime drama *Law & Order*, a police officer is killed in a gunfight and Detectives Lennie Briscoe (Jerry Orbach) and Mike Logan (Chris Noth) investigate. Though they identify the actual shooter fairly quickly, a controversy arises over the cops assigned as the officer's backup. It seems it took a lot longer for them to respond than it should have, and the shooter says he saw a cop car sitting right around the corner from the shooting.

When it turns out that the cop who was shot was gay, Briscoe and Logan become suspicious that the late backup was intentional. The 911 call report confirms that something was fishy about the communication by the dispatcher and the response of the officers. Logan tells the captain, "Donnie ... they left him out there to die."

After a sketchy investigation, it turns out that the whole precinct harbors anti-gay sentiments, and even sent around flyers announcing their discrimination against gay cops. The case goes to trial and, after the defense attorney realizes he cannot establish that the negligence wasn't intentional, he shifts to a positive defense: they did it, but they couldn't help it. The defense attorney enlists a psychologist to testify that homophobia is a culturally conditioned pathology that a person is not responsible for having or controlling. The defense attorney concludes from this testimony that the defendants should not be held responsible for any acts motivated by this culturally conditioned response. Unfortunately, the jury agrees and the defendants are acquitted.

Commentary: Is homophobia uncontrollable?

In this episode, the defense attorney's psychologist testifies as follows:

> The fear of homosexuals is common. ... [I]n our culture, defining masculinity is complicated. "What is it that makes a man?" ... Men are oftentimes afraid of gays making sexual overtures. Men make passes; women receive them. Somebody makes a pass at you, you feel like a woman, which, to most men, means "weak." ... A fear of seduction by another man makes them angry. Oftentimes this anger can turn into hatred.

When the defense attorney asks whether this is normal, the psychologist says he would call it "common." The defense attorney continues, "So these feelings are not voluntary or reckless?" to which the psychologist responds:

"Yes, that's right. 'Recklessness' implies its opposite: 'control.' You can't control these feelings."

Executive ADA Ben Stone (Michael Moriarty) asks the psychologist, "Are you saying that it is acceptable to hate homosexuals?" to which, he replies, "I'm saying that men who have these feelings have difficulty controlling them." Now, we should notice here a distinction between the conclusion the psychologist draws about this case and the one the defense attorney draws from the psychologist's testimony. The psychologist merely says that the defendants cannot control their anti-gay feelings. The defense attorney adds that they should not be held responsible for their actions because of their inability to control their feelings.

Stone says the psychologist makes it sound as if what the defendants did was permissible. But the psychologist replies: "I would never say that. Hatred of homosexuals is unfortunate, not to mention pathological. And, like any pathology, it's not voluntary." The defense attorney, on the other hand, tells the jury in his summation that holding the defendants responsible for their actions would be "unjust":

> Did these men act recklessly, or unconsciously – unaware of what they were doing.
>   What the prosecution demands is unjust: To find these men guilty of upholding the very values of the society that they've sworn to protect. Ladies and Gentlemen, in your deliberations, please, ask yourselves, are their values really so very different from your own?

The defense attorney argues that, because society has conditioned the emotions of the defendants so that they cannot help but hate homosexuals, their actions, while lamentable, are not punishable.

Might this conclusion be justified? If someone is predisposed to act a certain way, conditioned by education and culture, does this mitigate their blame for an action? It actually might.

Consider a person who is raised in a healthy, encouraging environment and taught right from wrong at an early age using clear and loving teaching techniques. If this person commits a heinous crime such as premeditated or serial murder, we would be incensed and horrified. We might say things like, "How could someone so privileged stoop so low?" or "He should have known better!" We might even think his punishment should be more severe than someone who was raised in an unhealthy, discouraging, and abusive environment.

On the other hand, if someone raised in an unhealthy, discouraging, and abusive home were to commit premeditated or serial murder, we might not be so surprised. We would be incensed, but we might say things like, "Well, what do you expect from someone raised in that environment?" or "There was no way he could have known better."

So, an environmental or biological predisposition might mitigate the *degree of punishment* for an action (see Episode 12 for more on the morality of punishment). But notice that it does not seem to mitigate the moral blame associated with committing the crime. Even if someone is raised in an unhealthy, abusive home, we do not expect that person to commit premeditated or serial murder. He cannot control his tendencies, but he can control his actions (if he is not mentally unstable or mentally handicapped). There is still a sense in which it is appropriate to say, "He should have known better," *while still believing* he has a moral obligation not to do it. Even though choosing to not commit a crime might be more *difficult* for a person with a disposition to commit crimes, we still expect that person to exert the necessary moral determination to refrain from that action. That is, we expect it *if* we believe that our actions are our own and not completely determined by our environments.

Is the defense attorney's argument a good one? No: he commits the naturalistic fallacy (see the "Pilot Episode," fallacy 6). Just because the officers have a certain disposition (if they really do) does not mean they *should* have this disposition or that they are *permitted* to act on it. Of course, we have to balance our moral judgment against the principle of "ought implies can." If the defendants, in fact, have the disposition to fear homosexuals, this is something they cannot control, and therefore, cannot be responsible for having. There is no moral obligation to do something you cannot possibly do – e.g., to not have a craving for ice cream, to not have a sexual desire of a certain sort. But there can be a moral obligation not to act on that disposition – to not eat too much ice cream, to not have sex with children or commit adultery. In this case, the defendants had an obligation to help their fellow officer, despite their disposition to hate homosexuals, but they chose to ignore this obligation. Unfortunately, the jury is unable to draw this technical, but crucial, moral distinction.

CASE STUDY 2: *Family Guy*, "You May Now Kiss the ... Uh ... Guy Who Receives," season 4

AVAILABILITY: NetFlix, iTunes

In this episode of the animated comedy *Family Guy*, Brian's gay cousin Jasper comes to visit with his boyfriend Ricardo. Jasper tells the family that he and Ricardo are planning to get married, and Lois discovers that she is unsure about the permissibility of gay marriage.

In the meantime, Mayor Adam West offers a tribute to the soldiers of Quahog by constructing a solid gold statue of the Sugar Smacks cereal mascot Dig 'Em. He also announces that there will be extreme budget cutbacks "having almost nothing to do with this solid gold statue." The town protests the statute and Mayor West, so West tries to find some issue to distract the town from his incompetence. He decides to pass a citywide bill banning gay marriage and the town seems to forget about the statue.

Brian, who told Jasper he could have the wedding at the Griffin house, petitions to stop Mayor West from signing the bill. Lois is still not sure why she opposes gay marriage, and goes to stay with her parents until after the wedding. Chris Griffin is coerced into burning Brian's petition, but Brian works for 24 hours straight to get 10,000 more signatures, and ends up holding Mayor West hostage at gunpoint to stop him from signing the bill.

When Lois finally realizes that her objections to gay marriage are merely cultural, she overcomes her objection and talks Brian out of the hostage situation. Mayor West agrees not to prosecute on the kidnapping charge, since the town was thoroughly distracted from the Dig 'Em scandal and the family has Jasper's wedding at their house.

Commentary: The morality of homosexuality has nothing to do with its legality

We have considered quite a bit, in this Episode, about the *moral* permissibility of homosexuality, but what, if anything, does this have to do with its *legal* permissibility? In this episode of *Family Guy*, Lois objects to gay marriage, though she's not sure why. She says she has nothing against homosexuals, yet "the idea of two men actually getting married, it just doesn't seem right." She tells Brian, "Well, they certainly have every right to be together, but marriage should be between a man and a woman."

We get a feel for the town's anti-gay sentiments, and some of their reasons for disapproving of gay marriage, when Brian takes his petition door-to-door. One character, Quagmire, refuses to sign, saying, in his raunchy fashion, "C'mon, two halves can't make a whole without a hole." Quagmire seems to think that, since homosexual intercourse cannot result in children, it is immoral. Herbert, the elderly man who is always making sexual advances toward Chris, calls Brian a "pervert" for supporting gay marriage. Mr Bottomtooth refuses on religious grounds, though, given his speech impediment, we can't quite make out his explanation. When Lois goes to a priest to help her sort through her feelings, he shows her a video about how to "tell when you've got a gay." The video explains that owning a Madonna album and having deadly corrosive acid instead of blood are sure signs that "you've got a gay."

As we saw earlier in the Episode, the inability to have children is not likely a sufficient reason to consider homosexuality immoral or gay marriage illegal, since it would also entail that sterile couples or elderly couples should not get married. Therefore, Quagmire's argument won't do.

It is certainly hypocritical for Herbert to oppose gay marriage on the grounds that it is "perverted," since we have ample reasons for believing he is a pedophile who prefers young boys. But hypocrisy is not a reason to believe someone's conclusion is false. This is called the "*tu quoque*" fallacy. For instance, if someone who regularly commits adultery tells you it is immoral and gives an excellent argument for believing so, merely pointing out that he is a hypocrite is not a sufficient response. He may fully acknowledge that he is acting immorally, but remind you that this does not undermine the force of his argument. You must respond to the argument to show whether he is wrong, not his actions. Unfortunately, Herbert doesn't give us any reasons for thinking that gay marriage is "perverted," so his comments won't do.

Mr Bottomtooth rejects gay marriage on religious grounds, but, again, we are not told precisely what those are. As we noted earlier, there may be a strong religious argument against it, but such an argument would have to presented clearly, and withstand objections. So, without more evidence, Mr Bottomtooth's mumbling rejection won't do, either.

And finally, the priest's video simply commits the "red herring" fallacy, which means introducing some irrelevant piece of information to distract you from the actual issue. The actual issue is whether gay marriage is legally permissible. The red herring is to ask (a) how can you tell whether someone is gay, and (b) to make it seem as if gay people are essentially effeminate or non-human (also a fallacious appeal to emotion). Since the video does not provide any legitimate reasons for thinking gay marriage is impermissible, its rejection won't do.

Where does Lois's soul-searching lead her on this issue? When her father begins ranting against gay marriage, Lois considers that two people who love each other should be able to be together. But her father says the issue is not about love, but about marriage, and implies that he doesn't love Lois's mother. Lois replies: "So two straight people who hate each other have more of a right to be together than two gay people who love each other?" Her mother explains: "That's what we raised you to believe." When Lois realizes that her opposition to gay marriage is merely based on a cultural bias instilled by her parents, she screams, "Oh, my God! I've made a terrible mistake! I've been brainwashed, like Elizabeth Smart!"

So Lois recognizes that her culturally conditioned *tendency* to act a certain way does not entail anything about the *moral permissibility* of actions motivated by that tendency – a similar conclusion to the one we reached in our case study from *Law & Order*. On reflection, Lois concludes that she is acting inappropriately toward the idea of gay marriage, and chooses to overcome her conditioned response against it.

It is important to see that, even if Lois believes that homosexuality is morally impermissible, she might be obligated to defend the legal permissibility of gay marriage. Everyone does immoral things from time to time: lying to one's mother for selfish gain, hitting one's dog when angry, cussing out a cashier for not giving the correct change, etc. But it is not clear that any of these things should be illegal. If they were, the legal system would be vastly overrun with frivolous claims, so there are practical reasons not to criminalize such acts. But there are also moral reasons. For instance, let's say I'm right that lying to one's mother for selfish gain is immoral, but you disagree. Who is to decide the issue? If I can get the law to agree with me that it is immoral and convince them to coerce you into not lying to your mother, have I won the argument? Is it therefore true that lying is immoral just because I can force you to comply? No. "Might" doesn't make "right." Unless you are actually hurting someone (which is the primary standard of legal action in the law), the only recourse I have is to convince you to believe as I do, with good arguments. So, if we disagree about homosexuality and there is no obvious harm (as there is with rape or pedophilia), my best and only recourse is to argue with you – not to try to coerce you by means of the government. Therefore, it is possible to hold both that homosexuality is immoral and that gay marriage is legally permissible.

STUDY QUESTIONS

1. Is it possible that the environment we were raised in instills us with dispositions to act a certain way? Do these dispositions justify the actions they inspire? Why or why not?
2. Think about any immoral tendencies you have. How do you control these tendencies?
3. Imagine that a scientist placed a microchip in your head that makes you form the intention to kill someone and carry out the intention. Are you morally responsible for that act? Why or why not? Imagine that the chip is in your head, but the scientist will only activate the

chip if you don't decide to kill the person. As it turns out, you decide to kill the person on your own, with no help from the chip. Now are you morally responsible for that act? Why or why not?

4. Construct a fallacious argument the jury might have used to justify their conclusion that the defendants are not guilty. Explain why your argument is fallacious.

5. Imagine that you are on the jury. How would you argue with your co-jurors about the conclusion to be drawn based on the evidence in this case? Make sure to include at least one moral reason in your argument.

6. How does Lois deal with her personal conflict over gay marriage? Is this a rational course of action? Why or why not?

7. Imagine that homosexuality is morally permissible. What bearing, if any, would this have on the question of whether gay marriage should be legal?

8. Imagine that some divine being (God, for instance) tells you personally that homosexuality is not how people were designed to relate to one another, and therefore, homosexuality is immoral. How might this influence your decision about the moral permissibility of homosexuality? If others knew about your experience, how would you justify your decision to them in light of your revelation?

9. If there are no good arguments for the moral permissibility of homosexuality, does this mean it is morally impermissible? Why or why not?

10. Brian commits several crimes when he takes Mayor West hostage. Do these actions hurt the pro-gay-marriage cause? Do these actions undermine any arguments for the legal permissibility of gay marriage?

ALTERNATIVE CASE STUDIES

1. *Cold Case*, "It's Raining Men," season 2
   (If an action appears to lead to great social harm, is it morally impermissible?)

2. *The Simpsons*, "There's Something about Marrying," season 16
   (Is this episode a "straw man" of the anti-gay-marriage movement?)

3. *All in the Family*, "Judging Books by Covers," season 1
   (Are judgments based solely on how someone looks immoral?)

EPISODE 12: PUNISHMENT AND CAPITAL PUNISHMENT

INTRODUCTION

What if someone does something immoral? What if it is abhorrent? To what extent should he or she be held accountable for those acts? In one episode of *Star Trek: The Next Generation*, the crew, tired from recently establishing a new colony on a planet, decides to take a period of shore leave on a newly discovered, inhabited, Earth-like planet ("Justice," season 1). The planet is beautiful, the people are very like humans, their civilization is

What's Good on TV?: Understanding Ethics Through Television, First Edition.
Jamie Carlin Watson and Robert Arp.
© 2011 Jamie Carlin Watson and Robert Arp. Published 2011 by Blackwell Publishing Ltd.

fairly advanced, and they are incredibly amorous, as Lieutenant Commander La Forge (LeVar Burton) notes: "And they make love at the drop of a hat." Captain Picard (Patrick Stewart) comments, ominously: "Let's just hope it's not too good to be true."

After contact is established and the crew is basking in the hospitality of the people known as the "Edo," Ensign Wesley Crusher (Wil Wheaton) is playing a game with some of the Edo youth and falls into a "punishment zone." Two law officers arrive and start to administer the punishment – death. According to the Edo, random punishment zones and extreme punishments deter everyone from willingly breaking the law. Thus, their crime rate is almost zero and life in the Edo civilization is almost ceaselessly happy. Should Wesley be put to death for this crime? Clearly the consequences of putting people to death for menial crimes has a tremendous benefit to the Edo society.

This episode of *Star Trek* raises some challenging questions about the morality of punishment. Is it morally permissible to punish someone for an immoral or illegal action? If it is permissible, why? And to what degree are we permitted to punish someone? Does the nature of the crime affect the degree of punishment or should we focus only on the social consequences of punishment? In this Episode, we will explore answers to each of these questions.

Before we address these questions directly, we should first ask: What does it mean to "punish" someone for acting immorally or illegally? Many of us grew up with the idea that punishment involves either inflicting harm (for example, depriving a person of something good, removing privileges, a prison sentence, etc.; physically causing pain – spanking, caning, the electric chair, etc.) or forcing reparations (for example, making someone give back something that was stolen) for an act that is deemed, by the appropriate authority (for example, parents, courts), as immoral or illegal. It is important to note that philosophers generally agree with this general idea. In an insightful article on the nature and justification of punishment, Hugo Bedau (2010) offers a similar definition:

> Punishment under law (punishment of children in the home, of students in schools, etc., being marginal rather than paradigmatic) is *the authorized imposition of deprivations – of freedom or privacy or other goods to which the person otherwise has a right, or the imposition of special burdens – because the person has been found guilty of some criminal violation, typically (though not invariably) involving harm to the innocent.* (Emphasis in original)

Bedau allows that "deprivations" might include the causing of pain (perhaps because pain deprives a person of a normal pain-free life). In addition, Bedau must allow that "criminal" be interpreted morally, since an infraction in the home (e.g., a child lying to her mother) would not constitute a "criminal" action in the legal sense, though it would in the moral sense. The central disagreement between our common-sense notion of punishment and that held among moral philosophers generally comes primarily when we ask the questions: "What is punishment for?" and "When is it justified?"

Answers to these questions are diverse and complex, but there are four well-established answers to the first question: the retributivist theory, the behaviorist/therapeutic theory, the utilitarian theory, and the liberal/ deterrence theory. We will briefly discuss each of these in turn and explain how they might inform the debate over the moral permissibility of capital punishment and then discuss the moral permissibility of the death penalty in light of Jeffrey Reiman's article, "The Morality of the Death Penalty in an Unjust World." Finally, we will apply the insights from this discussion to some difficult questions about punishment and capital punishment through the shows, *Star Trek: The Next Generation* and *Oz*.

THEORIES OF PUNISHMENT

The retributivist theory

Retributivism is the view that "retribution" (or "desert") is an essential aspect of moral blame. If a being has the capacity to understand and act on moral reasons, that being is morally responsible for its actions, and thus *deserving* of praise or blame. Praise and blame are considered a just and fair response to the behavior of agents with the capacity for moral reason. Praise often includes reward (whether general approbation or a token of gratitude) and blame often includes punishment (whether general disapprobation, forced restitution, or the intentional infliction of harm – which may be as mild as confinement or as extreme as execution).

Whether the retributivist theory is true depends on the truth of at least two other claims: (a) the guilty deserve to be punished; and (b) no other moral or epistemic considerations outweigh the guilty's desert of that punishment. There may be cases where (a) is false, that is, where immoral behavior does not entail that the guilty deserves punishment, for instance, if the guilty were mentally handicapped or a child. Similarly, there may be cases where (a) is true, but (b) is false because some moral considerations outweigh the guilty's desert. For instance, if someone is starving and steals bread to feed her family, then, after restitution is made, we may conclude that this moral good of her actions outweighs the need for punishment in this case. Also, there may be cases where (b) is false because some epistemic considerations outweigh the guilty's desert. For instance, crime shows often draw a distinction between a criminal's guilt and proof of that guilt. Even if a prosecuting attorney knows the person is guilty, given his commitment to the legal system, if there is not enough evidence to prove to a jury that the person is guilty, punishment may be unwarranted. If either (a) or (b) is false in a particular case, punishment is not deserved in that case. But, the retributivist argues, if (a) and (b) are true, punishment is just and, in some cases, is obligatory.

What reasons might justify this theory of punishment? The truth of any theory of punishment depends on two types of fact: the nature of moral agents and what makes actions right and wrong. If human actions are fully determined by our genetics and physical laws or if we are coerced by some other outside force, then, many argue, there is no rational sense in which an agent "deserves" punishment. However, if we are free to decide and have the rational capacity to choose based on reasons, then we are responsible for what we do.

In addition, if the wrong of an action is about the relationship between an action and the good of society, as with utilitarian and other consequentialist theories, then the type and degree of that agent's punishment is not determined by moral or epistemic considerations attaching to the agent, but to the community. On the other hand, if the wrong of an action is about the relationship between an agent and an obligation, as with deontological theories, then the type and degree of punishment is determined by the extent to which the punishment is "fitting" for the crime. Kant writes: "*Punishment by a court* ... can never be inflicted merely as a means to promote some other good for the criminal himself or for civil society. It must always be inflicted upon him only *because he has committed a crime*" (1996: 105; emphasis in the original). Therefore, if you believe that people are generally free and morally responsible and hold some version of deontology, you probably also hold a retributivist theory of punishment.

Notice that the Edo in the *Star Trek* episode do not seem to accept that people are morally responsible for their actions (or at least they don't seem to care). Since the laws are arbitrary and the crimes not associated with any negative consequences, "blame" and "retribution" would be foreign terms to them. And their theory of morality is that actions are only good or bad as they affect the rest of society; therefore, individual responsibility or "desert" is not taken into consideration in a punishment. The Edo are definitely not retributivists.

The behaviorist/therapeutic theory

In the late 1950s, many psychologists defended a psychological theory of human behavior known as "behaviorism." Behaviorism is the view that all of a person's actions are a product of that person's experiences and conditioned reactions to those experiences. Humans are, roughly, very complex stimulus-response mechanisms. We can understand and explain every human behavior (responses) simply by understanding the environment and experiences to which a person was exposed (stimuli).

Since, according to this view, people are merely products of their combined experiences, they cannot be morally responsible for their behaviors. People have no control over their upbringing or environment, and no control over how their brain processes these experiences and translates them into behavior. Therefore, if someone commits what the majority of people consider an "immoral" action, it would be irrational to "punish" that person (in the retributivist sense of punishment). Why? First, because our concepts of "moral" and "immoral" are simply products of our behavioral environment in the first place, and second, because, although the person is physically responsible for his actions, there is no legitimate sense in which he is *morally* responsible for his actions. Therefore, the behaviorist theory of punishment is the view that punishment is justified only insofar as it has the capacity to reform the (moral or legal) criminal.

According to the behaviorist theory of punishment, the only rational way to treat the criminal is re-train her to act more consistently with the opinions of her society. According to behaviorists, punishment should be viewed as therapy, not as retribution. In the wake of behaviorism, many prisons instituted policies of "reform" rather than harm. The term "prison" was often changed to "correctional facility," chain gangs and hard labor were traded in for soothing paint colors on the walls, educational programs, and counseling. Even though behaviorism has fallen out of favor with most psychologists, a number of these behavior modification strategies are still used in many "correctional facilities."

What reasons might justify this theory of punishment? Behaviorists deny that agents are sufficiently free to act on moral reasons to "deserve" punishment, therefore "blame" or "retribution" are not appropriate terms to use when speaking of a criminal or immoral person. As a result, their moral theory cannot be that the wrong of an action is about the relationship between an agent and an obligation – considerations of benefit or harm to society are essential. Behaviorists argue that punishment is justified because it contributes to the agent's behavioral conditioning, in order to produce a better society, so a primary consideration in punishment is the extent to which the punishment "rehabilitates" the criminal and "deters" future infractions. The tricky part is explaining why behaviorists' desire to punish is not, itself, merely a conditioned response to their respective environment, and therefore, why their concept of a "better" society is actually better than that of a criminal's. This explains part of the disillusionment with behaviorism.

The Edo, from our *Star Trek* episode, are concerned almost exclusively with deterrence, and they make no claims about the extent to which a person is responsible for her actions. The idea is simply that extreme punishment for arbitrary crimes prevents people from acting in socially unacceptable ways. Though the episode doesn't explain punishment in these terms, the Edo may hold some version of a behaviorist theory of punishment.

The utilitarian theory

The utilitarian theory of punishment follows directly from the utilitarian theory of morality. An action is moral if it reduces overall pain and increases overall happiness. Therefore, punishment is *for* what every action is for – increasing happiness and decreasing pain. Therefore, the utilitarian theory is the view that punishment is *justified* only insofar as it brings about better consequences for society than if there were no punishment.

In some cases, punishing someone might deter that person or others from committing a similar crime in the future. If this is case, then punishment is bringing about more good in the future than harm, and therefore, punishment is permissible. In other cases, punishing someone might make lots of people feel better, and reduce many social tragedies.

Whether the utilitarian theory of punishment is true depends on the truth of at least three other claims: (i) the utilitarian theory of morality is true; (ii) crime decreases overall happiness; and (iii) traditional punishments, such as fines and imprisonment, successfully deter crime. If any of these claims is false, the utilitarian theory of punishment is false. If it turns out that a particular punishment, say the death penalty, is no longer a successful deterrent of crime and the overall pains involves outweigh the overall goods, the death penalty is not a permissible punishment. (Obviously the death penalty is a deterrent for the criminal – he can no longer commit crimes. But the question of deterrence is about the effect the death penalty has on the frequency of similar crimes committed by other criminals. If this frequency is not affected by instituting or repealing the death penalty, then the death penalty does not deter similar crimes.) On the other hand, if the death penalty is the absolute best deterrent – as it seems to be in our *Star Trek* episode – then it might be obligatory.

A worry for this theory is that it seems to condone punishment in some cases where it should not. Consider a classic case called "The Drifter Dilemma" (which we already came across, in Episode 6):

> Suppose that a terrible murder has occurred in a small town and the townspeople are convinced that a lone drifter who happened to be in town at the time committed the crime. Many of the townspeople form a mob to hang the drifter. The sheriff, however, knows that there is no evidence at all linking the man to the crime and that in all likelihood he is completely innocent. He takes the man into protective custody, but the mob surrounds the jail and demands that the sheriff hand over the drifter. The sheriff realizes that a riot is in the works, and if that were to happen then many innocent people would be killed, including schoolchildren on their way home from school. The phone lines have been cut, so he can't call for help (and he doesn't have a cell phone!). What should he do? (Driver 2007: 63)

According to the retributivist, the sheriff should not punish the drifter even to prevent a riot in which innocent children would die – the drifter does not *deserve* to be punished. According to the utilitarian, however, the drifter's guilt is not the primary concern – bringing about overall happiness is. Since allowing the town to frame him for the crime will most likely bring about the greater happiness of the town (placating its rage), and reduce the suffering that would be caused by the riot, it is obligatory that he do so.

In response, Richard Brandt, a utilitarian who defends a utilitarian deterrence view of punishment, argues that this sort of case ignores certain assumptions, particularly that even the townspeople probably hold that someone should only be punished when there is evidence of wrongdoing. "Imagine the pleasure of driving an automobile if one knew one could be executed for running down a child whom it was absolutely impossible to avoid striking! One certainly does not maximize expectable utility by eliminating the traditional excuses" (1982: 244). The idea is that punishments cannot be completely arbitrary or depend always on the whim of the crowd, otherwise overall pleasure (what Brandt calls "expectable utility") would probably not increase. Therefore, a utilitarian theory of punishment would not likely condone intuitively immoral punishments in most cases. The remaining question, however, is: What justifies the "traditional excuses" if not the ethical theory that determines the moral value of your actions?

In our *Star Trek* episode, the Edo are preoccupied almost exclusively with pleasure, especially sexual pleasure. Therefore, the Edo may hold some version of a utilitarian theory of punishment. However, it is not clear that they would condone killing someone randomly if that would increase overall pleasure. They might, but it is not clear. If they did condone this, then they hold some version of a utilitarian theory of punishment, and not a behaviorist theory. If they would not, it is safer to conclude that they hold the behaviorist view.

The liberal deterrence theory

Deterrence theories need not be associated exclusively with utilitarianism. They may also be motivated by considerations of duty or virtue. One classic theory of punishment is derived from what is known as the classical liberal account of natural rights. As we explained in Episode 8, classical liberalism is the view that individual liberty takes precedence over the interests of the political state, its leaders, and any groups of its citizens. But this account of rights can be defended on utilitarian grounds (John Stuart Mill) or on deontological grounds (John Locke). According to the deontological version, a person should be free to pursue whatever life he or she perceives to be good, and the best measure of what is good for that person is *that person* – that is, not the government, church, family, or any other outside source of authority.

How is this view expressed in a social setting? Each individual's pursuit of the good is protected from infringement by anyone else's pursuit of the good (recall Baxter's "spheres of freedom criterion," from Episode 8). And if you violate another person's right to pursue what she perceives to be good, then we hold you morally and, sometimes, legally responsible. Thomas Hurka (1982) explains that the rights-based (liberal) political theories entail a "right to punish," which is "a right to inflict harms on persons who have successfully violated the rights of others."

According to the liberal deterrence theory, does a criminal "deserve" punishment? A classical liberal can accept this aspect of the retributivist theory, but places significant restrictions on the permissibility and degree of punishment. The classical liberal may, alternatively, choose to remain agnostic about the degree of actual "guilt" or "blame" involved in a crime. She may believe that it is possible that what she perceives to be immoral is really not. Because of this belief, punishment may be used simply to deter further behavior that, at this time, is considered to be immoral and/or illegal.

Hugo Bedau (2010) explains:

> Deserved punishment, insofar as it exists at all, thus emerges as a result of "pure procedural justice" (Rawls 1971). That is, we have only the vaguest idea of the just or deserved punishment for a given offender guilty of a given crime apart from the sentencing schedule provided by the laws of a just society (and thus laws that conform to the constraints above). The punishment deserved is the punishment authorized under a fair penalty schedule; no other conception of deserved punishment can be defended; the perennial lure of an illusory independent criterion for desert, founded ultimately on intuition, as well as of utilitarian calculations, must be resisted.

In a society that respects individual rights, it would be better to prevent crime than to restrict the freedom of an individual long enough to charge, try, and punish (or not) her. Therefore, rationally, the most plausible account of punishment is the deterrence account.

Like the retributivist view, and unlike the utilitarian view, the liberal deterrence view demands significant restrictions on what that punishment can be like for the individual being punished. Bedau offers a list that includes the following: punishment may not be "inhumane" or "cruel"; punishments must not violate legally granted rights – for example, due process and trial by peers; and the punishment should fit the crime.

What reasons might justify this view of punishment? Interestingly, many of the same reasons that justify the deontologist's view of moral agents. If there is good reason to believe that a person can understand and act on moral reasons, then we have a reason to believe that person is morally responsible for her actions. In addition, this view depends on being agnostic about whether we are strongly justified in our moral beliefs. Practically, we can punish on the grounds that a victim's rights have been violated without evaluating whether the criminal's actions are actually immoral.

Clearly, the Edo in the *Star Trek* episode do not respect individual rights. Their punishments are given out indiscriminately and in the most extreme degree. It is interesting to note, however, that the punishment zones are arbitrary, change regularly, and do not seem to include anything anyone would pursue as a good on a normal basis, at least, nothing they couldn't get elsewhere (in Wesley's case, it looks like a flower bed). It is not clear whether they would regard actions such as rape or child molestation as always immoral and punishable.

ARGUMENTS FOR AND AGAINST CAPITAL PUNISHMENT

Let's assume that one of the above theories is correct and that punishment is, under some circumstances, morally permissible and possibly obligatory. If punishment is justified, to what extent may we punish? Is death too harsh a punishment for any crime? Is it too lenient for some? Even those who defend capital punishment (the death penalty) typically argue that it should only be applied in the most heinous of murder cases. Therefore, the debate takes place over a very narrow, though important, set of circumstances – important especially to the person whose life is on the line.

Retributivists are famous for defending capital punishment. The primary motivation is that, for certain crimes, death is not only warranted, it is obligatory. If it also deters future murders, that is good, but that is not its primary purpose. Kant explains:

> If . . . he has committed a murder, he must *die*. Here there is no substitute that
> will satisfy justice. There is no *similarity* between life, however wretched it
> may be, and death, hence no likeness between the crime and the retribution
> unless death is judicially carried out upon the wrongdoer. (1996: 106;
> emphasis in original)

Kant is saying that, because punishment should fit the crime independently of the consequences of punishing or not punishing, if someone commits a murder, death is the only fitting punishment. In addition, the judicial system commits a crime against morality if it does not administer punishments that fit the crime.

Utilitarians are not convinced by retributivist arguments. If the death penalty does not deter crime or lead to more overall happiness than unhappiness, it is not permissible. However, if instituting the death penalty leads to a significant decrease in similar crimes, then, according to the utilitarian, capital punishment is permissible, and possibly obligatory.

Interestingly, there is a growing amount of evidence that suggests the death penalty is not an effective deterrent. Studies from 1970 to 2009 show that the death penalty has no effect on the rate of violent crime, especially murder, or at least no statistically significant effect. This almost conclusively places those who hold a deterrence theory of punishment, whether utilitarian or liberal, against the permissibility of the death penalty. (See, for example, Bedau 1970; Narayan and Smyth 2006; Land et al. 2009.)

These statistics are, of course, open to challenge. For instance, if a state government applies the death penalty in inconsistent ways in unclear cases, would-be criminals have no particular incentive to not commit a particular kind of crime. Whether they are sentenced to the death penalty will seem more a matter of luck than desert in those states. States that stipulate extremely technical conditions for applying the death penalty are not likely to provide a would-be criminal, who is likely uneducated and contemplating a crime (especially one of passion or necessity), sufficient reasons for refraining – he could not predict whether the crime he wants to commit fits those conditions. But even if these challenges are accurate, there remains the question of whether we could implement a policy of capital punishment in a way that *would* increase its effectiveness as a deterrent. If we could not, then the conclusion stands – it is not an effective deterrent.

If the death penalty is not an effective deterrent, might there be any additional utilitarian grounds on which to defend the death penalty? If it is significantly cheaper for a state to execute criminals, or if the policy generally leads to overall happiness, if not through decreased crime, through some other indirect means, then capital punishment may be morally permissible, even obligatory. As it turns out, capital punishment cases are quite a bit more expensive over the long run than sustaining a prisoner over a life sentence (see Baicker 2004). The costs of room and board are significantly less than the appeals process in a capital punishment case. Other pleasure versus pain trade-offs are more difficult to assess, but the utilitarian is committed to following this analysis wherever it leads.

If, however, the analysis shows that capital punishment elicits more harm than happiness, the utilitarian should be uniformly against it. The benefit of the utilitarian approach to punishment is that it is tied strongly to empirical results. If we can precisely formulate the trade-offs between pleasure and pain, we can run a utilitarian calculus to determine the moral permissibility of an action. If it is the case that capital punishment is not an effective deterrent and that the costs of sustaining inmates with a life sentence are lower than those for capital criminals, many utilitarians would be against the death penalty.

Are there any deontological reasons to object to the death penalty? It depends on how stringently you interpret Kant's account of the "good will." According to Kant, the good will is intrinsically good and *inviolable* – that is, there is nothing a person can do to forfeit her intrinsic value. In addition to these, a stringent Kantian interprets intrinsic goodness as unable to be overridden by any other considerations; that is, there are no moral considerations that can outweigh the rights entailed by a person's intrinsic goodness. If this more stringent reading is correct, then the death penalty is probably impermissible. The idea is that all moral agents are, as Kant calls them, lawmakers in the Kingdom of Ends, which means that beings with a good will are the primary source of understanding right from wrong, and the source of all other moral value in the universe. Therefore, we may imprison you based on the fact that we perceive you have committed a wrong act, but we cannot be sure we see your decision fully and clearly from your perspective. We are more sure that you are still intrinsically valuable than that you have done something that overrides that value – especially since the consequences of an action are not an indication of whether you are intrinsically valuable. A less stringent Kantian, however, may grant that intrinsic value is inviolable, but admit that there are moral concerns that could override it – for instance, self-defense.

Another deontological consideration against the death penalty is presented by the Roman Catholic Church. In 1999, Pope John Paul II addressed a youth rally in St Louis, Missouri, where he asked America to abolish the death penalty: "I renew the appeal I made most recently at Christmas for a consensus to end the death penalty, which is both cruel and unnecessary," he said. "Modern society has the means of protecting itself, without definitively denying criminals the chance to reform" (see Feister 1999). The Pope does not appeal here to any theological reasons for abolishing the death penalty, but he presupposes that criminals have an intrinsic moral standing that might allow them the opportunity to "reform," if given time and treatment. This intrinsic moral standing derives from his theological perspective on the nature of humanity as created in God's image, but it could just as easily derive from a Kantian appeal to the good will.

The difference between the Pope's appeal and a strict Kantian's is in the focus on the possibility of redeeming the criminal's moral character. The Pope fully acknowledges that the criminal is guilty, and perhaps even deserving of death. However, he is more concerned with the eternal soul of the individual than with whether the criminal receives the full measure of his punishment. The death penalty would deprive a priest of time to redeem the criminal's soul. Therefore, if you are Catholic and you believe there is a command that people should be given every opportunity possible to accept the redemption of God, then you will probably oppose the death penalty. Table 12.1 charts the arguments for and against the death penalty this way (each reason is followed by the theory or theories of punishment that would most likely motivate it).

Table 12.1

Arguments for capital punishment	*Arguments against capital punishment*
1. There are crimes for which death is the only just punishment (retributivist).	1. There are no crimes for which death is a just punishment (behaviorist).
2. The death penalty deters similar crimes by other would-be criminals (behaviorist, utilitarian, liberal deterrence).	2. The death penalty is not an effective deterrent of similar crimes by other would-be criminals(behaviorist, utilitarian, liberal deterrence).
3. The death penalty has great social benefit (utilitarian).	3. The social benefits of the death penalty do not outweigh the social harms (utilitarian).
	4. A person is intrinsically valuable no matter what she does, and this value cannot be overridden by any other considerations (strict Kantian).
	5. It is more important that a person has time to reform than that they experience their just punishment (Roman Catholic Church).

CAPITAL PUNISHMENT IS UNJUSTIFIED

Jeffrey Reiman, "The Justice of the Death Penalty in an Unjust World"

Jeffrey Reiman argues that there are two moral questions about the death penalty, which he calls, "The question of the justice of the death penalty *in principle*," which refers the permissibility of the capital punishment in general, and "The question of the justice of the death penalty *in practice*," which refers to the moral permissibility of a court's application of the penalty. Reiman writes: "Moral assessment of the way a penalty is actually going to be carried out is a necessary ingredient in any determination of the justice of adopting that penalty as our policy" (1992: 340).

When considered on grounds of justice alone, capital punishment may be fully justified. The punishment should fit the crime and death may be the only fitting crime for someone who has violated someone else's right to life. However, when considered on grounds of how the policy is administered, capital punishment may be unjustified. The punishment should fit the crime, but if there is some doubt about the charges or whether the penalty can be applied fairly, the death penalty is unjust. Reiman argues that, while there are compelling justifications for capital punishment in principle, in practice, it is immoral.

What reasons are there for thinking the application of the death penalty is immoral? Reiman offers four reasons; we will discuss two: first, the application of the death penalty is discriminatory; and second, the social conditions that foster murder are discriminatory.

The application of the death penalty is discriminatory

If the courts apply the death penalty in some cases but not in other similar cases, and if there is no justifiable principle that distinguishes these cases, then the court discriminates on arbitrary grounds. If this happens, Reiman argues, rather than administering justice, courts are introducing injustice into the world. In addition, Reiman offers evidence that "among equally guilty murderers, the death penalty is more likely to be given to blacks than whites, and to poor defendants than to well-off ones" (1992: 345). One study notes: "Among killers of whites [in Florida], blacks are five times more likely than whites to be sentenced to death" (1992: 345). From this and other similar studies, Reiman concludes that the death penalty is not applied in a manner consistent with justice.

An interesting response to this objection is that, in these cases, the injustice is not committed against blacks or the poor, but against those who are not executed. "Neither the argument from discrimination against black victims, nor the argument from discrimination against black murderers, has any bearing on the guilt of black murderers, or on the punishment they deserve" (Haag 1992: 352). If all are equally guilty, then those executed receive the proper response to their crimes. Those not executed, and society as a result, experience the injustice of their continuing to live.

The social conditions that foster murder are discriminatory

Reiman also argues that the social conditions that contribute to violent crimes, especially murder, constitute discrimination in the application of capital punishment. Independently of the legislative or legal system, the economic system of society places poor people at higher risk of being sentenced to death in murder cases. Reiman explains:

> For example, most defendants in capital cases cannot afford to hire their own lawyers and thus must have attorneys appointed by the state . . . . Accordingly, if discrimination in the handing down of death sentences was completely

eliminated, it is still likely that the overwhelming majority of death row inmates would come from the bottom of society. (1992: 347)

Reiman says that, even if we clean up the courts, and apply the death penalty consistently, on non-arbitrary grounds, the economic system of society might determine that poor people are more likely to be put to death than the rich for similar crimes.

Some might respond to this worry using the same argument as above. If someone commits a crime deserving of death and if the death penalty is permissible, then no injustice is committed. But in this case, there is a further question of whether the social conditions that encourage murder mitigate the blame of those who live in those conditions. Ernest van den Haag says, No:

> I grant that certain social conditions predictably produce crime more readily than others. Does it follow that those who commit crimes in criminogenic conditions are less responsible, or blameworthy, than they would be if they did not live in these conditions? Certainly not. Predictability does not reduce responsibility. (1992: 350)

Haag's point is that, if we believe people can act on moral and legal reasons independently of outside influences, then no encouragement short of coercion can mitigate the blame for an action. Of course, it is important to note that if you hold a behaviorist theory of punishment, you believe people are not fully responsible for their actions, and that behavior is a conditioned response to one's environment. If this is right and if Reiman is right, capital punishment is immoral. But if Haag is right, it is perfectly permissible.

CASE STUDY 1: *Star Trek: The Next Generation*, "The Hunted," season 3

AVAILABILITY: NetFlix, iTunes

In this episode, the crew act as ambassadors of the Federation of Planets to the planet Angosia III, which has expressed interest in becoming a member of the Federation. During their visit, a prisoner escapes from one of their maximum-security penal colonies. The crew of the *Enterprise* contribute their assistance in the pursuit of the fugitive. The prisoner proves especially difficult to capture, but ultimately no match for the *Enterprise*'s cunning officers.

The Prime Minister of the planet, Nayrock (James Cromwell), explains that the criminal, Roga Danar (Jeff McCarthy), is very dangerous and given to bouts of extreme violence. But after he is captured, the ship's counselor Deanna Troi (Marina Sirtis) (an "empathy" who is telepathic and able to sense a person's feelings) senses something inconsistent between what Nayrock told them and the feeling she has about the prisoner. Danar is angry, but deeply troubled about his crimes. Troi says there is a duality about him that she doesn't yet understand. When she asks Danar whether he is mistreated in prison, he tells her that the Angosians take good care of their prisoners: "I am comfortable, well fed and housed. . . . It's simply a matter of never being able to leave." Troi reports to Captain Picard (Patrick Stewart): "When I am with him I cannot believe that he is randomly and deliberately violent. In fact, inherently, he has a non-violent personality."

Troi's report spawns an investigation, which reveals that Danar was a soldier with an impeccable service record. It turns out that when he volunteered for military service, he and the other soldiers were put through "intense psychological manipulation and biochemical modifications" that rendered them too dangerous to return to society. They were imprisoned to prevent them from harming anyone. Rather than attempting to "reprogram" the soldiers returning from war, the Angosians simply exiled them to a penal colony.

After Danar escapes again, Captain Picard refuses to help the Angosians violently resist Danar's attack on the penal colony. When Nayrock explains that the prisoners are dangerous, Picard responds, "You are dangerous. They're only victims. You made them what they are. You asked them to defend your way of life and then you discarded them." The Prime Minister explains: "No one was happy with the solution. But we had to act for the greater good. . . . There was a referendum. The people weighed the costs involved. They chose the settlement solution."

Finally, the prisoners hold the Prime Minister hostage and demand their lives back. Picard says he has enough for his report on the Angosians' application to the Federation and that the Prime Minister has a decision to make: "Whether to try and force them back or welcome them back. In your own words – this is not our affair. . . . When you're ready for membership, the Federation would be please to consider your application."

Commentary: Is punishment justified in an unjust world?

There are two important issues relating to punishment in this episode: (1) Can someone be punished for an act for which they are not responsible? and (2) Are humans efficient at judging whether a punishment fits the crime?

1. Can someone be punished for an act for which they are not responsible?
The principle of "ought implies can" (see the "Pilot Episode") prevents us
from holding someone responsible for actions they cannot control. For instance, if someone has a natural urge to rape women, we might call
this unfortunate or improper or tragic, but we cannot call it immoral. It
is only his unwillingness to suppress this urge that we can call immoral. In
addition, someone who was forced at gunpoint to steal food would
be committing an immoral act, but could not be blameworthy for committing it.

In this episode, the Angosian government has instilled in their soldiers,
under certain conditions, the compulsion, not merely the tendency or urge,
to act violently, even to kill. Since these soldiers cannot be held morally
responsible for their actions, it seems immoral to "punish" them by placing
them in a penal colony. Even though the penal colony is a humane,
comfortable way of life, as Captain Picard notes, "even the most comfortable prison is still a prison."

But now a paradox is introduced. The government is responsible for any
of the prisoner's actions (because they are responsible for the conditioning), but the prisoners cannot act other than they do. The slightest
agitation between citizens may result in a murder; they really are a threat
to society. How should the government react? It is immoral to allow them
to harm society, but it is also immoral to imprison them for actions they
cannot help. This is quite a dilemma.

Deanna Troi suggests that the only resolution is to figure out a way to
reprogram the soldiers. As it happens, new technology would likely make
this possible. The Angosian Prime Minister is reluctant, though desperate.
But what if reprogramming were not possible? It would seem that such a
situation would be similar to the case of violent mentally handicapped
patients. If someone is not morally responsible for her actions, but her
actions are morally dangerous, there are good reasons to isolate that
person from society. We should not inflict retributive harm to that person,
since she does not have the capacity to intend moral harm, but it would
seem that isolation is justified. If this is right, and if the Angosian prisoners
cannot be reprogrammed, it would seem that the "settlement solution" is
the only acceptable solution, however damaging to the prisoners. This is
unsettling, especially since the soldiers seem more aware of their predic-
ament than many severely mentally handicapped criminals. Nevertheless,
it would seem that whatever decision is made, someone will be harmed
and, in the case of the Angosian soldiers, the government would bear
the responsibility.

2. Are humans efficient at judging whether a punishment fits the crime?
Prime Minister Nayrock explains that the population voted for the
"settlement solution." And though this was the morally best solution, it
is still not good, given the soldiers' innocence. This raises a question about
the fitness of humans to administer punishments on other humans. We are
not omniscient (all-knowing), and therefore cannot be absolutely certain
that a particular punishment is fitting for a particular crime. We cannot
know every aspect of the circumstances surrounding an action, and we
cannot know a suspect's mental states and intentions. Any of this may
mitigate the circumstances surrounding a crime.

In the episode, "The Hunted," it appears, at first, that Roga Danar is guilty
of the crime of escaping from a prison that he was justly imprisoned in. If he
was not justly imprisoned, it is difficult to consider his escape a "crime." And
it turns out that the justification for his imprisonment is questionable.

Translating this into our own culture, there are significant questions
about the criteria a court uses to apply judgments. Twelve regular people
with no legal or moral training are asked to determine the guilt of a
suspect for a crime they know little about. Therefore, even if someone is
guilty of a crime and deserves punishment, it is not clear that humans are
the best administrators of the type and degree of punishment fitting for
the crime.

Does this mean we should not punish? Not at all. Our knowledge is
limited in many areas of our lives, from buying a car, to signing a contract,
to purchasing insurance, to choosing a mate, to trying to raise a child, to
resisting in self-defense. But that our knowledge is limited does not mean
we should not act. We should, though our actions should be based on the
best evidence and made with the utmost respect for caution.

CASE STUDY 2: *Oz*, "Capital P," season 1

AVAILABILITY: **NetFlix, iTunes**

HBO's edgy prison drama *Oz* takes viewers into the nefarious world inside
the fictional maximum-security prison, Oswald State Correctional Facility,
nicknamed "Oz." Many of the episodes center on an experimental ward of
the prison, known as the "Emerald City," in which Unit Manager Tim
McManus (Terry Kinney) attempts a more comprehensive rehabilitation
and moral education program for the inmates. The program is never as
successful as McManus hopes.

In this episode, we are presented with the details of the capital punishment case of Jefferson Keane (Leon Robinson), from the moment of conviction to the moment of execution (with a few dramatic details in between). From the opening scenes we are given the traditional argument against the death penalty: it doesn't work as a deterrent. A reporter at a press conference asks the governor, "Even, Governor, if it's been proven that executions have no effect on the increase or decrease of crime whatsoever?" The governor responds, "Especially if it has no effect. These days, murders are random, senseless. Maybe the punishment should be, too."

Sister Peter Marie (Rita Moreno) objects to the death penalty and announces to the warden that she will stand with the anti-capital punishment protesters, a commitment for which she is fired until after the execution. Tobias Beecher (Lee Tergesen), a former lawyer and fellow inmate, discovers that there may be a surveillance video that shows that Keane killed the victim in self-defense, and therefore doesn't deserve the death penalty. After a few threats from racist inmates, Beecher asks to be put in protective custody while he continues his investigation.

When Beecher talks to Keane about his investigation, Keane, a recent convert to Islam, puts him off, explaining that if he dies now, he might go to heaven, but if he goes back to "Em City," he tells Beecher, "I might go back to my old ways. I might lose my faith, my soul. I'm at peace right now." Keane tells him he isn't concerned about his soul and that he will continue the investigation.

Unfortunately, the tape is destroyed by the guards. The only reprieve that Keane gets is a short leave to a hospital, where he donates a kidney to his extremely ill sister. But shortly afterward, amid growing controversy outside the walls of the prison, Keane is led to the lethal injection room. While the dead man is walking, the narrator lists some statistics about the death penalty:

> Three thousand men and women are sitting on death row, right now. Congress has denied state inmates access to federal courts. Congress has also eliminated finances to law offices for death row appeals. States themselves are shortening the appeals process. In this country, there is now one execution every single week. There were more executions this year than any time since the fifties. And we all know how righteous the fifties were.

Commentary: Capital punishment from the prisoner's perspective

In this episode we are presented with several of the major reasons that capital punishment should be prohibited: it is not an effective deterrent (the reporter); a person is intrinsically valuable despite their actions (Sister Peter

Marie); a person should be given as much time as possible to repent (Father Ray). But, in stark contrast to these objections, the episode raises the interesting possibility that prisoners might prefer capital punishment to life in prison.

When Beecher meets with Keane about his investigation, Keane welcomes the death penalty. Without it, he risks his commitment to a religion that promises a beautiful afterlife. In addition, he explains that his death might settle a feud in the prison that could lead to the deaths of many of his friends if not abated. Keane has weighed the costs and benefits of execution, and chooses execution. At the end of the episode, the show's narrator, prisoner 95H522, Augustus Hill (Harold Perrineau), explains that "life in prison without parole is a shitload worse than death. ... Death is the real mercy."

Do these considerations constitute reasons in favor of the death penalty? The retributivist would say, No. Regardless of what a prisoner wants, the punishment must fit the crime. No criminal wants to be punished – we hope, otherwise it wouldn't be "punishment" in any meaningful sense. But, that a prisoner would prefer one punishment to another should not affect the type or degree of punishment inflicted. The retributivist does not say, "We want whatever will make the criminal feel worse," but merely that, "The punishment should fit the crime." If life in prison fits the crime, that's what the punishment should be; if death, then death should be the punishment.

The situation is similar with the utilitarian. The prisoner's wishes are not the primary concern when determining a punishment; it is the measure of suffering caused, as opposed to the level of suffering relieved, that is at issue. However, if the death penalty does not increase overall happiness (because it is not an effective deterrent), and life in prison increases overall suffering, then perhaps the death penalty would be obligatory. It is not the prisoner's "preference" that counts as evidence, but the degree of the prisoner's suffering. If relieving his suffering outweighs the costs of the appeals process in a capital case, even if it doesn't deter similar crimes, the death penalty may be obligatory on a utilitarian theory of punishment.

An interesting dilemma: The case of Richard L'Italien

There is a strange paradox in the law. If a prisoner is convicted for one heinous crime and is sentenced to life in prison, or even the death penalty, if evidence surfaces that the prisoner is guilty of an additional crime, he might have to return to court to be tried for it. On one hand, this seems perfectly right. Without another trial, officially, those crimes are unsolved and the suspect is not guilty of them. So, if we are concerned with desert and appropriately assessing blame, then we should hold another trial. On the other hand, what if the suspect is already sentenced to death? Should we postpone carrying out the death sentence until all the crimes are appropriately added to his record? This is precisely the worry in another *Oz* episode, "Capital P," with prisoner 97L641, Richard L'Italien (Eric Roberts).

L'Italian was sentenced to death for suffocating a woman named Jennifer Miller. But the night before his execution, L'Italien lists 39 murder victims, by first and last name, for whom he claims responsibility. The problem is that if L'Italien is executed for the first murder, then the family of the first victim receives justice for their daughter. But the other 38 victims' families officially are left without reprieve. On the other hand, if the execution is stayed, pending trials for the other 38 victims, the first family's daughter is not avenged. Now, technically, since he dies either way, everyone receives justice – we can't take his life more than once. But legally, the debt is outstanding. So, there is a sense in which the moral question may be settled with his death, irrespective of the legal considerations. But since the legal question is tied to the issue of moral justice, and since the legal considerations leave us with a dilemma, the moral question might not yet be completely settled. The warden decides to keep the information private so that the execution takes place as planned. Perhaps he's hoping that the scales of moral justice will be balanced, even if the legal ones are not.

STUDY QUESTIONS

1. If they genuinely believed that there was no way to reprogram the soldiers, did the Angosian civilians make the best decision by starting the prison settlement? Why or why not?
2. If the Angosian citizens were aware of a way to reprogram the soldiers, but knew that it would cost a lot of money and take a long time, should they still have chosen the settlement instead? Explain why or why not.
3. Are there any cases where a person should be punished even though she is innocent? Explain from a retributivist perspective, and then explain from a utilitarian perspective.
4. How should our limited knowledge of the circumstances surrounding a crime affect whether and how we administer punishment?

5. According to the behaviorist theory of punishment, are the Angosians acting appropriately toward their prisoners? Explain the ways in which they are acting appropriately and the ways they aren't.
6. Is capital punishment justified if a prisoner would prefer the death penalty to life in prison?
7. According to the behaviorist theory of punishment, would it be permissible to execute a prisoner who committed a capital crime and could not, under any circumstances, be reformed?
8. Imagine that some new treatment became available that would reform prisoners who commit capital crimes. Would this undermine the retributivist argument for the death penalty? Why or why not?
9. At the beginning of this episode, in partial justification for reinstating the death penalty, the governor says that murders are random and senseless, so maybe the punishment should be too. Is this a sufficient justification of capital punishment? Explain why or why not.
10. Should Richard L'Italien's execution take place even though he confessed to 39 additional murders that will not, officially, be attributed to him if he is not tried for them?

ALTERNATIVE CASE STUDIES

1. *Foyle's War*, "Enemy Fire," set 3
   (Does Dr Wrenn deserve to be punished? If so, for what?)
2. *Cheers*, "Homicidal Ham," season 2
   (Was prison therapeutic for Andy? What implications does this have for developing a theory of punishment?)
3. *The Twilight Zone* (original), "The Lonely," season 1
   (How can we know whether a punishment is excessive?)

EPISODE 13: ASSISTED SUICIDE

EPISODE OUTLINE

Introduction
A Few Terms
Three Moral Arguments Against the Permissibility of Assisted
   Suicide
Moral and Practical Arguments for the Permissibility of Assisted
   Suicide
The good of society depends on assisted suicide
   Daniel Callahan, "Aging and the Ends of Medicine"
Case study 1: *Picket Fences*, "Abominable Snowman," season 2
Case study 2: *Scrubs*, "My Jiggly Ball," season 5
Study questions
Alternative case studies

INTRODUCTION

In one episode of *Gray's Anatomy*, a patient in the fictional Grace-Mercy West Hospital wants to die ("Death Defying," season 6). She has stage-four lung cancer which has spread to various organs and breathing is becoming increasingly difficult. Dr Hunt (Kevin McKidd) explains: "Dying isn't easy. The body was designed to stay alive. Thick skulls,

What's Good on TV?: Understanding Ethics Through Television, First Edition.
Jamie Carlin Watson and Robert Arp.
© 2011 Jamie Carlin Watson and Robert Arp. Published 2011 by Blackwell Publishing Ltd.

strong hearts, keen senses." Modern medicine is aimed at preserving life, not taking it, just as the body is organized to fight off predators and reproduce its own kind. So what happens when the body and modern medicine disagree?

To what degree is my life my own? Do I have any duties to myself or society that morally prohibit taking my own life? In Episodes 8, 9, and 10, we began each discussion with the assumption that *mature, human beings have a right to life*, and then asked whether there are any reasons to extend this right to rainforests, dogs, fetuses, or infants. But in this Episode, we are dealing with mature human beings, presumably with a right to life it would be wrong to rob them of. Do any moral considerations override or undermine a person's right to life such that they have *a right to die*?

In this Episode, we will define some confusing terms, consider some arguments for and against assisted suicide, discuss an article in which a philosopher argues we should refuse medical treatment from some patients later in life, and then entertain some unusual questions about these arguments in light of episodes from *Picket Fences* and *Scrubs*.

A FEW TERMS

"Suicide" is the intentional taking of one's own life. "Assisted suicide" is often called "euthanasia." But we think conflating the terms does more to confuse the debate than clarify it. "Euthanasia" is derived from a Greek word meaning "good death." (The prefix "eu-" means "good," as in "eucharist" – good grace – and "eulogy" – good word; the word "thanatos" means "death.") A "good death," in ancient cultures, was considered a dignified death. So, for example, for a soldier to die in battle or as a prisoner of war was a *eu-thanatos*, a good death. But to die while running away or for treason was an undignified death. Some people refer to assisted suicide as a good death because a person makes the decision to die while she is in control of her mental faculties – she does not wait until she has dementia or incapacitated from disease. But the meaning of "euthanasia" does not imply anything with respect to taking your own life or the moral permissibility of suicide. So, of course, the *moral* question remains: is *suicide* ever a dignified, or "good," death?

To make matters cloudier, "euthanasia" has come to mean, in common usage, "mercy killing," that is, someone taking someone else's life as an act of mercy, for instance, if they are in terrible pain from a terminal illness. For a common example of a mercy killing, imagine a battlefield, where one soldier is mortally wounded but not dead and he asks a fellow soldier to "end it quickly" so he doesn't have to suffer for the final few minutes. The mortally wounded soldier asks to be killed, but it is the other soldier who commits the act.

"Assisted suicide," on the other hand, refers to cases where one person helps another person take his life, but doesn't commit the act. For instance, consider the battlefield scenario again, but in this case, instead of the mortally wounded soldier asking his fellow soldier to kill him, he just asks him to hand him a gun, so he can do it himself. The fellow soldier merely helps his friend commit suicide. "Physician-assisted suicide" refers to cases where a doctor helps a patient commit suicide by either prescribing deadly drugs or setting up drugs that a patient can inject herself.

To make matters worse, still, James Rachels calls mercy killing, "active euthanasia," and respecting a patient's decision to refuse treatment, "passive euthanasia." We imagine he would lump mercy killing and assisted suicide together under "active euthanasia." It is unclear from Rachels whether a patient need be able to consent for mercy killing to be morally persmissible.

Therefore, to help keep things clear, we will use the following terms in the following ways:

- *euthanasia*: a dignified death
- *suicide*: the intentional taking of one's own life
- *assisted suicide*: the intentional taking of one's own life with the help of someone else (e.g., either to prescribe drugs or prepare an injection)
- *passive assisted suicide*: withholding or withdrawing life sustaining treatment from someone who requests to die (e.g., a patient who refuses treatment or food)
- *active assisted suicide*: the intentional taking of someone else's life by that person's request (e.g., the battlefield scenario)
- *mercy killing*: the intentional taking of someone else's life, with or without their consent, for reasons of compassion for the alleviation of suffering (e.g., refers to both active assisted suicide and the intentional taking of someone else's life without that person's consent for reasons of compassion)

THREE MORAL ARGUMENTS AGAINST THE PERMISSIBILITY OF ASSISTED SUICIDE

J. Gay-Williams (2008) offers versions of three prominent moral arguments against suicide in general, all of which, if successful, have implications for assisted suicide in particular. (Gay-Williams argues against "euthanasia," but since he makes no distinctions among how the killing takes place or for what reasons, we use "suicide" instead.)

The religious argument against suicide of any kind

Some argue that humans are created by God and, therefore, our lives do not belong wholly to us. We are merely stewards of a trust, and that trust has certain rules. And one of those rules is that we have no right to end our own lives. If this is right, any type of suicide is morally impermissible. Imagine someone asks you to watch their dog for a couple of weeks. You are free to do a lot of things with the dog – you can play with it, walk it, take it for a car ride, curl up with it to watch TV, etc. But the dog is not yours; the owner has the right to expect certain things from you – that you will not feed it table scraps, that you will not let it on the couch, that you will not kill it, etc. If our lives are remotely similar to having responsibility over someone else's property, then suicide might be impermissible.

Gay-Williams offers the following version of this argument:

1. God created man.
2. Therefore, God is man's rightful possessor, and to whatever extent man is autonomous, he is merely a trustee, and not a co-owner.
3. God commands we hold life sacred and never take it without just and compelling cause.

4. Therefore, suicide is impermissible.

In order to accept this conclusion, we need reasons for believing the premises are true. To justify premise (1), we would need a compelling argument for God's existence and creative activity. Premise (3) is plausible, since it is likely true that we should only take a life when there is a just and compelling cause even if God doesn't exist or didn't create us. But even if premise (3) were true, it is not clear whether some cases of assisted suicide have a just and compelling cause.

And even if we were to grant premises (1) and (3) for the sake of argument, it is not clear how we would justify (2). Premise (2) might be true, or our lives might be a gift to us. If it is a gift, God has no further claim on it. Therefore, the religious argument against suicide is likely insufficient.

The natural argument against suicide of any kind

Gay-Williams also argues that observations of nature suggest an argument against the permissibility of suicide. For instance, our bodies are naturally disposed to preserve themselves: our reflexes help us fend off attacks of various kinds; if we are cut, platelets seal our bodies to shut out harmful micro-organisms; and, even without help, our bodies start healing any wounds that we receive. Nature tells us that our bodies have a natural inclination to survive.

In addition, virtue comes through seeking the goals we are designed to achieve. From these two premises, Gay-Williams offers the following argument:

1. Moral dignity comes from seeking our ends.
2. Every human being has a natural inclination to continue living.
3. Therefore, survival is one of our ends.
4. Suicide does violence to this natural end.
5. Therefore, suicide violates our dignity.
6. Therefore, suicide is impermissible.

If premises (1) and (2) are true, the conclusion follows fairly strongly. Unfortunately, it is not clear whether we should believe (1) and (2). Like Aristotle's virtue ethics, premise (1) presupposes that our ends are morally valuable; but why suppose this? Perhaps one of the ends my body is best suited for is killing other humans. Is it morally good that I go around killing people just because it is my natural tendency? Not at all. Therefore, as it stands, this argument commits the naturalistic fallacy (see the" Pilot Episode," fallacy 6).

In addition, premise (2) is sometimes false. In some cases, the body turns against itself: congenital defects threaten organs and defense systems; the body, consistent with the laws of physics, breaks down over time; and the body resists getting stronger by making muscles sore, deceiving you into thinking you've harmed it and should not continue exercising. Therefore, if premise (1) were true, the conclusion might be false, since, in some cases, my natural ends are to dispense with living.

The argument from self-interest against assisted suicide

A prominent motivation for suicide or assisted suicide is to avoid the immense pain or inconvenience or indignity of a certain type of illness, especially a terminal illness. Those who are motivated by such considerations presumably value life of a certain quality. While you might not value extended hospital stays and painful treatments, you value the *object* of these inconveniences, namely, the freedom to go and do as you please. Gay-Williams argues that, if your life is morally valuable to you, there are certain considerations that should lead you to oppose suicide, even if your life is very painful or inconvenient at the moment.

We can formulate his argument like this:

1. Suicide is final and irreversible.
2. A mistaken diagnosis is possible so that you might think you're dying when you're not.
3. Even if your disease is terminal, an experimental procedure might soon become available.
4. In many cases, spontaneous remission (or a miracle) occurs.
5. Suicide denies you of these possible opportunities.

6. Therefore, suicide should not be committed.

Since suicide is irreversible, if there is some significant degree of probability that you will regain your preferred quality of life, then suicide should not be a consideration. Even if the probability of any of premises (2), (3), or (4) is fairly low, combined, he argues, they provide a sufficient reason to reject suicide.

Though we are getting better at determining when a disease is terminal, doctors still make mistakes. For instance, some people have malignant cancer for years without exhibiting any painful symptoms. And even if doctors get it right, medical research is advancing at lightning speed, so a better treatment for your disease might soon become available. And sometimes, something known as "spontaneous remission" occurs, which means that cancer just disappears for no explainable reason. Since any of these is possible, and the combination, depending on the case, might amount to a significant degree of probability, and since suicide would drop your probability to zero, suicide is not in your self-interest.

While this argument has some strength, there are certain illnesses where these probabilities are significantly mitigated. For instance, melanoma of the brain and small cell lung cancer are incredibly aggressive forms of cancer that do not respond well to treatment. Though new research is under way, the amount of time a person has to live until these cancers kill the patient is very short. As it turns out, these cancers are not associated with excruciating pain as some are, and so not many patients would be motivated to request early termination of their lives. But imagine a relatively aggressive disease that is very painful and has a low spontaneous remission rate. In this case, premise (2) is likely false, since you are directly experiencing the diagnosis, and the probability of premise (4) is low or inscrutable. How willing would you be to hang around "just to see" if a cure becomes available? So, where-as this argument may be quite compelling in many cases, there are some exceptions.

MORAL AND PRACTICAL ARGUMENTS FOR THE PERMISSIBILITY OF ASSISTED SUICIDE

There are at least two important arguments for the permissibility of assisted suicide:

The individual rights argument

If a person has rights that no one else can violate, then that person has a unique moral standing. It is morally permissible for her and her alone to dictate what happens to all that she owns, including her body. If this is right, then it would seem that she also has a right to take her own life. We might formulate this argument as follows:

1. A person is intrinsically valuable.
2. Intrinsic value entails certain rights, including exclusive use of property that person has justly obtained.
3. A person's body is hers essentially, and therefore justly.
4. Therefore, she has a right to do whatever she wants with her body, including kill it.

Therefore, even if God created me and wants me to live, if he gave me the sole rights over my body, then I am morally free to do with it as I wish.

The only worry with this argument is the extent to which individuals can extend rights over their bodies to others. For instance, on this view you cannot sell yourself into slavery since, by definition, this undermines your freedom to do as you please. If it is not permissible for an individual to enter into a contract to end her life, then, while suicide and assisted suicide are probably morally permissible, active assisted suicide is not.

A consequentialist argument

If we set aside concerns over rights, it might be the case that some people should die, so that others can live a better quality of life. If one person's life is not worth any more than any other, and the happiness of the whole is the primary concern, then it is permissible that a few are sacrificed for the many. Therefore, a consequentialist argument for the permissibility of assisted suicide might go like this:

1. One person is no more valuable than any other.
2. Actions that increase happiness and decrease pain are morally best.

3. In some cases, one person's death would bring about the happiness of many others.

4. Therefore, in some cases it is permissible, and in some obligatory, that one person dies for the sake of overall well-being.

Consequentialist arguments like this would weigh the suffering of the patient against the goods that would result from his death. If the death would lead to more overall happiness than any alternative, his death is obligatory.

What goods might result from a person's death? Primarily, the resources of medical care. There is a finite number of medical resources – hospital beds, medicines, doctors, money to pay for it, etc. Therefore, when considering the costs and benefits of a treatment and suicide, many terminally ill patients may make the world a better place by dying earlier than their disease would dictate. Daniel Callahan offers an argument along these lines.

THE GOOD OF SOCIETY DEPENDS ON ASSISTED SUICIDE

Daniel Callahan, "Aging and the Ends of Medicine"

Daniel Callahan argues that there are certain cases in which it is morally justified to refuse medical treatment to a person, regardless of that person's consent. He asks, given these scarcities: "How will it be possible . . . to keep pace with the growing number of elderly in even providing present levels of care, much less in ridding the system of its present inadequacies and inequities – and, at the same time, furiously adding expensive new technology?" (2009: 273). He answers that it will not be possible, and will probably cause, rather than relieve, more harm to try than to pursue an alternative.

Callahan notes three major concerns of an increasing number of elderly patients: (i) "an increasingly large share of health care is going to the elderly in comparison with the benefits going to children"; (ii) "the elderly dying consume a disproportionate share of health care costs"; and (iii) new medical technology is being applied primarily to the elderly, though much of it was not intended for this age group (2009: 273). Notice that these concerns presuppose significant government assistance with healthcare costs; this will become relevant shortly.

To assuage these concerns, Callahan suggests an alternative approach to healthcare distribution. "The future goal of medicine in the care of the aged should be that of improving the quality of their life [*sic*], not in seeking ways to extend that life. In its longstanding ambition to forestall death, medicine has in the care of the aged reached its last frontier" (2009: 275). If we help people recognize that a longer life is not necessarily a better life, then help them understand that the best quality of life often includes much less medical treatment, we can then implement a healthcare policy that respects the limits of the benefits of medical treatment. Callahan explains: "[G] overnment has a duty, based on our collective social obligations to each other, to help people live out a natural life span but not actively to help medically extend life beyond that point," and "beyond the point of natural life span, government should provide only the means necessary for the relief of suffering, not life-extending technology" (2009: 276).

Callahan basically asks us to run a cost-benefit analysis on the effectiveness of medical care beyond a certain age and stage of illness. Once an average "normal life span" has been calculated, he suggests that the government stop subsidizing treatments intended to extend life beyond that point. With such a policy, those who are of advanced age or terminally ill will likely have a better quality of life near the end, and society will benefit from increased access to medical resources.

One worry with Callahan's view is that he believes the government has an "obligation" to supply healthcare resources to its citizens. This is not at all obvious, especially since the government will probably have to levy taxes on healthy people to pay for the healthcare of the sick. So, there is already a worry about the fairness of Callahan's system.

A second worry is that he suggests that the government devise an artificial "natural life span," according to which, some people would not qualify for government medical assistance because of their age and/or medical condition. This might meant that a routine surgery would be covered for an 85-year old, but not for an 86-year old, even if the older person is in better overall health. This would seem to make the distribution of medical resources arbitrary in many cases.

CASE STUDY 1: *Picket Fences*, "Abominable Snowman," season 2

AVAILABILITY: iTunes, NetFlix, available free at: http://www.flixster.com/watch-tv/picket-fences–abominable-snowman

Picket Fences was a show about the residents of a fictional community in Rome, Wisconsin, including especially Dr Jill Brock (Kathy Baker) and her husband Sheriff Jimmy Brock (Tom Skerritt). The show ran from 1992 to 1996, but, despite its controversial topics, such as abortion, transsexuality, and spontaneous human combustion, it was not able to maintain a stable audience.

In this episode, townsperson Kevin Buss (Time Winters) has a heart attack, and Dr Brock discovers that he has congenital heart failure and needs a transplant – otherwise, he will die within the next three weeks. His father, Harold Buss (Robert Cornthwaite), is in the middle stages of Alzheimer's disease and has begun to experience "sundowning," which is when mental faculties start to fade later in the day. Despite his illness, there are many times when he is lucid and engaged.

Early in the episode, when it looks as if the hospital will not be able to find a heart for Kevin, Harold comes to Dr Brock and asks her to transplant his heart into his son's. He explains, "My brain is rotting away. Kevin is 40, with small children." Dr Brock, afraid that Howard is confused, says, "Howard, we can't just remove your heart. You'll die." But Howard explains, clearly, "Yes, with some dignity. And I could give my son life. . . . I've done my living, Jill. I've been happy. I don't want my last memory to be my son's funeral."

Dr Brock takes Howard's case to court, so she can avoid any murder charges the hospital might attract in this delicate political and moral case. But later, when Howard shows up at the Brocks' house confused and appears surprised to learn that his son is sick, Dr Brock doubts whether he is mentally fit enough to consent to the transplant.

Nevertheless, the court hearing goes forward. The judge carefully considers the testimony of Howard's attorney, the US attorney representing the state of Wisconsin, and even the testimony of Howard himself, who comes to the judge's chambers late one evening. But although it is clear from the medical testimony that Howard will die a grueling death from Alzheimer's and that his son could live with a transplant, the judge ultimately rules against Howard's request on the following grounds:

> Yes, you could very well deteriorate from the Alzheimer's and be dead in a year, even three months, I don't know. But I do know, today, each day, you wake up with the capacity to live, and to love. You're embraced by life. You're still made rich by it. And I have absolutely no doubt: life continues to be made more rich by you. I will pray for your son. But I will not sit up here as a judge and deem your life worthy of termination. That job belongs to a much higher power.

Commentary: Who has the right to decide who dies?

When Dr Brock takes the stand to defend Howard's decision to give his heart to his son, she explains the horrors of dying from Alzheimer's and argues that dying now would be morally better than suffering this fate. But the judge asks her: "What about the next person who comes to me with cancer? Or the amputee who tells me he doesn't want to live if he can't walk? Or ... the patient with clinical depression? They may all want to die. Do we assist them?"

There are a number of interconnected considerations to consider when deciding whether assisted suicide is permissible. Is mere desire to die, even if someone is not dying of a terminal disease or would not face a great deal of pain, sufficient of justify suicide? Can just *anyone* make this decision, or do you have to have a certain mental capacity? In light of these complicated issues, Dr Brock responds: "Well, your honor. I think we need to look at each individual case." But even to evaluate individual cases, we need some general principles; otherwise, our decision in each case might be arbitrary. Are there any such general principles to help us decide whether someone in a particular case is morally permitted to die, or whether it is morally permissible for someone to take another's life?

If we agree that mature adults have rights, then "consent" is a primary consideration in assisted suicide cases. If someone does not or cannot consent to dying, it is immoral to take her life from her. Some utilitarians disagree that humans have this sort of inviolable right to life, but without it, the utilitarian faces some strange counterexamples, such as "The Drifter Dilemma" (see Episode 12). But if we hold the principle of consent fixed, then mercy killing without consent is immoral.

Consent requires that a person have the cognitive ability to make moral decisions. For instance, children and mentally handicapped people cannot consent to medical procedures or take part in binding contracts; their guardians or surrogates must do that for them. In this episode of *Picket Fences*, Harold consents and, as far as we can tell, still has enough control over his faculties to do so. Nevertheless, in asking someone for help to choose between two lives, there remains a worry that the outside person cannot understand the issues clearly enough to make the best decision.

Do humans have the ability to sit in judgment on the value of someone else's life? We may think it is easy to say, "That person is in pain; I would never want to live like that." But are we therefore justified in taking that life from her? Even if she consents? This is the worry expressed by the US attorney. After getting Dr Brock to admit that she has a deep emotional investment in Harold, he says: "Well perhaps this is why we should not let doctors play God. Doctors are human, with human emotions."

But doctors are called on to make these decisions every day. Howard's attorney explains:

Before any transplant, medical committees convene to determine who's the best candidate. One guy gets the organ, the next guy loses out. Doctors make the call. We separate Siamese twins knowing that one is going to live and the other one's going to die. A person becomes vegetative, many times we pull the plug. Every single day, in every hospital across this country, doctors decide who lives and who doesn't. It's a reality. Well, here's another one. Howard and Kevin Buss are both dying. Howard can't be saved. But Kevin could be, if he could find a new heart. His father wants to give him his.

There are cases where doctors are forced to make decisions about who lives and who dies. But, interestingly, it is not clear whether this is one of them. The problem in this case is not the permissibility of suicide, but of enlisting the help of someone to commit it. It is not the permissibility of saving Kevin's life, but the permissibility of taking Howard's, even with his consent. Howard may be fully within his moral rights to take his own life. But it is still not clear that we have the right to enlist others in taking our own.

Of course, if we fall back on the individual rights argument from above, we might be able to argue that these rights also include the right to enter into fair contracts. If one of those fair contracts involves my death, it is not clear that any court has the right to stop it. If I am mentally competent and consent to my own death, and someone is willing to take something in compensation for carrying out my death, then it seems we have a fair contract. If I have the right to take my own life, it seems perfectly reasonable that I could extend this right to someone else. The worry, of course, is determining when such a contract has been reached fairly and when a murder has been committed. But this is an epistemic issue for courts to sort out. I may have a moral right to hire someone to kill me even if the courts do not recognize that right.

In his final decision, the judge invokes the principle of caution (see the "Pilot Episode"). Though it may seem simple to judge that one dying man can be sacrificed to save someone who might not die, the value of a human life can only be evaluated from a limited human perspective. And from within that scope, the judge perceives that Howard's life is valuable, not only to himself, but also to the community in general. With this shred of value left, the judge cannot choose to eliminate it for the sake of another person with a right to life. The value of one innocent person's life does not override that of another, though, in some tough cases, sometimes one must decide between two innocent people.

CASE STUDY 2: *Scrubs*, "My Jiggly Ball," season 5

AVAILABILITY: NetFlix, iTunes, YouTube

Scrubs is a comedy about working in the fictional teaching hospital, Sacred Heart. Doctor John "J.D." Dorian (Zach Braff), his best friend surgeon Chris Turk (Donald Faison), and fellow doctor Elliot Reed (Sarah Chalke) spend time daydreaming, playing games, and dating while tending to patients under the watchful but cantankerous eye of Dr Perry Cox (John C. McGinley) and avoiding the penny-pinching Chief of Medicine, Bob Kelso (Ken Jenkins).

This episode is indirectly about how the hospital treats two patients, Mr Morrison (Duane R. Shepard, Sr.) and Mr Franks (uncredited). Mr Morrison has a brain tumor and Dr Cox tells him that there is an experimental drug trial he will try to get him into. When Dr Kelso finds out that Mr Franks is rich, but before he finds out his condition, he tells J.D. and Cox: "Listen up, bozos. That gentleman over there is basically a cash piñata waiting to be whacked open. So how about someone diagnoses him so I can get my candy." Due to recent budgetary constraints, Kelso announces that he has to close the mobile prenatal unit. Ever the miser, he sees dollar signs when he looks at Mr Franks. Cox takes this as an opportunity to make a deal with Kelso: "I'll be glad to do it, Bob, if you'll do me a favor and put *my* patient, Mr Morrison, in that experimental drug trial." Kelso agrees and Cox runs some tests.

As it turns out, Mr Franks has the same type of brain tumor as Mr Morrison and there is only one spot left open in the drug trial. J.D. and Cox run to Mr Franks's room only to find what they expected – he is away at the drug trial, while Mr Morrison is still in his room. J.D. says, "I think we both knew that we couldn't change anything. Because given a choice between a rich guy and a poor guy, it was pretty obvious who Bob Kelso would put in the drug trial, and who he'd leave behind."

When Cox forces Kelso to face Mr Morrison, Kelso takes Cox aside and explains: "There was one spot open in the study. I gave it to the rich guy because with the money he's now donating, I can reopen the prenatal unit." Cox responds, "What really bothers me is that you can look in there, at John Morrison, a guy that you essentially gave a death sentence to, and just not care." Kelso just says, "It's not my job to care, Perry."

In the end, Mr Morrison dies, Mr. Franks gets the experimental treatment, and the mobile prenatal unit reopens. In J.D.'s final commentary, he notes: "As far as Bob Kelso goes, I know even some of the good things he does are for the wrong reasons. ... Still, I also know that I wouldn't want to have to make any of the decisions he makes."

Commentary: Should other people's happiness determine my medical care?

Aside from questions about whether to refuse care to patients because of a horrible condition for the sake of compassion, doctors are already allowed to make decisions that affect our lives that have nothing to do with our condition, but are determined by factors independent of us – including the well-being of others. Is this morally permissible?

Dr Cox is incensed that Dr Kelso would let a good person die just because he had less money than someone else. Cox cares deeply for each of his patients and cannot understand why Kelso seems so cold and indifferent to their plight. But what Cox doesn't seem to understand is that Kelso didn't let one person die *just* because he had less money. There were a number of moral considerations that figured into Kelso's decision.

Both patients have a right to life, and both are going to die without a successful new treatment. A new treatment is available that might be successful, but there is only room for one of the two patients. If you're the doctor, how do you decide which one? By not choosing one patient, you, in effect, condemn him to die. To be sure, the other patient might die, too, but he is at least given a chance. What do our moral theories have to contribute?

The Kantian is in quite a corner, here. Both patients are intrinsically valuable and the consequences of the decision cannot affect whether the decision should be made. But surely, we shouldn't do nothing and allow both to die. So, should the Kantian just flip a coin? Given the excellent consequences of putting the rich man in the trial (the prenatal unit reopens, so Kelso gets fame, so the hospital gets fame, so the hospital gets more resources), it would seem odd to suggest putting the poor guy in the trial. Since the Kantian cannot take consequences into account in moral decision-making, this case constitutes a problem for that theory.

On the other hand, a utilitarian can easily justify Kelso's decision. The consequences of putting the rich guy in the trial far outweigh the consequences of putting the poor guy in. Since both would die without the treatment, Kelso is not acting immorally toward Mr. Morrison. Not only will the hospital benefit from his donation along, perhaps, with any further treatment, should the trial prove successful, Kelso will be able to use this money to re-open the prenatal unit, which will positively contribute to the welfare of innumerable families.

Of course, the worry with the utilitarian theory is that it would seem to justify even immoral actions toward Mr Morrison. Imagine that, instead of both men having a certain disease, the rich man needs an organ or he will die, and none is available. The poor man, who, let's say, has no family or friends, has a different disease, one that is not life-threatening. As it happens, the poor man has an organ the rich man could use, though it would kill the poor man to take it. Nevertheless, if the rich man gets the transplant, all the same good consequences will ensue as they do in our *Scrubs* episode. It would seem that killing the poor man to reap the benefits of saving the rich man is consistent with a utilitarian theory of morality.

So, in this episode of *Scrubs*, it seems the utilitarian has a more intuitive answer to the dilemma than the Kantian. If the Kantian cannot overcome the problem of having arbitrarily to choose between the two, there may be reasons for doubting or modifying the theory.

"My Jiggly Ball," highlights ways in which doctors have control over our lives independently of our consent. There are some decisions doctors have to make about our lives that we cannot, even in principle, consent to. Which Siamese twin do we save when separating them? How many chemotherapy treatments until the patient dies from the chemo instead of the disease? How many milligrams of this drug can this particular patient handle without going into cardiac arrest? Is this vegetative state permanent or merely temporary? We cannot help doctors make these decisions (1) because we are not trained in medicine, and (2) because we have a vested interest in the outcome, which other moral considerations may override. Almost all the cancer doctors we have met or heard about have seemed more like Bob Kelso than Perry Cox. However, at least in this episode, it seems Kelso made the right decision.

STUDY QUESTIONS

1. In the Picket Fences case, Harold Buss consents to allow Dr Brock to take his life. Is consent enough to make it permissible for Dr Brock to kill Harold?

2. What worries does Harold's Alzheimer's raise for his ability to consent? If it undermines his ability to consent, is someone else morally responsible for making decisions for him? If so, could they even consent to his death?

3. Howard argues that, in allowing himself to be killed, he is dying with "dignity." How might this influence (that is, would it strengthen/ weaken) an argument for the moral permissibility of assisted suicide?

4. Why does Howard's attorney think that the fact that other doctors regularly make decisions about who is permitted to live and die should count as evidence in favor of allowing Howard to decide to die?
5. What does the judge mean when he says: "You're embraced by life. You're still made rich by it. And ... life continues to be made more rich by you"? How is this supposed to count as evidence in support of his ruling?
6. In the *Scrubs* case, in response to Perry's worry about his heartlessness, Kelso says, "It's not my job to care." Is this consistent or inconsistent with a Kantian perspective on morality? Explain your answer.
7. Does Kelso's desire to re-open the prenatal unit justify his giving the open spot in the drug trial to the rich patient over the poor patient? Why or why not? Which moral theory is more consistent with this decision?
8. Are there any additional considerations a Kantian could introduce in order to help make the decision between the rich patient and the poor patient? Are there any reasons for thinking that a contemporary Kantian could agree with Kelso's decision?
9. If you were in Perry's position, would you have acted differently? Why or why not? Is there any argument you would have given Kelso in attempt to change his mind?
10. If you were Mr Morrison's attorney, and you were asked to provide an argument as to why Mr Morrison, the poor patient, should be allowed the spot on the drug trial, what sort of argument might you offer? Which moral considerations would you highlight, if any?

ALTERNATIVE CASE STUDIES

1. *Law and Order*, "The Reaper's Helper," season 1
   (Is mercy killing morally permissible?)
2. *CSI: NY*, "What Schemes May Come," season 3
   (What are the social implications of the legal permissibility of assisted dying?)
3. *House, M.D.*, "Son of a Coma Guy," season 3
   (Is it morally permissible to talk a terminally ill person into committing suicide to save the life of another person?)

THE EPILOGUE: DOES TV ERODE OUR VALUES?

THE MORAL INFLUENCE OF TELEVISION

Sages and mothers have long noted that humans, especially young humans, are impressionable. It is supposed that the environment that one inhabits plays a large role in a child's behavioral and moral development. Jamie's mother used to tell him, "Garbage in, garbage out," implying that, whatever you expose yourself to will be reflected in your thoughts and

What's Good on TV?: Understanding Ethics Through Television, First Edition.
Jamie Carlin Watson and Robert Arp.
© 2011 Jamie Carlin Watson and Robert Arp. Published 2011 by Blackwell Publishing Ltd.

actions. And it's pretty obvious that Tony Soprano didn't become a mobster for the job security. Research into this claim has produced some support, as psychologists now tell us that about 50 percent of our behavioral tendencies are due to environmental pressures (see, for example, Alexander 2010). If this is correct, there is something to be said for keeping certain information found on TV and in other media such as film, games, books, etc. away from children until they are old enough to understand, evaluate, and appreciate or reject it.

Although such experiments are now deemed immoral (which goes a long way in supporting the idea that kids are impressionable), there is a famous experiment from the 1960s called the "Bobo doll experiment." In this experiment, several children watch a video where a person is beating the pulp out of one of those wobbly-but-won't-fall-down, plastic, blow-up toys with a clown drawn on it, called a "Bobo doll." Nowadays, you might see one with Batman, Spiderman, or The Joker drawn on it in the toy section of a department store. The person in the video beat the clown Bobo doll with a mallet, threw it to the floor, kicked it, flung it into the air, smacked it with balls, and did other nasty things. After the video, the children were placed in a room with identical clown Bobo dolls and other toys. Guess what happened? Some 88 percent of the children beat the pulp out of the Bobo doll in ways similar to the person in the video. Even some eight months later, 40 percent of the same children reproduced the violent behavior that they witnessed in the Bobo doll video (see Bandura 1962, 1975).

THE DEBATE OVER CENSORSHIP

Some have argued that TV sex and violence are directly responsible for cases of sex and violent crimes committed by kids in the real world. As a result, these same people want to see laws enacted that limit the production and sale of, or ban altogether, "rated M for Mature" kinds of TV shows, movies, books, and violent video games. A parody of this occurs on the show, *Family Guy*, where concerned mother, Lois, notes: "You gotta be careful about what you put on your network. You know how impressionable children are. Remember what happened after Chris [her son] saw Jackie Mason?" In a hilarious flashback, Chris goes around talking just like Jackie Mason (which is hilarious, but probably only if you're old enough to have seen Jackie Mason skits and bits).

Now, there seem to be individual cases where a sexual or violent TV show, game, or other form of media has been partially – note *partially* – influential in causing some kid to act out in the real world. Watch out all you Bobo dolls! But, can we draw the general conclusion that simulated sex and violence, even if viewed by kids, are bad for *all* kids, from evidence that supports the fact that they're bad for *some* kids? Further, should we ban these things altogether, even if kids view and engage them, especially since they are so popular for adults? Hmmm. (For discussions of violence in relation to TV, video games, movies, and the like in the media, see Grossman and Degaetano 1999; Thompson 2005; Kirsh 2006.)

So, there is a further question about the limits to which TV affects *adults* in their thinking, attitudes, and character. This is where the real debate comes in concerning *moral censorship*, which is the government-enforced suppression or removal of material in a society (usually through some law) that has been deemed morally objectionable or harmful to members of that society. Most of us realize that kids do, in fact, imitate much of what they see and much of what is done to them by other kids, parents, uncles, teachers, and other role models – positive or negative. So, most of us find no problem with censoring TV and other material so that kids don't experience it. Robert Arp edited book *South Park and Philosophy* (2006), but he would never let his 6-year old daughter read the book (because of the curse words alone!) or watch *South Park* episodes, for obvious reasons. But what about the adult citizens of some society? Should we censor what they watch? Besides the "kids watching adult programs problem," the effects of negative programming on adult citizens of some society is usually the basis for any kind of TV censorship in a particular culture.

A KANTIAN REASON NOT TO CENSOR

There is a long and strong tradition, going back to Immanuel Kant (see Episode 5), in which adults in a society are seen as autonomous, rational beings who are free to make choices for themselves, unimpeded by any coercion. Fundamental rights such as freedom of thought, respect for privacy, and the freedom to watch and do what one wants to without harming someone else are all viewed as traceable to Kant's claim that humans are rational and capable of action on moral reasons independently of external influence. The freedom to watch and do what one wants to without harming someone else is what is central here, and today this translates into: If adults watch horrible and crazy stuff on TV, as long as they *do not actually do* any of that horrible and crazy stuff out in the real world, it would be immoral to prevent them from watching it. There should not be any kind of censorship of TV or any other material for adults – no matter how graphic, grisly, grotesque, or gross – because they themselves should be respected as their own censors (see O'Neill 1990; Hill 1991; Korsgaard 1996; Madigan 1998).

CASE STUDY 1: *Family Guy*, "PTV," season 4

AVAILABILITY: **Netflix, iTunes**

The *Family Guy* episode, "PTV," expresses clearly the Kantian reason that censorship is immoral. In protest at the US Federal Communication Commission's (FCC) heightened censorship, the buffoon father of the Griffin family, Peter, starts his own television station, *PTV*, "[w]here you get to watch your favorite shows as nature intended them: with all the sex, violence, swearing, and farts intact." *PTV* includes quality, wholesome programming like "The Side Boob Hour," "Dogs Humping," and "Douchebags." When his wife Lois has had enough of this nonsense, she calls the FCC to shut *PTV* down. At one point the head of the FCC claims: "We're tired of you infecting people with your smut. This is an epidemic and it must be contained."

As his broadcasting equipment is being confiscated, Peter exclaims that, though the FCC can shut down *PTV*, they cannot keep people from being who they are. In response, the FCC decides to censor real life and starts by hovering over the Griffin family with blackout placards and air horns and forcing people to wear a device that converts all fart sounds into Steven Wright jokes (again, YouTube this). Lois finally concedes that Peter is right about the FCC when the censorship begins interfering with their sex life. So she and Peter and the family head to Washington, DC to confront Congress with the problem. The ban is finally lifted when Peter convinces Congress that all the monuments in Washington, DC somehow reflect the more base aspects of humanity: the Washington Monument looks like a penis, the Capitol Building looks like a large boob, and the Pentagon looks like an anus.

The satirical possibility that the FCC might actually try to censor someone's real life – even their sex life – should lead us to question the extent to which government is permitted to interfere in one's personal decisions. No adult wants to be treated like a child, being told what they can and cannot watch on TV by the government. Similarly, radio personality and "shock jock" Howard Stern has had his share of run-ins with the FCC, and he actually left terrestrial radio (regular radio) for satellite radio so that he could do all of the lusty, lurid, lewd, and lasciviously entertaining things he does. Thus, Kant, the writers of this *Family Guy* episode, and Howard Stern are all on the same page regarding the thought that, "Hey, I'm an adult, and not some kid; I have the right to watch whatever I want to watch on TV (or listen to on the radio)."

UTILITARIAN REASONS NOT TO CENSOR

Besides the Kantian reason that TV censorship is immoral for adults, there are a couple of utilitarian reasons that can be traced back to the work of John Stuart Mill, whose moral theory we explored in Episode 6. If you recall, according to the utilitarian moral theory, the consequences of actions for everyone involved become significant when making a moral decision. The rule is essentially this: if an action likely will bring about good consequences (pleasure, benefits, good results, etc.) for the person or persons affected over a longer period of time than any other possible decision, then that action is morally obligatory. On the other hand, if an action likely will bring about more bad consequences (pain, detriments, bad results, etc.) for the person or persons affected over a longer period of time, then that action is impermissible (see also Quinton 1989).

A utilitarian could offer at least two reasons that censorship is immoral. First, if the sex, violence, and other crazy stuff on TV brings a significant amount of pleasure to a society, and if this pleasure outweighs any of the negative consequences of watching this content, then by the utilitarian's calculus of "what brings the most pleasure to the most people," television should not be censored – period. If utilitarians are correct that people are motivated to pursue what they find most pleasurable, then the immense popularity of trashy, garbage-y TV shows constitutes a moral reason to not censor.

Second, a utilitarian might also argue that all the bad stuff on TV acts as a foil to real life, teaching folks lessons about how *not* to treat people. For example, there's a lot of lust on TV. Now, consider patterns of social development, like the proverbial "sowing of wild oats," courting rituals, rites of passage to adulthood. We might learn more about healthier forms of love by watching very real expressions of lust. This is nothing new, as we "hear it through the grapevine" that "there was this one guy who" or "this one gal who" was in a situation where his or her action caused an immense amount of heartache and suffering. We learn from their inappropriate behavior how to act appropriately. Watching lusty trash on TV – and trash of all kinds – then, could have the good consequence of teaching the multitude a moral lesson or forming our characters. In fact, this kind of "moral of the story" thinking has been the muse behind screenplays, staged dramas, epic poetry, and song since humans began producing such works. Think of stories in the Bible, the plays of Aristophanes, Aesop's Fables, Shakespeare's tragedies, Tolstoy's novels, or the show *The Hills* (though, we worry there is something wrong with including *The Hills* in a list that includes the Bible and Shakespeare). This is heavily dependent on empirical research. But, if it turns out that people make better moral decisions after watching other people fail miserably, the greater good of a moral education through smutty television may be worth the price of not censoring TV trash.

MORAL REASONS TO CENSOR

Are there any good reasons for thinking censorship is morally permissible? We have already seen reasons for thinking it is permissible for parents to censor what children watch. What if there are adults who, like children, do not have the capacity to make moral decisions for themselves?

Unfortunately, even after a person is legally an "adult," she may still act like a child. There is a genuine concern among some psychologists that many people do not, or cannot, achieve the capacity, envisioned by Kant, to understand and act on moral reasons. Philosophers and psychologists have noted for centuries that there are certain people in society who simply do not have this ability. Shouldn't these people, at least, be sheltered from the crazy stuff on TV and other media? If there were empirical evidence that people could not make moral decisions for themselves, then the Kantian reason against censorship would fail.

And, if there are a large number of people in a society who can't make Kantian-style moral decisions, and if the effects of TV violence on adults is similar to that in children, then the utilitarian argument against censorship becomes an argument *in favor of* censorship. If the negative stuff on TV and other media are a major source of violent or sexually deviant imitations for many in a society, then, given that these are negative consequences, the utilitarian would say, "Ban the garbage on TV to promote peace and harmony in our society!"

Therefore, whether the Kantian and the utilitarian theories support or reject censorship depends on certain facts about people. Are people able to make their own moral decisions independently of external stimuli? If they are, censorship is morally impermissible – the Kantian moral agent will not be affected by it, and the utilitarian moral agent will watch whatever shows produce more pleasure and less pain. And, if people cannot make their own moral decisions independently of external stimuli, and if watching certain shows leads to negative consequences, censorship is morally permissible – the Kantian moral agent doesn't have the capacity to care and the utilitarian moral agent will likely be happier.

There may be another reason that censorship is morally permissible that is independent of any of these considerations. Recall the virtue ethics theory of Aristotle (see Episode 7). The virtue ethicists' central idea is that, if one has a virtuous character, then not only will one likely perform morally right actions, but also these actions likely will have good consequences (see MacIntyre 1984). And, after all, we want not only to perform right actions (Kant's deontology) and actions that have good consequences (Mill's utilitarianism), we also want to be *virtuous persons*. You can get a demon to do the right thing, and that right thing may lead to good consequences; however, he is still a demon.

Followers of Aristotle see virtue as a good habit whereby one fosters a kind of balance in one's character. The idea is to promote the "not too much" and "not too little" – the "just right" – in our characters so that our actions and reactions to situations reflect this hitting of a mean between two extremes. The virtuous person has cultivated the kind of character whereby she knows how to act and react in the right way, at the right time, in the right manner, and for the right reasons in each moral decision she encounters. Don't go rashly into war, but don't run away scared either; don't give away all your money, but don't be miserly either; don't eat six pieces of cake or no cake at all, just have one small piece; and so on.

However, a primary way in which one cultivates a virtuous character is through *watching other virtuous people* and choosing actions that are conducive to building that virtuous character. One need not experience, or even witness, vicious behaviors; one need only witness virtuous behaviors and then act virtuously oneself. This makes sense, since there are many horrible actions we need not actually experience or commit to know that they are horrible – for example, murder, rape, and fraud. Given that watching others perform positive actions leads to virtuous characters (actions that are honest, courageous, prudential, generous, and respectful, to name just a few), it could be argued that censorship on witnessing certain kinds of vicious behaviors is justified from a virtue ethics perspective.

To determine whether this is a sufficient reason for censoring television, we would need to understand what constitutes virtuous behavior and why. If the reasons turn out to be deontological or utilitarian, then we can refer to our arguments above. If there is some additional, independent reason, this would need to be defended.

EXPLOITATION, OBJECTIFICATION, AND TV

Let's assume, for the sake of argument, that censorship of adults by the government is immoral – for either deontological or utilitarian reasons. There may yet be things that should not be portrayed on television. For example, murder is generally considered immoral. If someone happened to film a murder, it seems wrong to think that it might be portrayed on television. This is not an argument against watching it – if it's on television, given our assumption that censorship is immoral, we have every right to watch it. But it doesn't seem like it should even be on television. But why?

Some argue that certain images are exploitative. "Exploitation" is the using or taking advantage of some person or persons by another person or persons, in a way that is unjust. It's unjust because the exploit*er* gets the majority, or all, of the pleasure, benefits, good results, etc., while the exploit*ed* gets minimal or no pay-off. Obvious examples include various forms of slavery, sweatshops, and sex-shopping, where slave owner, sweatshop owner, or pimp is the exploiter, while slave, sweatshop worker, or prostitute is the exploited.

Others argue that some images are objectifying. "Objectification," in this context, means treating a human like an object, rather than as a moral equal. This has an obvious connection with exploitation in that the exploited is usually objectified. When a villain or jerk on a TV show uses someone for sex, or to get information, or to climb the corporate ladder, the person being used in that way is being treated like an object. Now, most of us think that exploitation and objectification are wrong, but *why* are they wrong? We can point to three reasons based in the work of Kant, Mill, and Aristotle.

As we have discussed already in Episode 5, followers of Immanuel Kant ground moral decision-making in the fact that persons are rational beings, capable of making their own informed and free decisions. In this sense, persons are *autonomous* beings who not only have an innate worth and dignity that ought to be respected, but also must be treated as ends in themselves and never used as means to some end. In other words, because they are rational, autonomous beings, persons are unique in having an *intrinsic* value (as ends) and not an *instrumental* value (as means to some end) like some object, tool, thing, or instrument to be used, manipulated, or exploited in any way.

From this perspective, moral decisions are those decisions where a person is treated as an end, and immoral decisions are those where someone is treated as a mere instrument or means to an end. Characters on TV constantly are portrayed as having instrumental value, to be used like mere things. For example, a basic element of the show, *Survivor*, is that contestants need to use one another to ultimately try to be the lone survivor who wins a million bucks.

A second reason not to exploit and objectify is grounded in Mill's utilitarianism. If consequences are the key to determining whether exploitation and objectification are morally wrong for the utilitarian, then we can see that treating persons as objects has negative ramifications and, hence, is morally unacceptable. Think of all of the instances of slavery throughout human history where one group of persons has been subjugated by another group, and all of the negative consequences of such horrible situations. Or, think of all of the instances of totalitarian regimes – like Stalin's Soviet Union or Hitler's Third Reich – where persons were tortured, tormented, displaced from their homes, manipulated, and murdered all for the greater "good" of some state or ideal. Further, think of the consequences to our communities of treating women or men like sex objects, the way in which this is done in TV shows, advertising, movies, and other media. Such objectification has been linked to violence against women, date-rape, eating disorders, and a general disrespect for the sanctity of intimate relationships (see the resources, videos, and articles at www.vawnet.org; also Barry 1995; Dwyer 1995; Tessman 2001). These examples of slavery, the Soviet Union, and sex – where persons are treated as objects – have yielded negative consequences for majorities of persons. Hence, on utilitarian grounds, one can argue that these forms of exploitation and objectification are immoral and should be condemned.

Third, there is the virtue ethics view inspired by Aristotle and his followers that sees morally right actions as stemming from virtuous characters. Here, objectification would be considered immoral because of its stemming from, and contribution to, a non-virtuous (vicious) character.

Virtue ethicists have a general list of virtues, including honesty, courage, prudence, generosity, integrity, affability, and respect, to name just a few. Respect is the key virtue for our purposes here, and several virtue ethicists have argued that objectification stems from a disordered or unbalanced character. The person who has cultivated respect for persons in her/his character naturally will not objectify another person. When one exploits a person or treats a person as an object, one empties another of their intrinsic dignity, value, and worth, affecting both the one doing the exploiting/objectifying and the one being exploited or objectified. In effect, the problem lies in the psychological ill-effects of treating another as less than a person (see Friedman 1993; Andrew 2001; Tessman 2001; Brake 2003).

Reality TV and real exploitation and objectification

TV shows and other media that present *fictional* characters exploiting and objectifying other fictional people are one thing; TV shows that *actually* exploit and objectify people are another thing altogether. In fictional shows, exploitation is intentional and obvious. But when real people are involved, it is not always clear whether someone is being exploited. Especially in cases where people consent to participate in the show – in particular, game shows like *Survivor* and *Wipe Out*.

Most people who participate in reality television are compensated for their time. But is this compensation make up for the fact that, technically, they are being exploited for placing their lives in front of the camera? Which measurement could determine what counts as enough? The same problem applies outside the television studio. Who determines how much someone should pay a clothing maker in Indonesia? Fifty cents a day would be far too little in the US. But is it too little to pay in Indonesia? We are not in a position to say, and we don't know whether that's the only job available there. It may be an excellent thing to earn fifty cents a day in some countries.

Despite these difficulties, there are a few clear cases where we can appeal to moral principles and judge that an action is exploitative. These primarily involve children and the mentally handicapped. Consider the reality show *Toddlers & Tiaras*.

CASE STUDY 2: *Toddlers & Tiaras* (any episode)

AVAILABILITY: clips available on Discovery.com and YouTube

Toddlers & Tiaras chronicles the life and times of parents who place their children on the US toddler beauty pageant competition circuit. Toddlers are dressed up to look like little dolls or adults and engage in performances of their various talents. Their performances can be cute and child-like or sexual and adult-like. These performances can lead parents to say either, "Aw, how cute!" and "What a cute little lady!" or "That's disgusting and wrong!" and "A toddler has no business wearing make-up, being in high heels, and being paraded around onstage!"

With respect to *Toddlers & Tiaras*, it could be argued that exploitation and objectification occur in the following ways:

1. The kids are exploited by their parents insofar as it is really the *parents'* desire for success, fame, and fortune that effectively coerces these kids into competing – a competition which negatively impacts psychological development. So, the kids are being exploited by their own parents, which many of us find *doubly* immoral. Also, there are plenty of instances – several of which are displayed on the show itself – where a child does not want to engage in competition, but is coaxed, manipulated, or even forced to compete anyway by her parent.
2. The parents and the kids are exploited by the producers of the show and the TV network itself insofar as the producers and network not only (a) air the trials and tribulations of the parents and kids for all the world to see, but also (b) generate monetary benefits that always *far* outweigh what the parents and kids are receiving as compensation for doing the show in the first place.
3. The advertisers who support the show and network could be considered exploiters as well, since they stand to gain huge monetary benefits from the viewers who watch the trials and tribulations of the parents and kids.

One common response to these objections is that "My kid *wants* to be in the pageant, and I don't force her. The moment she does not want to do this anymore is the moment we'll stop competing." Rob heard this kind of response first-hand from the mother of a would-be child actor, as the two were on their way to Hollywood for "little Ry-Ry's" (the kid's name was Ryan) auditions.

The problem with this response is that it assumes the child has the mental capacity to make morally informed decisions. Not even Kant thought that! Given the incredible emotional and psychological influence that a parent has over a child, entering a child into pageants, sports, plays, or cub scouts is effectively a parental decision for which parents are responsible for the consequences. As a parent you have the moral responsibility to do only what is in your child's best interests. Children do not know what is in their best interests (and parents may not, either, but they are responsible for not knowing – the children are not). Therefore, this response grossly misses its target, and thus does not justify the exploitation of a child that is associated with child beauty pageants.

Reasons to exploit or objectify

Exploiting kids is one thing, and relatively easy to identify; exploiting *knowing and willing adults* is another, and much more difficult to identify. This is where the arguments concerning reality TV and exploitation/ objectification become complicated. Adults should know better, right?

The show *Survivor* comes to mind as one of the more obvious examples of reality TV whereby a person is encouraged to exploit, use, objectify, manipulate, emotionally harm, and/or psychologically harm another person just to win a competition (plus a million dollars, but put that aside). And *Jerry Springer* is an obvious example of a show whereby the producers of the show, the network, and the advertisers stand to benefit from the misery of the show's participants. However, believe it or not, there are actually a couple of arguments that fully rational (and apparently uncoerced) people offer in defense of the moral permissibility of self-exploitation.

First, some post-Kantian thinkers have made a slight adjustment to Kant's system. Since a person's innate value is tied to rational autonomy, some Kantians argue that what is most significant in making a moral decision is whether a person's "autonomy," that is, *freedom in decision-making*, has been respected (see Hill 1991; Korsgaard 1996; Madigan 1998). The word *autonomy* is made up of two Greek words meaning "self" (*auto*) and "law" (*nomos*), and refers to beings that can act independently of outside influences. They are "self-ruling" and their decisions should be respected. The idea here is that if a fully rational person chooses to engage in some action – as long as the action does not harm anyone else – then it is morally permissible for that person to make the decision, even if the decision puts that person in the position of being exploited or objectified by another person or group of persons. These philosophers hold, unlike Kant, that there are no duties to yourself that cannot be overridden by yourself.

As examples, think of fully rational adults who join the military knowing they may be sacrificed for the sake of that nation's war. Or, think of persons who are hired at large corporations with full knowledge that the goal of the company is to make money, and that they may lose their jobs in a down-sizing event in order to keep the corporation solvent. This is also part of the classical liberal argument that prostitution should be legalized everywhere. It is perfectly morally permissible for one rational adult to sell sex to another as long as there is no deceit, coercion, or harm in the transaction. Finally, think of reality TV show participants who not only get paid for being on the show, but willingly participate in it, knowing full well that they will be used, manipulated, objectified, and/or exploited.

In other words, as long as these fully rational folks all freely and autonomously agree to engage in these behaviors, then there is nothing morally wrong in their decision-making. In fact, these same folks might argue that to deny a person the freedom to choose to be of use to, exploited by, or objectified by someone else *would itself be immoral* because such a denial violates a person's autonomy as a rational, wholly-free decision-maker (see Garry 1993; Madigan 1998; Schwarzenbach 1998).

Besides this Kantian justification for exploitation and objectification, there is another reason to defend self-exploitation that is derived from a version of virtue ethics – though not the virtue ethics of Aristotle, which cherishes virtues such as honesty, courage, prudence, generosity, integrity, affability, and respect. Some philosophers have argued for a set of virtues that differ significantly from Aristotle's, including social and political "power" prominently in their list. These thinkers link certain types of exploitation and objectification with psychological, social, and economic power, and conclude that exploitation can enhance an agent's virtue (see Whelehan 1995; Hohmann 1998).

Philosophers like Thomas Hobbes (1588–1679), Niccolo Machiavelli (1469–1527), and Friedrich Nietzsche (1844–1900) have argued that power can be cultivated in one's character and, if exercised in the right way, can be conducive to a well-balanced character (see Hobbes 1982; Machiavelli 1984; Nietzsche 1966, 1967). Here, power can be understood in the context of a dominating master/slave relationship. Different people have different psychological dispositions, an idea that can be traced back to Plato's *Republic*. Some people have the disposition to be in power, control others, or rule, while others have the disposition to be powerless, controlled by others, and ruled. A well-balanced character is cultivated by a person being what he is naturally disposed to be. To be something you are not would be the result of a disordered character, and also conducive to forming a disordered character.

This being the case, a master exhibits the virtue of power and rightly subjugates, controls, and objectifies those persons who would be considered as powerless slaves. In fact, all of this exploitation and objectification is right and good since masters are fulfilling their natural station in life as exploiters/objectifiers, while the folks being used are fulfilling their natural stations in life as slaves and the ones being exploited/objectified. So, if you do not have the skills to become a professional basketball player, for example, then don't bother beating yourself up – you'll never make it as a pro and, instead, will only find misery. In the same way, if you are naturally a master or a slave, then just go with it; be *who* you are as a master or a slave.

However, this may be where the power-master virtue ethics perspective of Hobbes et al. relies too much upon what *is* the case, and neglects what *ought* to be the case (recall the naturalistic fallacy from the "Pilot Episode"). It seems that, even if you are destined to be slave-like, people around you should not treat you as such (and someone could cite Aristotelian virtue-ethical, as well as Kantian or utilitarian, reasons for this). To help decide this issue, we might honestly consider these four questions:

1. As a fully rational and autonomous person, may I treat myself or another fully rational and autonomous person as a means, rather than as end in her or himself? (The Kantian perspective)
2. What kinds of consequences will result for other persons affected by my action, and for me, if I do decide to treat myself or another fully rational and autonomous person as a means, rather than as an end in him or herself? (The utilitarian perspective)
3. Do I want to foster a virtue in myself, my kids, my family, my community, and/or in my world whereby others are seen as persons worthy of respect, fundamentally equal to myself, making it such that one person is not permitted to objectify another person? (The Aristotelian virtue ethics perspective)
4. Do I want to foster a virtue in myself, my kids, my family, my community, and/or in my world whereby certain others are seen as emptied of the intrinsic dignity, value, and worth afforded to me as one of the lucky persons who happens to be endowed with a naturally powerful disposition, such that I am permitted to objectify another unlucky person? (The power-master virtue ethics perspective)

Of course, these questions are loaded – we want you to agree with us that exploitation is a morally bad thing, so we have included phrases with that rhetorical flourish. But our hope, ultimately, is to make clear the moral implications of each view for objectification, so that all our decisions will be better informed. It seems that, if (1) and (2) do not halt us in our tracks and get us to think twice about exploiting and objectifying ourselves or another, then (3) and (4) may give us pause to consider what kind of person we would become if we continually exploit and objectify.

REALITY TV AND PSYCHOLOGICAL HARM

We do both have to admit that, like most other people on the planet, we love to see people placed in comical situations where they are being filmed without knowing it. We all love a good prank. There was a TV show called *Candid Camera* where people were "pranked" by being placed in unusual and often uncomfortable situations. At the end of a segment, usually at the height of confusion, frustration, discomfort, or humiliation on the part of the person pranked, the show's creator, Alan Funt, would reveal himself and say, "Smile, you're on *Candid Camera*!" This was followed by the person being pranked expressing either shock, relief, laughter, or some combination thereof. This show probably might be the earliest ancestor of reality TV, since it started in the late 1940s (and ran on and off until 1996).

   Was *Candid Camera* exploitative? People who were pranked on *Candid Camera* were not physically harmed, and if there was psychological or emotional harm, it was minimal. (There was one case where someone sued *Candid Camera*, and won, for having received a bruise on the leg after having fallen off of a conveyor belt at an airport.) However, people were entertained at their expense and because they were not in on it – they could not consent to be pranked, in principle, otherwise it wouldn't be a genuine prank. Coercion and deception are essential features of exploitation, so even if they caused no residual harm, even *Candid Camera* might cross moral boundaries.

From Candid Camera *to* Punk'd

But now take a show like *Candid Camera* and up the intensity. Consider *Punk'd*, the Ashton Kutcher-hosted gem where celebrities are placed in grossly uncomfortable, sometimes traumatic, situations culminating in Kutcher revealing himself and the prank. The show ran from 2003 to 2007 on MTV, but full episodes can still be found on MTV's website. *Punk'd* is just above *Candid Camera* on the intensity scale. In episode 807, season 8, Ashton punks rap star Pitbull. Pitbull goes to a boys' and girls' club to hand out free turkeys to the needy on Thanksgiving, but Ashton tricks him into thinking he has given out spoiled turkeys to children, one of whom (an actor) begins crying uncontrollably because he doesn't want to give up the turkey for his large family. Workers at the club try to convince Pitbull to trick the boy into giving up the turkey. Thankfully, Pitbull refuses to trick the boy. But the ensuing argument becomes very traumatic when, after they get the turkey away from him, the boy starts screaming, "They're trying to kill me!" over and over. All the tension is relieved when Pitbull discovers he's been punk'd, but there is a worry that harm might last long after the trick. In addition, there may be some violation of Pitbull's intrinsic moral value, as the producers use him as a means to the audience's end, namely, entertainment.

As a spoof of the intensity of *Punk'd*, and the potential harm that might ensue, *Saturday Night Live* did a skit called "Pranksters" featuring Christopher Walken (season 28, available through NetFlix and iTunes). In the skit, Walken plays Larry Hobson, who pranks a guy at his work named Phil (who always takes Larry's parking spot) by jumping out from behind Phil's car and beating him to death with a rusty tire iron. The host of the show is completely shocked, and when the host expresses some criticism, Larry warns him that he may "prank" him if he's not careful. It's a must-see, and it causes us to question the moral permissibility of placing people in an apparently real-life situation in which they can't, in principle, consent, and where they experience serious discomfort through a prank.

From Punk'd *to* Scare Tactics

And finally, ramp up the intensity one more notch, and consider a show like *Scare Tactics*, where unsuspecting victims are placed in terrifying situations that cause them to beg, plead, swear, scream, cry, and even punch and kick – all while being filmed by multiple hidden cameras. Rob has to admit that he thought the pilot episode was one of the coolest things he had ever seen on TV at the time. He enjoyed it, and gleefully relayed every detail to his wife after he saw the show. By the end of the second episode, however, he was thinking, "This is not right."

A victim on the show is lured to some location, invited there by people he or she knows (friends or even relatives, if you can believe it!), where there are actors who are involved in setting up some frightening scene for the unsuspecting victim. Then, with the help of the actors, the victim experiences some kind of terrifying event such as a horrible accident, a violent crime, or even some ghostly presence or strange monster. Analogous to "Smile, you're on *Candid Camera*," at the very height of terror, one of the actors asks the victim, "Are you scared?" The victim says, "Yes," and the actor always responds, "You shouldn't be! You're on *Scare Tactics!*"

As we hinted above, in the very midst of these scare tactics the victims not only are psychologically and emotionally traumatized – who wouldn't be, given that they *truly believe* that they are in harm's way? – but they will also resort to swearing at, begging and pleading with, and punching or kicking the actors. In one scene, a "psycho hitchhiker" actor is picked up at night by three people – a girl, her brother, and the girl's friend – who are supposedly "driving to a rave in the middle of the desert." The brother is the unsuspecting victim in the back seat next to his sister who has set him up, and when the hitchhiker sitting in the front seat pulls out a knife and threatens to kill everyone in the car, the brother commences whaling on him from the back seat until his sister's friend reveals that he's on *Scare Tactics*. Other *Scare Tactics* episodes include: "Buried Alive," "Camp Kill," "Flatline," "Lab Spill," "Serial Killer," "Hellride," "Body in Trunk," "Chainsaw Attack," "Massacre under the House," and "Home Invasion."

The titles themselves indicate the terror involved, and one can easily imagine the psychological and emotional trauma that these people experience. Psychologists tell us that such terror has the potential to haunt people in their dreams, and may even alter parts of their emotional response mechanisms to perfectly normal stimuli. Now, there is a basic moral principle that says something like, "One should not needlessly harm someone; indeed, one should prevent needless harm, if possible." Utilitarians hold this principle as the fundamental criterion of the moral permissibility of an action. Deontologists often argue that it is a *prima facie* duty.

One could easily argue that a show like *Scare Tactics* not only violates this principle, but, given what was said earlier in this Episode, also exploits and objectifies the show's participants for the viewer's pleasure, as well as the producers', network's, and advertisers' monetary benefits. These are the reasons why Rob was thinking, "This is not right," by the end of the second episode.

THAT'S ALL FOLKS!

TV is a powerful medium, not only for entertainment, but also for communicating influential ideas. We hope we have used it to enhance both your moral and your cultural education. There are many other issues we could have discussed, not least of which is whether we should censor violent or graphic events in the real world recorded by news reporters, such as shootings, auto accidents, explosions, and various natural disasters, and whether it is permissible to use television shows to disseminate propaganda. But in the end, we hope we've provided you with a few tools to clarify and inform any moral question or decision you face. May all your TV viewing – whether partially censored or censor-free – be happy!

STUDY QUESTIONS

1. What is the point of the Bobo doll experiment? How might the findings of this experiment influence the debate over censorship?
2. Define *moral censorship*. What reasons might a Kantian offer against censorship?

3. Watch a few episodes of the show *Family Guy* and then complete the following exercises:
   (i) Should *Family Guy* itself be censored? If so, what are your reasons? If not, what are your reasons? Should PTV shows like "The Side Boob Hour" and "Dogs Humping" be censored? If so, what are your reasons? If not, what are your reasons?
   (ii) In the *Family Guy* episode "PTV" the family dog, Brian, claims that "responsibility lies with the parents. There are plenty of things that are much worse for children than television." (Yes, Brian can talk.) First, given Brian's claim that "responsibility lies with the parents," lay out what you think Brian's argument is for why we should not censor TV. Second, a fallacy is an error in reasoning whereby a conclusion does not follow from a premise in an argument, but the speaker intends the conclusion to follow. If part of Brian's argument includes these claims, "responsibility lies with the parents. There are plenty of things that are much worse for children than television," then there is fallacious thinking involved. Can you explain the fallacy?
   (iii) Act like a Kantian and mount an argument for why PTV should not be censored.
   (iv) Act like a utilitarian and put forward two reasons why PTV should not be censored.
   (v) Now, give two reasons why PTV should be censored.
   (vi) Of the arguments you constructed for (iii), (iv), and (v), which do you find most compelling? Why?
4. What is the virtue ethical reason to censor spoken about in this Episode?
5. What are three ways one could argue that exploitation and objectification are committed by the show *Toddlers & Tiaras*?

REFERENCES

Adams, Robert M. 1996. "Ethics and the Commands of God," in Michael Peterson et al. (eds.), *Philosophy of Religion: Selected Readings* (New York: Oxford University Press), pp. 527–536.

Alexander, Rudolph 2010. *Human Behavior in the Social Environment: A Macro, National and International Perspective* (Thousand Oaks, CA: Sage Publications).

Andrew, Barbara 2001. "Angels, Rubbish Collectors, and Pursuers of Erotic Joy: The Image of Ethical Women," in Peggy DesAutels and Joanne Waugh (eds.), *Feminists Doing Ethics* (Lanham, MD: Rowman and Littlefield), pp. 119–134.

Aristotle 2001. *Nicomachean Ethics*, in Richard McKeon (ed.), *The Basic Works of Aristotle* (New York: The Modern Library), pp. 935–1126. (Abbreviated as *NE* in text references.)

Arp, Robert (ed.) 2006. *South Park and Philosophy: You Know, I Learned Something Today* (Oxford: Wiley-Blackwell).

Baicker, Katherine 2004. "The Budgetary Repercussions of Capital Convictions," *Advances in Economic Analysis and Policy* 4/1 (B.E. Press).

Bandura Albert 1962. *Social Learning Through Imitation* (Lincoln, NE: University of Nebraska Press).

Bandura, Albert 1975. *Social Learning and Personality Development* (New York: Holt, Rinehart & Winston).

Barras, Colin 2007. "Lobster Pain May Prick Diners' Consciences," *New Scientist* 2629.

Barry, Kathleen 1995. *The Prostitution of Sexuality* (New York: New York University Press).

Baxter, William 2008. "People or Penguins," in Lewis Vaughn (ed.), *Doing Ethics: Moral Reasoning and Contemporary Issues* (New York: W. W. Norton & Co.), pp. 370–373; originally published in *People or Penguins: The Case for Optimal Pollution* (New York: Columbia University Press, 1974).

Bedau, Hugo 1970. "Deterrence and the Death Penalty: A Reconsideration," *Journal of Criminal Law, Criminology and Police Science 61/4*: 539–548.

Bedau, Hugo 2010. "Punishment," *Stanford Encyclopedia of Philosophy*; http://plato.stanford.edu/entries/punishment/.

Benedict, Ruth 2003. "A Defense of Ethical Relativism," a selection from "Anthropology and the Abnormal," in William F. Lawhead (ed.), *Philosophical Questions* (New York: McGraw Hill), pp. 420–426; originally published in *The Journal of General Psychology*, 10 (1934).

Brake, Elizabeth 2003. "Sexual Objectification and Kantian Ethics," *Proceedings and Addresses of the American Philosophical Association, 76*: 120–131.

Brandt, Richard B. 1982. Excerpts from *Ethical Theory: The Problems of Normative and Critical Ethics*, in Raziel Abelson and Marie-Louise Friquegnon (eds.), *Ethics for Modern Life*, 2nd edn. (New York: St Martin's Press), pp. 240–251; originally published 1959 (Englewood Cliffs, NJ: Prentice-Hall).

Callahan, Daniel 2009. "Aging and the Ends of Medicine," in John Arthur and Steven Scalet (eds.), *Morality and Moral Controversies*, 8th edn. (Upper Saddle River, NJ: Pearson/Prentice Hall), pp. 272–278; originally published in *Annals of the New York Academy of Sciences* 530 (June 15, 1988).

Cooper, John M. (ed.) 1997. *Plato: Complete Works* (Indianapolis: Hackett Publishing).

De Silva, Lily 2001. "The Buddhist Attitude Towards Nature," in Louis P. Pojman (ed.), *Environmental Ethics* (Stamford, CT: Wadsworth, 2001), pp. 256–260; originally published in K. Sandell (ed.), *Buddhist Perspectives on the Ecocrisis* (Sri Lanka: Buddhist Publication Society, 1987).

Doyle, Arthur Conan 2010. *The Sign of the Four* (London: Bibliolis); originally published in 1890.

Driver, Julia 2007. *Ethics: The Fundamentals* (Malden, MA: Blackwell), p. 63. The original "drifter case" was constructed by H. J. McCloskey in "A Non-Utilitarian Approach to Punishment," *Inquiry* 8 (1965): 249–263.

Dwyer, Susan 1995. *The Problems of Pornography* (Belmont, CA: Wadsworth).

Feister, John Bookser 1999. "The Pope Visits St Louis," *St Anthony Messenger*; http://www.americancatholic.org/Messenger/Apr1999/feature1.asp#F6.

Friedman, Marilyn 1993. *What Are Friends For? Feminist Perspectives on Personal Relationships and Moral Theory* (Ithaca, NY: Cornell University Press).

Garry, Ann 1993. "Pornography and Respect for Women," in John Arthur (ed.), *Morality and Moral Controversies* (Upper Saddle River, NJ: Prentice-Hall), pp. 395–421.

Gay-Williams, J. 2008. "The Wrongfulness of Euthanasia," in Lewis Vaughn (ed.), *Doing Ethics: Moral Reasoning and Contemporary Issues* (New York: W. W. Norton & Co.); originally published 1979.

Geisler, Norman 1989. *Christian Ethics: Options and Issues* (Grand Rapids, MI: Baker Books).

George, Robert P. and Gerard V. Bradley 1995. "Marriage and the Liberal Imagination," *Georgetown Law Journal 84*: 301–320.

Grossman, Dave and Gloria Degaetano 1999. *Stop Teaching Our Kids to Kill: A Call to Action Against TV, Movie and Video Game Violence* (New York: Crown).

Haag, Ernest van den 1992. "Refuting Reiman and Nathanson," in Steven Luper-Foy and Curtis Brown (eds.), *The Moral Life* (Fort Worth, TX: Harcourt Brace Jovanovich College Publishers, 1992), pp. 350–353.

Harman, Gilbert 2000. *Explaining Value and Other Essays in Moral Philosophy* (Oxford: Clarendon Press).

Hill, Thomas 1991. *Autonomy and Self Respect* (New York: Cambridge University Press).

Hobbes, Thomas 1982. *Leviathan* (New York: Penguin Books, 1982).

Hohmann, Marti 1998. "Prostitution and Sex-Positive Feminism," in James Elias, Vern Bullough, Veronica Elias, and Gwen Brewer (eds.), *Prostitution: On Whores, Hustlers, and Johns* (New York: Prometheus Books), pp. 354–360.

Holmes, Arthur F. 1984. *Ethics: Approaching Moral Decisions* (Downers Grove, IL: InterVarsity Press).

The Holy Bible 2001. *English Standard Version* (Wheaton, IL: Crossway Bibles).

Hume, David 2006. *A Treatise of Human Nature*, ed. David Fate Norton and Mary J. Norton (Oxford: Clarendon Press).

Hurka, Thomas 1982. "Rights and Capital Punishment," *Dialogue* 21; repr.in Michael D. Bayles and Kenneth Henley (eds.), *Right Conduct: Theories and Applications*, 2nd edn. (New York: Random House, 1989), pp. 210–217.

Jaffa, Harry V. 2004. *Original Intent and The Framers of the Constitution: A Disputed Question* (Washington, DC: Regnery Publishing).

Johnson, Robert 2008. "Kant's Moral Philosophy," *Stanford Encyclopedia of Philosophy;* http://plato.stanford.edu/entries/kant-moral/.

Kant, Immanuel 1964. *Groundwork of the Metaphysics of Morals*, trans. and ed. H. J. Paton (New York: Harper & Row); originally published 1785.

Kant, Immanuel 1996. *The Metaphysics of Morals*, ed. Mary Gregor (Cambridge: Cambridge University Press); originally published 1797.

Kant, Immanuel 2008. "The Fundamental Principles of the Metaphysic of Morals," trans. Thomas K. Abbott (1873), in John Arthur and Steven Scalet (eds.), *Morality and Moral Controversies: Readings in Moral, Social, and Political Philosophy*, 8th edn. (Upper Saddle River, NJ: Prentice Hall), pp. 56–65.

Kirsh, Steven 2006. *Children, Adolescents and Media Violence: A Critical Look at the Research* (Sage Publications).

Korsgaard, Christine 1996. *The Sources of Normativity* (New York: Cambridge University Press).

Land, Kenneth C., Raymond H. C. Teske, Jr., and Hui Zheng 2009. "The Short-Term Effects of Executions on Homicides: Deterrence, Displacement, or Both?" *Criminology* 47/4: 1009–1043.

Levitt, Steven and Stephen Dubner 2005. *Freakonomics* (New York: William Morrow).

Lewis, C. S. 1996. *Mere Christianity* (New York: Touchstone Books); originally published 1942–4.

Lewis, C. S. 2001. "Divine Goodness" (ch. 3) and "Human Pain" (ch. 6), in *The Problem of Pain* (New York: HarperCollins); originally published 1940.

Macedo, Stephen 1995. "Homosexuality and the Conservative Mind," *Georgetown Law Journal 84*: 261–300.

Machiavelli, Niccolo 1984. *The Prince*, trans. Daniel Donno (New York: Bantam Classics).

MacIntyre, Alasdair 1984. *After Virtue*, 2nd edn. (Notre Dame, IN: University of Notre Dame Press).

Mackie J. L. 1977. *Ethics: Inventing Right and Wrong* (Harmondsworth: Penguin).

Madigan, Timothy 1998. "The Discarded Lemon: Kant, Prostitution and Respect for Persons," *Philosophy Now 21*: 14–16.

Mansfield, Harvey C. 1993. "Saving Liberalism from Liberals," *The Harvard Crimson*, November 8; http://www.thecrimson.com/article/1993/11/8/saving-liberalism-from-liberals-pbmby-friend/?print=1.

Marquis, Don 2008. "Why Abortion is Immoral," in Lewis Vaughn (ed.), *Doing Ethics: Moral Reasoning and Contemporary Issues* (New York: W. W. Norton & Co.), pp. 192–204; originally published in *The Journal of Philosophy*, 86/4 (April 1989).

McNaughton, David 1988. *Moral Vision: An Introduction to Ethics* (Oxford: Blackwell Publishers).

Mill, John Stuart 2002a. *On Liberty*, in J. B. Schneewind and Dale E. Miller (eds.), *The Basic Writings of John Stuart Mill* (New York: The Modern Library: 2002); originally published 1969.

Mill, John Stuart 2002b. *Utilitarianism*, in J. B. Schneewind and Dale E. Miller (eds.), *The Basic Writings of John Stuart Mill* (New York: The Modern Library, 2002).

Moore, G. E. 1993. *Principia Ethica*, rev. and ed. Thomas Baldwin (Cambridge: Cambridge University Press); originally published 1903.

Naess, Arne 1973. "The Shallow and the Deep, Long-Range Ecology Movement," *Inquiry* 16: 95–100.

Narayan, Paresh and Russell Smyth 2006. "Dead Man Walking: An Empirical Reassessment of the Deterrent Effect of Capital Punishment Using the Bounds Testing Approach to Cointegration," *Applied Economics 38/17* (September): 1975–1989.

Nietzsche, Friedrich 1966. *Beyond Good and Evil*, trans. Walter Kaufmann (New York: Random House).

Nietzsche, Friedrich 1967. *The Will To Power*, trans. Walter Kaufmann (New York: Random House).

O'Neill, Onora 1975. *Acting on Principle* (New York: Columbia University Press).

O'Neill, Onora 1990. *Constructions of Reason: Explorations of Kant's Practical Philosophy* (Cambridge: Cambridge University Press).

O'Neill, Onora 2009. "A Simplified Account of Kant's Ethics," in John Arthur and Steven Scalet (eds.), *Morality and Moral Controversies*, 8th edn. (Upper Saddle River, NJ: Pearson), pp. 78–83; originally published in Tom Regan (ed.), *Matters of Life and Death* (New York: McGraw-Hill, 1986).

Plato 1997. Republic, in John M. Cooper (ed.), *Plato: Complete Works* (Indianapolis, IN: Hackett Publishing), pp. 971–1223.

Pojman, Louis P. (1990) *Ethics: Discovering Right and Wrong* (Belmont, CA: Wadsworth Publishing).

Quinton Anthony 1989. *Utilitarian Ethics* (LaSalle, IL: Open Court Publishing Company).

Rachels, James 2003. *The Elements of Moral Philosophy*, 4th edn. (Boston: McGraw-Hill).

Rachels, James 2008. "Drawing Lines," in Lewis Vaughn (ed.), *Doing Ethics: Moral Reasoning and Contemporary Issues* (New York: W. W. Norton), pp. 435–443; originally published in Cass Sunstein and Martha Nussbaum(eds.), *Animal Rights* (New York: Oxford University Press, 2004), pp. 162–174.

Railton, Peter 2003. *Facts, Values, and Norms: Essays toward a Morality of Consequence* (Cambridge: Cambridge University Press).

Rawls, John 1971. *A Theory of Justice* (Cambridge, MA: Harvard University Press).

Rawls, John 1976. "Legal Obligation and the Duty of Fair Play," in James Rachels (ed.), *Understanding Moral Philosophy* (Encino, CA: Dickenson Publishing), pp. 370–379; originally published in Sidney Hook(ed.), *Law and Philosophy: A Symposium* (New York: New York University Press, 1964).

Rawls, John 1989. "Themes in Kant's Moral Philosophy," in E. Förster (ed.), *Kant's Transcendental Deductions* (Stanford: CA: Stanford University Press), pp. 81–113.

Rawls, John 2000. *Lectures on the History of Moral Philosophy*, ed. Barbara Herman (Cambridge, MA: Harvard University Press).

Regan, Tom (ed.) 1993. *Matters of Life and Death: New Introductory Essays in Moral Philosophy*, 3rd edn. (New York: McGraw-Hill).

Regan, Tom 2001. *Defending Animal Rights* (Urbana: University of Illinois Press).

Regan, Tom 2008. "The Case for Animal Rights," in Lewis Vaughn (ed.), *Doing Ethics: Moral Reasoning and Contemporary Issues* (New York: W. W. Norton & Co.,), pp. 421–428; originally published in Peter Singer (ed.), *In Defense of Animals* (Oxford: Blackwell, 1985), pp. 13–26.

Reiman, Jeffrey 1992. "The Justice of the Death Penalty in an Unjust World," in Steven Luper-Foy and Curtis Brown (eds.), *The Moral Life* (Fort Worth, TX: Harcourt Brace Jovanovich College Publishers, 1992), pp. 340–350; originally published in K. Haas and J. Inciardi (eds.), *Challenging Capital Punishment: Legal and Social Science Approaches* (Newbury Park, CA: Sage Publications, 1988).

Ross, W. D. 2002. *The Right and the Good*, ed. Philip Stratton-Lake (Oxford: Oxford University Press); originally published 1930.

Ruse, Michael and Edward O. Wilson 2001. "Moral Philosophy as Applied Science," in Elliott Sober (ed.), *Conceptual Issues in Evolutionary Biology*, 2nd edn. (Cambridge, MA: MIT Press), pp. 421–438; originally published in *Philosophy* 61 (1986): 173–192.

Sample, Ian 2007. "Blow For Fans of Boiled Lobster: Crustaceans Feel Pain, Study Says," *Guardian*, 8 November.

Schwarzenbach, Sibyl 1998. "On Owning the Body," in James Elias, Vern Bullough, Veronica Elias,and Gwen Brewer (eds.), *Prostitution: On Whores, Hustlers, and Johns* (New York: Prometheus Books), pp. 345–351.

Singer, Peter 1993. *Practical Ethics*, 2nd edn. (Cambridge: Cambridge University Press).

Singer, Peter 2008. "All Animals are Equal," in Lewis Vaughn (ed.), *Doing Ethics: Moral Reasoning and Contemporary Issues* (New York: W. W. Norton & Co.), pp. 411–421; originally published in *Philosophical Exchange* 1 (1974): 103–16.

Taylor, Paul W. 2008. "The Ethics of Respect for Nature," in Lewis Vaughn (ed.), *Doing Ethics: Moral Reasoning and Contemporary Issues* (New York: W. W. Norton & Co.), pp. 374–388; originally published in *Environmental Ethics* 3/3 (1981).

Tessman, Lisa 2001. "Critical Virtue Ethics: Understanding Oppression as Morally Damaging," in Peggy DesAutels and Joanne Waugh (eds.), *Feminists Doing Ethics* (Lanham, MD: Rowman and Littlefield), pp. 79–99.

Thompson, Jack 2005. *Out of Harm's Way* (New York: Tyndale).

Thomson, Judith Jarvis 2008. "A Defense of Abortion," in Lewis Vaughn (ed.), *Doing Ethics: Moral Reasoning and Contemporary Issues* (New York: W. W. Norton & Co.), pp. 173–183; originally published in *Philosophy and Public Affairs* 1/1 (1971).

Warren, Mary Anne 2008a. "Difficulties with the Strong Rights Position," in Lewis Vaughn (ed.), *Doing Ethics: Moral Reasoning and Contemporary Issues* (New York: W. W. Norton & Co.), pp. 428–434; a selection from "A Critique of Regan's Animal Rights Theory," *Between the Species* 2/4 (Fall 1987).

Warren, Mary Anne 2008b. "On the Moral and Legal Status of Abortion," in Lewis Vaughn (ed.), *Doing Ethics: Moral Reasoning and Contemporary Issues* (New York: W. W. Norton & Company), pp. 183–192; originally published in *The Monist* 57/4 (1973): 43–61.

Whelehan, Imelda 1995. *Modern Feminist Thought: From Second Wave to "Post-Feminism"* (New York: New York University Press).

INDEX

What's Good on TV?: Understanding Ethics Through Television, First Edition.
Jamie Carlin Watson and Robert Arp.
© 2011 Jamie Carlin Watson and Robert Arp. Published 2011 by Blackwell Publishing Ltd.

PEDRO

PEDRO'S
MONSTER

WITHDRAWN

by Fran Manushkin

illustrated by
Tammie Lyon

PICTURE WINDOW BOOKS
a capstone imprint

Pedro is published by Picture Window Books,
A Capstone Imprint
1710 Roe Crest Drive
North Mankato, Minnesota 56003
www.capstonepub.com

Text © 2019 Fran Manushkin
Illustrations © 2019 Picture Window Books

Library of Congress Cataloging-in-Publication Data
Names: Manushkin, Fran, author. | Lyon, Tammie, illustrator.
Title: Pedro's monster / by Fran Manushkin ; illustrated by Tammie Lyon.
Description: North Mankato, Minnesota : Picture Window Books, [2018] |
  Series: Pedro | Summary: Despite his father's reassurances, Pedro is
  frightened by the monsters in his dreams—until he finds a way to use his
  love of monster trucks to defeat his dream monsters.
Identifiers: LCCN 2018002733 (print) | LCCN 2018004451 (ebook) |
  ISBN 9781515828372 (eBook pdf) | ISBN 9781515828211 (hardcover) |
  ISBN 9781515828266 (pbk.)
Subjects: LCSH: Hispanic American boys—Juvenile fiction. | Dreams—Juvenile
  fiction. | Fear—Juvenile fiction. | Monster trucks—Juvenile fiction. |
  CYAC: Monster trucks—Fiction. | Trucks—Fiction. | Monsters—Fiction. |
  Dreams—Fiction. | Fear—Fiction. | Hispanic Americans—Fiction.
Classification: LCC PZ7.M3195 (ebook) | LCC PZ7.M3195 Pcm 2018 (print) | DDC
  813.54 [E]—dc23
LC record available at https://lccn.loc.gov/2018002733

Designer: Kayla Rossow
Design Elements by Shutterstock

Printed and bound in the USA
PA021

Table of Contents

Chapter 1
Bad Dreams

Pedro was dreaming.

He dreamed that a creepy

green dragon was chasing

him. The dragon was blowing

flames!

Pedro told his dad about
his dream.

His dad said, "Don't worry
about it. Dream dragons can't
hurt you."

Pedro tried to forget his dream. He raced his trucks all over the yard.

He and his brother Paco did speedy donuts, going around and around. They got nice and dizzy.

Pedro told Paco, "Now I'll

jump over the highest hill."

Oops! Pedro went flying

and landed in the mud.

"Cool!" he yelled.

The next night, Pedro

had another bad dream. He

dreamed that a long slimy

worm was creeping up his leg!

Pedro's dad told him,
"Dream worms cannot hurt
you. And I have a nice surprise.
I'm taking you and your friends
to a monster truck rally."

"Yay!" yelled Pedro. "Cool!"

Pedro and Katie and JoJo

painted posters for the rally.

BASH AND SMASH!

MASH AND SMASH!

CRUSH! CRUSH! CRUSH!

They were ready to cheer

on the truck drivers.

Chapter 2
Rally Time

The next day was the rally. The first truck did a somersault and landed in the mud. *THUD! SPLASH!*

"Awesome!" Pedro yelled. "I did that too."

A gigantic school bus
crushed three cars!

"I'd like to drive that,"
shouted Katie.

JoJo smiled. "You *would!*"

The trucks were fierce,

roaring and doing wheelies

around each other.

"Super awesome!" yelled

Pedro.

The next day at school,
Pedro wrote a story about
monster trucks. He could not
stop thinking about them.

But Pedro kept having bad

dreams. Each night before

bedtime, Pedro ate cookies,

hoping to have sweet dreams.

He didn't.

Each day after school,

Pedro raced his trucks. He

went faster and roared louder.

"Go, BIG THUNDER!"

cheered Katie.

"That's you!" shouted JoJo.

"BIG THUNDER!"

"Right!" yelled Pedro. "I am
noisy, and I am fast! Nothing
can stop me."

Pedro kept smiling. He
smiled all through dinner.

Chapter 3
Big Thunder

That night at bedtime, Pedro told himself, "I am strong! I am powerful! I am BIG THUNDER!"

Pedro said it again and again until he fell asleep.

Then it happened!

Pedro had a horrible

dream. That creepy green

dragon began chasing him!

The dragon roared and blew

his scary flames!

But Pedro didn't run away.
He roared back—loud as
thunder. Pedro chased that
dragon around in circles and
into the mud!

The dragon's fire went out!

He cried and cried, saying,

"You are so fierce!"

Then he ran away.

Katie and JoJo cheered,

"Way to go, BIG THUNDER!"

Pedro woke up smiling.

He told his mom and dad

about his dream.

"You were great, Pedro!"

said his mom.

"Way to go!" said his dad.

Pedro couldn't stop smiling.

"You were right," he told his dad. "Dream monsters cannot hurt me."

Then Pedro gobbled up his breakfast—Chocolate Crunch!

CHOCOLATE CRUNCH

About the Author

Fran Manushkin is the author of many popular picture books, including *Happy in Our Skin; Baby, Come Out!; Latkes and Applesauce: A Hanukkah Story; The Tushy Book; Big Girl Panties; Big Boy Underpants;* and *Bamboo for Me, Bamboo for You!* There is a real Katie Woo—she's Fran's great-niece—but she never gets in half the trouble of the Katie Woo in the books. Fran writes on her beloved Mac computer in New York City, without the help of her two naughty cats, Chaim and Goldy.

About the Illustrator

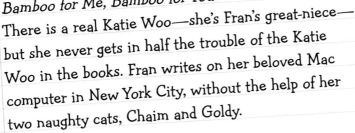

Tammie Lyon began her love for drawing at a young age while sitting at the kitchen table with her dad. She continued her love of art and eventually attended the Columbus College of Art and Design, where she earned a bachelor's degree in fine art. After a brief career as a professional ballet dancer, she decided to devote herself full time to illustration. Today she lives with her husband, Lee, in Cincinnati, Ohio. Her dogs, Gus and Dudley, keep her company as she works in her studio.

Glossary

awesome (AW-suhm)—extremely good

dizzy (DIZ-ee)—having a feeling of being unsteady or having a spinning head

donuts (DOH-nuhts)—motions that send vehicles spinning around in tight circles

fierce (FEERS)—daring and dangerous

gigantic (jye-GAN-tik)—huge

monster truck rally (MON-stur TRUHK RAL-ee)—a competition where monster trucks race and perform tricks

slimy (SLY-mee)—covered with or producing slime

somersault (SUHM-ur-sawlt)—a stunt where the back end of a monster truck rolls forward and over the top of the front end until the truck is back on its four wheels

speedy (SPEE-dee)—very fast

wheelies (WEE-lees)—a trick where the truck drives forward with its front wheels off the ground

Let's Talk

1. Describe the dreams Pedro had. Compare them with your own dreams. Have you ever had any dreams that were similar to Pedro's?

2. What things did Pedro try to do to avoid bad dreams? What finally worked?

3. Pedro gets a new nickname in this story. What is it? Explain why it is a good nickname for him.

Let's Write

1. Using the internet, look at photos of monster trucks or watch videos of them. Then write three sentences to describe monster trucks.

2. Pretend you are going to a monster truck rally and create your own poster. Be sure to include a chant or saying on the poster.

3. Draw your own monster truck, then write a paragraph about it. Be sure to include its name and what its most famous trick is.

- **Where do you get dragon milk?**
from a cow with short legs

- **Why do dragons sleep during the day?**
So they can fight knights.

- **Do monsters eat popcorn with their fingers?**
No, they eat the fingers separately.

- **What's big and scary and has three wheels?**
a monster riding on a tricycle

WITH PEDRO!

- What do you say when you meet a two-headed monster? "Bye-bye."

- What's the best way to talk to a monster? from a long ways away

- What kind of horses do monsters ride? night mares

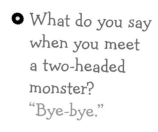

THE FUN DOESN'T STOP HERE!

Discover more at www.capstonekids.com

- Videos & Contests
- Games & Puzzles
- Friends & Favorites
- Authors & Illustrators

Find cool websites and more books like this one at www.facthound.com. Just type in the Book ID: 9781515828211 and you're ready to go!